The ABCs of IPOs

The ABCs of IPOs

✦

Investment Strategies and Tactics for New Issue Securities

Robert Anthony Chechile

iUniverse, Inc.
New York Lincoln Shanghai

The ABCs of IPOs
Investment Strategies and Tactics for New Issue Securities

Copyright © 2004 by Robert A. Chechile

iUniverse books may be ordered through booksellers or by contacting:

iUniverse
2021 Pine Lake Road, Suite 100
Lincoln, NE 68512
www.iuniverse.com
1-800-Authors (1-800-288-4677)

ISBN: 0-595-31118-0 (pbk)
ISBN: 0-595-76587-4 (cloth)

Printed in the United States of America

Contents

Introduction

I have always considered myself a teacher. My first exposure to imparting my knowledge to others eager to learn was while pursuing an MS degree in Mechanical Engineering from the Worcester Polytechnic Institute in Worcester, Massachusetts. Of all the duties required of a Graduate Assistant, teaching academic courses to undergraduates was my primary responsibility. After graduation, I was employed by a major petroleum producer in New Jersey, although I quickly returned to teaching when offered an Assistant Professorship in 1963 at a start-up engineering college in New England.

The contest to see which country could send the first men to the Moon and return them safely was a challenge that I simply could not resist. In 1965, I was recruited by a division of United Technologies Inc. for high-tech systems development. This included guidance systems for space vehicles: initially for the manned Lunar Lander, and later for the first Martian Landers. However, I did maintain ties to academia by continuing as an adjunct lecturer at the college.

I relocated to the West Coast in 1978 to manage development projects, for Litton Systems Inc., on guidance systems for military aircraft applications. I then earned an MBA from the California Lutheran University in 1982, as a necessary requirement for engineering management. However, the end of the Cold War forced a mid-life career change at age 58, after 28 years in technology development. The not-so-obvious choice was the securities industry.

The change was completed in 1992 by becoming a Registered General Securities Sales Representative (stockbroker) and later a Registered Principal with a West Coast, securities underwriter. I also became licensed with the State of California as both a life insurance agent and income tax preparer. With these credentials, I could then be able to offer clients life insurance and annuities, where appropriate, as well as being able to give authoritative tax advice on investments. In 1994, I was able to satisfy latent pedagogical instincts by being selected to conduct a formal training course for individuals desiring to pursue careers in the securities industry for my employer. In addition, I was recruited to teach a series of courses on securities investments at a local adult education school. Eventually, I became aware of the various ways that investors can be manipulated by some not-so-scrupulous sales reps in pursuit of commissions.

In 1997, I retired from the securities industry after only five years, and moved to a desert area of California. A few clients refused to accept my retirement, and persuaded me to manage their securities accounts under personal service contracts. Having time to explore the Internet, I realized the even greater potential for cyber-space securities fraud for risk-taking investors, especially when coupled with typical investor ignorance of high-risk securities.

Therefore, I began writing *The ABCs of IPOs* from material that I used for both the stockbroker-training course and the adult education investment courses, as well as from the great wealth of information available on the Internet. Additional sources were the Securities and Exchange Commission, the National Association of Securities Dealers, the New York Stock Exchange, and other government agencies.

Of all the IPO deals brought public each year, those whose price explode out of the "box" and continue to skyrocket in price can be counted on only one hand. Unfortunately, most investors don't realize that the average individual is unable to "get in" at the offering price of well touted offerings, but only at inflated market prices when the issue starts trading; unintentionally fulfilling their "intended" role. However, I do explain how one can be successful with IPOs—despite all the disadvantages to the average investor—and also with other new issue securities for the risk-neutral type person, which includes limited partnerships and convertible securities. Moreover, I show how to avoid money traps by explaining every aspect of public offerings; from how to determine beforehand whether an IPO has the potential for explosive capital appreciation, to how to evaluate the fair value of securities offerings touted as an income security.

Each of the ten chapters of this book explains a different aspect of new issue capitalization securities. The new issue securities industry, and investment strategies and tactics are explained, all of which should be fully understood, especially by the risk-seeking type personality. It is presented as if it were a text for a course on IPOs offered at a school of business and finance, because it leads the reader by the hand through every facet of new issue security distribution. As a result, the content is summarized in the following paragraphs.

The expectancy vs. reality of those who pursue investments in IPOs is discussed in Chapter One. It describes typical price performance characteristics of new issue securities illustrated by several well touted, IPO examples. The "hot," new issue distributions, by their explosive price increases, are explained as being in the realm of the *accredited investor* (institutions and high net worth individuals with high annual incomes). The chapter also explains that the intended role for the average individual is to provide sufficient demand to drive stock prices up in the marketplace.

Chapter Two describes the means investors use to accumulate wealth. It explains the various kinds of existing business organizations, and the various types of securities that are issued for business capitalization purposes. The reader will realize why it is extremely important that potential investors fully understand both the type of business organization that is being touted as a great investment opportunity, as well as the type of security that is actually being offered. Some securities cannot have ownership transferred and are therefore illiquid. Average individuals should not purchase investments that they cannot sell should the need arise, or simply whenever they feel the desire to sell.

Opportunities for investors interested in new issue securities depend on the type of securities dealer that is used to purchase securities. Therefore, all the "players" are characterized in Chapter Three. The roles of the different types of securities dealers as well as investors are discussed. I also explain why, in the absence of outright fraud, securities regulations designed to protect most individual investors do not apply to securities offered to *accredited* investors. However, these opportunities are frequently touted to the average individual by cold-calling salespersons. Therefore, all investors should beware of touts of unbelievably lucrative opportunities. There is absolute truth to the adage: If it sounds unbelievable, it probably is.

Every investor should be aware of the rules and regulations for the securities industry. Therefore, Chapter Four describes the securities trading environment before regulations were enacted following the 1929 Market Crash as a basis for understanding the "rules of the game." It also discusses the roles and responsibilities of everyone associated with the industry.

The securities trading arenas are detailed in Chapter Five. These include both the stock exchanges and the multi-tiered, over-the-counter markets. Most public securities trade in a stock market and therefore are liquid (the ability to sell whenever one decides to sell), but many securities cannot be traded because they do not have a market on which to exchange ownership interests. These include "restricted" securities such as "private placements" and most "direct participation program" limited partnerships, as well as stock listed on the "Bulletin Board" and "Pink Sheets."

All publicly traded securities (with exception of open-end mutual fund shares) can only be bought and sold in a securities account through a registered securities dealer. Consequently, Chapter Six describes the various types of ownership forms that are available for securities accounts, and also explains the differences between the types of accounts available: cash, margin, and retirement accounts.

The probability of success for many new issue equity securities can be detected by the type of legal relationship between the issuer and the underwriters participating in the offering, as well as from the required disclosure material presented in the prospectus. Accordingly, Chapter Seven discusses the different kinds of underwriting agreements, the information required to be presented in the prospectus, as well as the underwriting process and the roles of the different securities dealers involved. It also describes the various "exempt" security offerings: new issues that are exempt from Securities and Exchange Commission (SEC) registration.

Business organizations have a life cycle, and the type of security offered to the public will reflect not only the type of business organization, but also the current life cycle stage of the organization. However, the life cycle stage is secondary to the financial condition. Therefore, Chapter Eight not only illustrates the typical stages of the business life cycle but also clarifies the various financial statements typically issued by business organizations. In addition, it details the rudiments of "fundamental" and "intrinsic value" analyses and shows the reader how to assess the financial condition of a business organization and the "fair value" of the securities offered.

Although there are no magic formulas to guarantee the success of a new issue security, using specified guidelines can help avoid making an investment mistake. Since greed is what clouds the reasoning of otherwise rational individuals, Chapter Nine explains risk and reward, and also gives capital allocation guidelines to mitigate the possibility of going broke in the pursuit of wealth with speculative investments. It also presents specific selection guidelines for all the different types of new issue securities: from common stock to limited partnerships and more.

The success or failure of a new issue investment is not under control of the individual. Nevertheless, using appropriate tactics can either minimize any losses or lock in any gains that may have occurred. Therefore, Chapter Ten describes tactical maneuvers for new issues, which are different from conventional wisdom for most public securities investments, especially when the stock offering may be bundled with warrants. These different tactics are discussed for both fixed-income new issues as well as for new issues for capital appreciation.

During the publication process, an editorial reviewer stated that the material presented here was "dense" and in need of "punching up," which I took as a recommendation to transform it to be easily read. My intent has always been for this work to be a "sourcebook," an uncommon book on new issue securities in general and IPOs in particular. I felt that any attempt at "lightning up" the material would result in a common book on new issues, of which there are too many of these available. For the risk-taking novice investor, one who may invest in mutual funds and in company stock purchase plans, I recommend reading the entire book. The financially sophisticated investor must read chapters one, two, and seven through ten, although I do recommend reading chapters three through six also.

Finally, throughout the writing of this book I could not help reflecting on personal experiences with securities salespersons, as well as those of various acquaintances. One vivid reflection, before making the career change into the securities industry, was a friend and colleague in the aerospace industry, who I will call here "Pete." For many years, we shared adjoining offices where with the doors usually being opened, phone conversations could be overheard. Being a risk-seeker, Pete typically would engage every cold-calling securities salesperson touting financial bonanzas. One outrageous offering was for an illiquid limited partnership that had a 50% sales charge. Overhearing these discussions would give me a headache thinking that Pete might be actually persuaded to take advantage of such "opportunities."

Another reflection was a cold call I received one evening from a secretary to the President of a regional closed corporation offering private placement shares in the company. The young woman was only trying to be a good employee, and was stunned when I informed her that because I had never had a connection with the company or its officers, what she was doing was illegal and that she could be liable for a severe fine or imprisonment. I wonder how many receptive individuals that she convinced to accept an offering circular for the security before she called me?

As a stockbroker and personal finance instructor, too many potential clients would seek my help to repair previously deceptive securities transactions with other firms that would typically no longer be in business. Very few of these had any reasonable solutions. "Let the buyer beware" still reigns despite all the securities laws enacted to prevent fraud.

The vulnerability of the average individual has been paramount in the writing of this book. Everyone should realize that the only person that can really care about his or her financial health is ones' self. Therefore, this requires that each investor understand securities investments in general, and new issues in particular. For a case in point, my own brother some time ago admonished me to, "Just inform people how to get rich in 10 steps. Better still, it would be much easier if it could be reduced to five." How could I be so wrong?

Robert Chechile
April 2004

List of Tables and Figures

List of Tables

List of Figures

Table of Abbreviations and Acronyms

ADR . . . . American depositary receipt

AON . . . . All-or-none

AMEX . . . . American Stock Exchange

CB . . . . Credit balance

DPO . . . . Direct initial public offering

DPP . . . . Direct participation program

DRIP . . . . Dividend reinvestment plan

ECN . . . . Electronic communication network

FRB . . . . Federal Reserve Board

FOK . . . . Fill-or-cancel

GTC . . . . Good-until-cancelled

IPO . . . . Initial public offering

IRA . . . . Individual retirement account

LMV . . . . Long market value

LP . . . . Limited partnership

MSRB . . . . Municipal Securities Rulemaking Board

NASD . . . . National Association of Securities Dealers

NASDAQ . . . . NASD's Automated Quotation System

NASDAQ NM . . . . NASDAQ's National Market System

NYSE . . . . New York Stock Exchange

OC . . . . Immediate or cancel

OID . . . . Original Issue Discount

OTC . . . . Over-the-counter

REIT . . . . Real estate investment trust

SEC . . . . Securities and Exchange Commission

SIAC . . . . Securities Industry Automation Corp.

SCOR . . . . Small Company Offering Registration

SMA . . . . Special Memorandum Account

SMV . . . . Short market value

SOES . . . . Small Order Execution System

SuperDot . . . . NYSE electronic routing system

UIT . . . . Unit investment trust

UTMA . . . . Uniform Transfer to Minors Act

YTM . . . . Yield to maturity

A man once said, "Bulls make money, bears make money;
but pigs just get slaughtered!"

Anonymous

One
Getting Rich Quickly

✦

Reality Rarely Meets Expectation!

Businesses and governments raise capital by issuing securities. The offerings can be either debt obligations (contractual obligations between issuers and investors) or ownership interests in the business. Governments can only offer debt obligation securities, whereas businesses can offer either type security. Debt obligations are of interest mainly to individuals seeking income, while ownership interests are sought by those seeking capital appreciation (an increase in dollar value per ownership unit) and commonly called "growth" securities.

Generally, each security offering is considered as a new issue; however, the new issue security of primary interest to the risk-seeking individual is the *initial public offering* (IPO). IPOs represent ownership interests in corporations that consist of common stock shares being offered to the public for the very first time. They are perceived as the best type of investment security to achieve nearly instant wealth by the individual investor. This distorted view has been generated by intense media hype of the first day's price increase for occasional "hot" IPOs. Unfortunately, the belief that all IPOs behave this way is a fallacy.

The widely reported explosive price increases of new issue securities represent a small fraction of the new issues offered to the public. Furthermore, although theoretically available to suitable clients of the underwriting securities dealers, chances that the average individual will have ready access to hot IPOs at the offering price is next to nil; but not totally impossible. In addition to IPOs, individual investors have a variety of legitimate new issue securities readily available that can offer growth as well as income. However, new issues that may be offered to individual investors on the Internet or by cold-calling sales persons are typically unsuitable for the average individual.

NEW ISSUE GROWTH SECURITIES

Growth securities typically consist of common stock of public, for-profit, corporations whose business activities, as represented by annual revenues, are generally expected to increase substantially year-after-year. By definition, IPOs are new issue securities being offered for the first time. However, not every new issue is an IPO. A public company may decide to raise additional capital by issuing a new issue of the same class shares already held by the public. Sometimes it will offer a different class stock that differs from a previously issued share class. Even though both are defined as a new issue, neither of these offerings can be called an IPO. Consequently, new issue offerings typically represent additional shares of a company that are widely held by the public. Whereas, IPO shares going public on the effective date represent the only company shares available for trading.

Underwriting securities dealers (also called investment bankers) establish the offering price for the new issue security offering. This price is consistent with expectations for acceptance by the investing public as well as the amount of capitalization desired by the issuing corporation. However, the success of a new issue is governed by the marketplace demand for the securities. Heavy demand will result in explosive price increases, while a lack of demand will cause the market price to fall below the public offering price. Therefore, being able to judge the potential demand for new issue securities, independently of touts by securities dealers' representatives, can provide sufficient indication to the probable success of new issue securities. The demand can be gauged by:

1. the type of security being offered
2. the kind of underwriting commitment, or sponsorship
3. the stage of the business life cycle of the issuing company
4. the market on which the securities are to be traded
5. an estimate of the value of the securities being offered, and
6. a sense for the magnitude of potential investor excitement that is generated by reading the prospectus

The individual investor should also follow generally accepted guidelines to avoid potentially unsuccessful offerings called "turkeys." Relying on tips and touts by securities sales representatives and on information posted over the worldwide-web can be expected to end in failure. Once committed, subscribers should make appropriate tactical maneuvering transactions with these new issue offerings after the effective date to quickly minimize losses incurred with falling market prices, and conversely to take some profits when market prices increase.

IPO Price Explosions Entice Risk-Seekers

IPOs, as previously stated, represent common stock shares offered to the public for the first time. Some issues create such a demand with both the public and institutional investors that the explosive first day's price appreciation is typically widely reported by the media. The media heralding of such events attracts the risk-seeking type personality as well as the unassuming individual investor who may be astounded at the instant wealth being generated.

The spectacular first day's performance of IPOs can be illustrated with a select number of widely touted IPO issues, as shown below in Table 1-1, "Select First Day IPO Price Appreciation." The results shown in Table 1-1 are impressive and can seduce most any investor.

Table 1-1
Select First Day IPO Price Appreciation

IPO	IPO Date	First Day Price Appreciation, %
Callaway Golf	Feb. 1992	60
Boston Chicken	Nov. 1993	142
Netscape	Aug. 1995	108
Pixar	Nov. 1995	86
Sycamore Networks	Oct. 1999	430
United Parcel Service	Nov. 1999	164
VA Linux Systems	Dec. 1999	626
Krispy Kreme Doughnuts	Apr. 2000	76

However, phenomenal, multi-digit percentage, first day, price appreciation is rare! Moreover, issues that initially experience rapid increases in market price typically peak at about three months, and then decline to a level below the offering price sometime after a year. Those who are unable to buy in at the IPO price are disadvantaged. Purchasing shares in the marketplace on the first day of trading typically does not produce good results in the short-term, and usually results in a steep loss long-term. This is illustrated below by Figure 1-1, "Average IPO Stock Price Performance," which shows average price appreciation for IPOs for a normal expansion period. The data were obtained by William Powell during the years prior to the "dot-com" bubble expansion period of the late 1990s and presented in *The Wall Street Journal*. The historical share prices for the issues shown above in Table 1-1 illustrate the tendency shown in Figure 1-1.

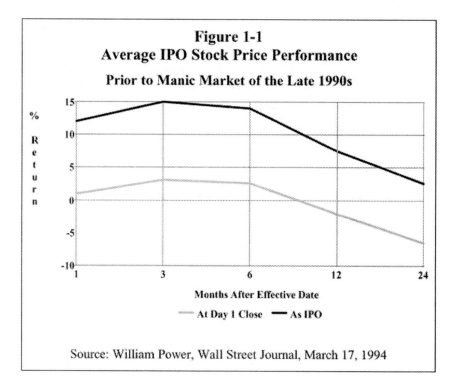

Figure 1-1
Average IPO Stock Price Performance
Prior to Manic Market of the Late 1990s

Months After Effective Date

‑‑‑ At Day 1 Close ▬ As IPO

Source: William Power, Wall Street Journal, March 17, 1994

Typical IPO Stock Price Performance

Historically, the majority of IPOs should be considered speculative, short-term investments. Very few IPOs turn out to become profitable long-term investments. Those subscribing to IPO securities need to pay extra attention to market price action. Both initial price declines below the offering price as well as price increases require that shares be sold. In the first instance, the holder needs to sell out completely, while in the second case one should take some profits by selling sufficient shares to try at least to get the initial investment back. These actions are contrary to the normal inclination of the average individual, which is to take no action whatever; only continue to wish up declining market prices, or sit around and watch onetime profits decline and turn to losses.

The share price history of Boston Chicken, a chain of fried chicken restaurants, is typical of many of the initially successful IPOs. The IPO for Boston Chicken was offered at a split-adjusted price of $10 per share in November 1993, which increased by 142% to $24 on the first day of trading. Three years later, in December of 1996, the share price hit $41½, which represented an annual return of 60% per year. One could dream of unimagined wealth holding on to this IPO.

However, by 1998, the share price had declined to 50¢, and Boston Chicken filed for bankruptcy. An IPO investor would have had the highest rate of return during the first month, and a respectable high rate of return even at three years. But the entire investment would be lost at five years. The company would later be acquired as a wholly owned subsidiary of McDonalds Corp. who changed the name to Boston Market to reflect an expanding product line of frozen meals.

The IPO for Pixar, a digital animation studio creating animated feature films, also illustrates typical, price performance history with its first day, price increase as shown in Table 1-1. Pixar issued an IPO for 6.9 million shares at $22 per share in November 1995 by underwriter Robertson, Stephens & Co. The first day, price appreciation at the market close was 86%; however, it would not sustain this price level. At one month, the appreciation would slip to 67%, and at three months, an IPO subscriber would have had a loss of 10%. Share prices would continue to decrease resulting in a loss of 31% at one year. It would take several years for the market price to recover to a level above the offer price. At five years, a long-suffering investor would finally have a 23% profit that when annualized, would have been a meager 4.2% per year. However, at eight years, the patient long-term IPO investor's gain would eventually have been 200%, resulting in an annualized appreciation of 15% per year.

Abnormal IPO Stock Price Performers

IPOs issued during manic markets that are initially very successful, can also quickly reverse course as the marketplace itself becomes depressive. Two examples of these types of IPOs are VA Linux and Sycamore Networks, whose first day, explosive, price gains (as illustrated above in Table 1-1) initially enjoyed phenomenal price appreciations of 626% and 430% respectively.

Linux, an application software company, issued 4.4 million shares at $30 through Credit Suisse First Boston. On the first day of public trading, the stock closed at over $220. However, this lofty price would not be maintained. For the next three months, as the technology issues reached their peak in March of 2000, the appreciation declined from 626% on the first day, to 256%. Within one year, share prices would drop below the offering price, and IPO subscribers still holding shares at that time would experience a loss of 72% of their investment. At two years, the loss would increase to 90%, and would continue at that low price for an additional two years.

Sycamore Networks, is a developer of voice and data traffic equipment for existing fiber optic transmission lines. It issued an IPO for 22.5 million shares at price of $12.67 (3:1 split adjusted) in October 1999 through the underwriter Morgan Stanley Dean Witter. This issue's initial success was demonstrated not only by the first day, price appreciation of 430%, but also by the increase to 629% within three months (January 2000). Consequently, a public offering for an additional 10.2 million shares at $150 was issued in March 2000, only five months after the initial public offering. However, within two years of the IPO effective date, the phenomenal price gains would turn into phenomenal losses! IPO subscribers would have lost 68%, while the subscribers to the public offering in March 2000 would have lost 94%. Those who bought shares at the closing price on the first day of public trading would have experienced even greater losses, should they have pointlessly held onto their shares.

Successful IPO Examples

Most IPO subscribers expect to become rich overnight, but the most successful, long-term, IPO investments are those that can stir the imagination of investors as something that is unique. These IPOs do not usually create an immediate public demand for shares, and most do not have phenomenal, double-digit, stock price escalation at the start of trading. No one, especially the average individual, can know in advance just how successful a particular offering will be, let alone to have access to the issue at the offering price. However, contrary to the typical admonition for buying shares of IPOs in the marketplace after the effective date, certain issues have unique qualities that continue to attract investors (as opposed to speculators). Over time, these will result in an excellent long-term investment. Two such examples, which have purposely been chosen outside of the explosive, high-tech industry, are the IPOs for Callaway Golf Co. and Krispy Kreme Doughnut Inc. These IPOs had first day price gains of 60% and 76% respectively, as are shown in Table 1-1. They are the dream of IPO investors and are called "no-brainers" (requiring no thought) by those in securities sales.

Callaway Golf manufactures high quality, innovative, golf clubs and balls. An IPO was issued in February 1992 for a split adjusted 20.8 million shares at $2.50 per share (2:1 stock splits were issued in 1993, 1994, and 1995) through Merrill Lynch. On the effective date of the IPO, about 37 million split-adjusted shares of a previously issued, preferred stock private placement were converted to common stock. This "liquidity event" allowed previously private investors (venture capitalists) to take profits by being able to sell these shares in the marketplace.

The success of the IPO could have been the popularity of their "Big Bertha" club, their market niche story. It certainly helped to have the good fortune of being offered at the start of the 1990's economic expansion, which permitted increased amounts of disposable income to be spent on leisure-time activities. In any event, the company issued a public offering for an additional 11 million shares at $3.38 (split adjusted) through Montgomery Securities in November 1992, nine months after the IPO. Subscribers of the IPO would have had a 215% profit at one year, and 550% at two years after the effective date. Subscribers of the IPO who did not take short-term profits would still have experienced a return of about 30% per year on their investment.

The failures of many initially successful technology IPOs offered in the late stages of the manic market of the 1990s were previously illustrated by the examples given for VA Linux and Sycamore Networks. However, the IPO for Krispy Kreme Doughnut reveals that some IPOs can be successful even when offered at the peak of a manic market and at the start of an economic recession. The IPO for Krispy Kreme, a national chain of premium quality doughnuts, was distributed by Deutsche Bank Alex Brown for a split adjusted 12 million shares at $5.25 in April 2000 (2:1 stock splits were made in March and June of 2001). The 76% price appreciation on the first day, shown in Table 1-1, would increase to 114% at one month, 238% at 3 months, and 311% at six months. Krispy Kreme, because of this success, then issued a public offering for an additional 9.2 million shares at $16.75, split adjusted, in January 2001. The return for IPO investors would be 738% by the end of 2001 (which represents an annualized gain of 224% per year), and subscribers to the January 2001 offering would have experienced a gain of 162%. The stock can be considered as having *graduated* to "tradable stock" status since 2003, because the price has traded in a range between a low of $27 and high price of $49.

IPOs ARE FOR ACCREDITED INVESTORS

IPO investing is not intended, nor is it suitable, for the average individual investor, risk-seeking personality or not! It is the playground of the financial institutions (investment partnerships, pension plans, hedge funds, and mutual funds) and professional *accredited* individual investors (individuals with high-incomes and high net worth). These deep-pocketed investors are invited to *road shows* set up by underwriters during the indication-of-interest phase of the offering process. Here these investors can meet company executives to assess the quality of management and get the opportunity to ask them questions. The purpose of these road shows is to encourage these deep-pocketed investors to subscribe to large block quantities of 100,000 shares or more with the underwriter's "principals" (senior management with multiple connections within the industry).

Average individual risk-takers, however, *can* find access to legitimate IPOs. Chapter Nine explains that the investor must have sufficient speculative capital to open one, or more, speculative objective securities accounts with major securities dealers that are also major underwriters. The investor then needs to demonstrate to each firm that he or she is a first serious investor by making sufficient trades that generate substantial commission dollars. Eventually, the investor's active trading history, as well as the commissions generated for the firm, should allow the client to get access to future IPOs underwritten by the firm. (Online new issue offerings are mostly illiquid securities offerings and should be avoided.)

The Non-Accredited, Risk-Taker's Role

The securities sales representatives in the retail side of underwriting securities dealers, as well as sales representatives for the selling group members, offer copies of the preliminary prospectus to accredited investors and other suitable clients who have specified that at least one their investment objectives is "speculation." The objective is to generate interest with all clients, not only to potential IPO investors. Most individuals who give an "indication of interest" (IOI) in the issue frequently find that they have not been allocated IPO shares requested. Some may get a partial fill of their order, while others may be shutout completely.

The primary goal of the retail securities sales representative (stockbroker) is to generate frantic interest among all their retail clients. In turn, they earn a fee on the IPO shares distributed, and a commission on shares bought (and sold) later in the marketplace. Consequently, clients who are shutout, or given partial fills, are then encouraged by brokers to place buy orders to purchase shares in the marketplace on the day of issue. The excessive demand coupled with a limited supply causes share prices to explode in the marketplace resulting in a successful launch of the IPO.

Explosive prices in the marketplace may cause one to ask, "Why didn't the underwriter set the offering price for shares of hot issues higher?" The answer is that the underwriter is required to perform "due diligence" on each issue, which includes investigating all mitigating factors that may affect the financial condition of the company. The result of these investigations then establishes a legitimate offering price range based on the business potential and financial strength. The range is then stated in the preliminary prospectus, well before solicitations can be made and the potential demand generated for the issue can be assessed. More-over, the underwriter also desires an attractive price to ensure that the issue will be fully subscribed so that unsubscribed shares will not have to be purchased by the underwriters.

Issues that indicate heavy investor interest will be price at, or slightly above, the top of the price range given in the preliminary prospectus. Issues with little interest will then be priced at, or slightly below, the bottom of the price range. The final offering price is an excellent indicator of the probable success of the new issue when compared to the preliminary prospectus offering price range. However, the final offering price is only disclosed on the effective date, and often being finalized as late as the evening of the previous day.

IPO Disadvantages for the Individual Investor

The average individual investor interested in new issue securities endures several other disadvantages in addition to being used to create demand for new issue securities offerings. The first is having limited access to new issue offerings through a single securities dealer. Most wage earning investors typically have only one securities account, which is likely to be with one of the discount securities dealers. These type securities dealers do not underwrite new issues, and they rarely participate as selling group members in distributing new issues. Moreover, many full-service securities dealers do not engage in securities underwriting. Therefore, the average individual is typically forced to purchase hot IPOs in the marketplace, at much higher prices than the offering price.

Another disadvantage is access to appropriate investment advice. Securities personnel cannot tout nor make any projections, or give information not explic-itly stated in the prospectus, either during the offering phase or for a limited period after the issue becomes public. Commercial, IPO advisory services are available by subscription, but these tend to be too expensive for the average individual. Therefore, the potential new issue investor must rely on his or her ability to understand and evaluate the information provided in the prospectus, as well as to be able to reject issues whose "story" does not create any internal excitement.

Understanding the Risk-Seeking Personality

Risk-seekers, otherwise called "gamblers," are individual investors that employ various means to achieve the greatest possible return in the shortest time in their search for *get-rich-quick* schemes. Gamblers desire the *luck-of-the-draw* action available in Las Vegas, Atlantic City, or at any of the numerous Indian gaming casinos. However, many of these venturesome personalities also seek riches with investment securities that use leverage to expedite capital appreciation. In addition to IPOs, hot investments include a variety of securities that are also attractive to the compulsive risk-taker in addition to table action at casinos.

Stock option contracts on individual stock, as well as option and futures contracts on various stock indexes, interest rates, foreign currencies and commodities, all provide the requisite short-term potential for huge rewards. However, the vast majority of risk-seeking individuals in these investments eventually go broke. They really do not understand either the extent of the risk involved, or when to take profits or to cut losses. In fact, many of these *so-called investments* can result in a financial liability far greater than the initial, required, investment deposit. Therefore, gambling personalities should stick with the action provided by the gaming casinos, since they can only lose whatever money they bring to the table.

Some risk-seeking investors may consider that the admonition on gambling with securities does not apply to IPO securities since they must be paid in full. These individuals should understand that the IPOs that explode in price in the marketplace are rare. It has been shown that about half of all IPOs will have a market price lower than the offering price after five years. Moreover, IPOs on average under perform the S&P 500 Index with lower annual price appreciation in bull markets, and greater price declines in bear markets. Therefore, both the odds and payout ratios at gambling casinos may be better. Nevertheless, the risk-seeking investor is invariably attracted to IPOs.

NEW ISSUES TYPICALLY AVAILABLE TO THE PUBLIC

Public solicitation for new issues often occurs for offerings in which the distributing securities dealer only acts as an agent, and does not having a firm underwriting commitment with the issuer. The reason is usually that the firm feels that the issue, or company, may be faulty or too risky to give a firm underwriting commitment. These are called "agency distributions" where the underwriter gets a sales fee for any shares actually sold and has nothing to lose. Agency distribution arrangements typically have high sales distribution charges, which are typically 20%, or even higher. (The author has observed one limited partnership offering with a 50% sales charge.)

These offerings represent less popular and even less understood type securities such as limited partnership units, intrastate offerings, small capitalization offerings, and private placements. These securities have additional disadvantages, beside high distribution expenses, and are they are not recommended for the average individual investor. The severest is the lack of liquidity: having no market on which shares or units can be traded. They have the greatest potential for fraud because registration with the Securities Exchange Commission (SEC), the industry watchdog, is not required and information disclosure is typically limited.

Growth Debt Obligations

Debt obligations that are offered to the public at a discount to the face value are also considered growth securities. They make no interest payments during their lifetime, and are only obligated to pay the face value at maturity. These are commonly called "zero-coupon" obligations, but are more accurately referred to as "original issue discount" obligations (OIDs). Since corporate OID obligations typically represent financially risky corporations, only government issued OIDs should be considered because they are backed by the taxing power of the government, either state, or federal. OIDs do not offer explosive price appreciation and are of interest to the risk-averse investor seeking relatively secure capital appreciation over the lifetime of the issue. Consequently, a discussion of these securities is considered not within the scope of this work.

Investing for Income Requires Alternative Securities

Investors seeking income have a choice of either corporate and government debt obligations, corporate preferred stock, unit investment trust units offering income, and also real estate investment trust units. These securities are collectively classified as "fixed-income" securities. Other fixed-income securities are convertible preferred stock and convertible debentures (bonds), which offer both income, and capital appreciation with the potential conversion to common stock. However, the long-term success of a new issue, fixed-income security with income as the primary investment objective, depends upon the financial quality of the issuer. This may cast some uncertainty for the ability to make consistent income payments, and return the invested principal at maturity. Therefore, individual investors strictly seeking income should consider one or more of the many mutual funds available as an alternative. These securities can provide safety through diversification, and relative consistency of the dividend income.

A discussion of new issue fixed-income securities is also not within the scope of this work. However, convertible fixed-income securities (convertible preferred stock and convertible debentures) are discussed herein because they provide the opportunity for conversion into common stock, which is of interest to the conservative growth objective individual.

Two
Business Capitalization Securities

◆

The Means to Accumulate Wealth!

Many sophisticated, risk-taking investors attempt to achieve windfall capital appreciation through new issue equity securities offered by business organizations as the hot investment security of choice. Business organizations offer a wide variety of new issue equity and fixed-income securities that provides the capital required for starting, expanding, or maintaining business operations. Equity securities offer an ownership interest, and the potential opportunity for both capital appreciation and dividend income. Fixed-income securities typically offer income, either from interest paying debt obligations or from "promised" fixed dividend payments of preferred stocks.

The type of security offered the public to raise desired capital depends upon the type of the business organization issuing the securities (many of which are not suitable to every individual), and the life cycle stage of the business. Not all business organizations are corporations offering common stock. Therefore, it is essential for the new issue investor to understand the type of business organization seeking capitalization, and the type of security that is being offered to the public. This chapter discusses the various forms of business organizations offering securities to the public, and the types of securities that are typically offered by these organizations. (The effect of the business life cycle on the type of capitalization securities offered is discussed in Chapter Eight, "Business Life Cycles, Financial Statements and Analyses.")

Federal, state, and local municipal governments, as well as business organizations offer new issue debt obligations to raise capital to fund particular projects. Governments can only issue debt obligations; however, business organizations can also offer ownership interests. Debt obligations typically pay semi-annual interest to the owner as a legal obligation of the issuer. Along with preferred stock (an equity security), these types of new issue securities are collectively called *fixed-income* securities, which are of interest only to those seeking income, not capital appreciation. (Some investors seeking capital appreciation trade fixed-income securities in the marketplace. They speculate on potential changes in market prices that would be associated with anticipated interest rate changes by purchasing previously issued fixed-income securities trading in the marketplace.) Most fixed-income securities offer periodic income payments, and do not have explosive price increases. Therefore, a discussion of new issue fixed-income securities is considered as not being within the scope of this work.

However, convertible fixed-income securities (convertible preferred stock and convertible debentures) are discussed herein because they provide the opportunity for capital appreciation by conversion into common stock. These type securities are of interest to risk-seeking personalities having a low-risk tolerance (those who cannot afford capital losses).

BUSINESS ORGANIZATIONS

Various business organizations offer new issue securities to the public as means of raising capital. To be able to make a reasonably successful securities investment, it is very important that investors understand both the differences between these organizations, and the securities that are publicly offered. The typical types of business organizations consist of:

1. the *for profit* business corporation, of which common stock is the most popular form of ownership security, but who also may offer fixed-income securities such as preferred stock and debt obligations

2. the closed-end investment management company, which is a mutual fund whose common stock is traded in the securities markets

3. the real estate investment trust, which provides capital for the real estate industry

4. the unit investment trust, which offers a variety of limited life, investment objective strategies

5. the limited partnership, which raises capital for a variety of business operations by typically offering illiquid, limited life, investment interests

6. the sole proprietor or general partnership, of which ownership interests are not usually offered to the public

The Private Business Organization

The *sole proprietorship* (individual engaged in business) and *general partnership* (business conducted by more than one individual owner) are private business organizations. Every person with an ownership interest has a share in the profits. However, each owner is usually legally responsible for *all* liabilities of the organization. Partners may share profits by agreement, but each individual partner may be held liable for all business debt (including legal judgments). Since this type of business organization does not offer ownership interests to the public, no further discussion of such organizations will be presented as they are considered to be not within the scope of this work. However, some corporations are private business organizations that offer ownership interests to a select class of individuals. A discussion of the private corporation and its securities offerings is presented below.

The Corporation

Corporations are legal business entities with indefinite lifetimes. They are initiated by a group of original incorporators who file Articles of Incorporation with the Secretary of State (or the state Department of Corporations) of the chosen state of incorporation. This is a formal document stating the business purpose, the number and names of the directors, the type of capitalization securities authorized to be issued, and the name of an individual to act as agent for legal service and processing of legal documents.

The Board of Directors is empowered to adopt the corporate by-laws, which defines how the business is to function. The Board also elects corporate officers, and decides the types and amounts of authorized capitalization securities to be offered to the public, which can include common stock, preferred stock, debt obligations, and convertible fixed-income securities (see "Capitalization Securities" discussed below).

Not all corporations are public corporations, but all corporations must be incorporated by a state to do business. Ownership of a private corporation is typically held by a small number of shareholders. Public corporations have a substantial number of shares issued and held by the public (called the "float"), who are persons having no other connection to the corporation or its directors and officers. Publicly held shares are called the "floating supply." All securities (common and preferred stock and debt obligations) issued by public corporations and offered to investors in multiple states must be registered with the Securities and Exchange Commission (SEC) before being offered to the public.

A *domestic* corporation is, for state tax purposes, one that does business only in the state of incorporation. It also refers to a national corporation who does business within the U. S. and whose securities are both registered with the SEC and trade on one of the domestic securities markets.

A *foreign* corporation is incorporated outside the U. S. and trades in a foreign market. Nonetheless, foreign corporation securities may trade on one of the U. S. securities markets, if the securities issued are registered with the SEC.

Public corporations, as mentioned previously, are initially capitalized with a common stock offering called an initial public offering (IPO). Additional capitalization can be raised with a *rights offering*. Rights offerings authorize additional shares of the same class common stock to be offered first to existing shareholders. If the shareholders do not participate fully in the offering, the remaining shares are then offered to the public. Corporations can obtain additional capitalization, as they evolve from the development stage into a mature growth stage (business life cycle stages are discussed in Chapter Eight "Business Life Cycles, Financial Statements and Analyses") by offering a different class common stock, different classes of preferred stock, and debt obligations

Common stock shareholders have an ownership interest in the business, but since the company is a legal entity, their liability is limited to the capital invested. They typically have voting rights and are entitled to a share of distributed earnings (called dividends) when declared by the Board of Directors.

Preferred stock shareholders are considered as having an ownership interest without voting rights. They are promised a fixed, periodic dividend payment, which is not a legal obligation of the corporation as are interest payments for debt obligations. Convertible preferred shareholders have the right to convert the security into common stock at a fixed number of common shares per preferred share.

Corporate debt obligation holders are creditors of the corporation, and have a legal right to receive the stated semi-annual interest payments (unless initially offered at a discount to the face value and thus called a "zero-coupon" obligation) and payment of the face value at maturity. Like convertible preferred stock, debt obligations that are offered with a convertible feature permit the holders to convert the debt security into common stock at a fixed exchange rate. The various forms of common and preferred stock (including convertible preferred stock and convertible debentures), as well as other securities, are discussed below under "Capitalization Securities."

All corporate dividend and interest payments are funded by corporate profits, which are taxable to the federal government as well as being taxable to most state, and some municipal governments. Therefore, corporations with inconsistent earnings or no earnings at all, typically do not offer debt obligations or preferred stock.

Private Corporation

A *private* corporation (also called *closed or privately held*) is a non-public entity chartered by a state to transact business, whose ownership interests number less than 35 shareholders. The common stock distributed between owners represents a single class ownership security that can be issued for either cash, property contributions, or for proprietary expertise by one, or more, of the owners. This stock is exempt from state and SEC registration; as a result, there is no public market for these shares since they have not been publicly issued. Any isolated sale of stock is considered as a private transaction. Either the seller is required to know the financial status of the buyer and have had a prior business relationship, or the buyer would be required to be an accredited investor.

Public Corporation

A *public* corporation is an entity that has been chartered by the state of incorporation to transact business, and who offers securities to the public that have been registered with both the SEC and the state, or states, in which stock is to be offered.

An *investment banker,* who is also called an *underwriter,* is a securities dealer that is hired by the corporation to distribute authorized shares to the public in compliance with both SEC and state regulations. Public offering securities are sold strictly by prospectus, for cash only. Once distributed by a public offering, these securities are traded in one of the various securities markets (described in Chapter Five) through registered securities dealers.

The *transfer agent* maintains a record of current shareholders; cancels certificates that have been sold, if they are found to be in *good delivery* (properly signed and not mutilated); issues new certificates to the buyers; and resolves problems with lost, stolen, or destroyed certificates. A commercial bank typically contracts with the company to execute this function, but the corporation may perform this by itself.

The *registrar* is a commercial bank that acts as an agent for the corporation issuing securities. Its function is to insure the issuing of only registered public shares. The transfer agent may also perform the function of the registrar if it is a commercial bank. However, for obvious reasons, the company cannot perform both functions else, they would be tempted to issue unregistered securities.

Closely-Held Corporation

A *closely held* corporation is a public company with a small number of shares being held by a small number of public shareholders. There is very little trading in these stocks; therefore, they are called *thinly traded* stocks (less than 5000 shares traded daily). There are usually an insufficient number of market makers to permit public trading in the over-the-counter market, and thus the issue may be relegated to a listing on either the Over-The-Counter Bulletin Board or the National Quotation Bureau's Pink Sheets, which are explained in Chapter Five, "Securities Markets."

The Closed-End Investment Management Company

The *closed-end* investment management company (closed-end mutual fund) can be either a corporation or an indefinite life trust, both of which are organized as a mutual fund under the requirements of the Investment Company Act of 1940. A closed-end mutual fund is similar to, but different than, the *open-end* investment management company, which is usually to what most people refer when they speak of a "mutual fund." Closed-end fund assets are typically 100% invested, unlike open-end funds, because there is no need to have cash available for shareholder redemption. There are a fixed number of shares outstanding, which are exchanged in one of the securities markets. New issue, closed-end fund stock will not have any appreciable price appreciation in the marketplace simply because they represent an investment money pool holding shares of publicly traded companies. (An explanation of mutual funds is beyond the scope of this work.) These offerings are of interest to long-term investors rather than risk-takers.

However, major securities underwriters frequently offer new issue, closed-end fund shares to the public, because they are not high risk. Therefore, the following discussion is presented to acquaint the reader with the basics for these securities.

The closed-end fund is capitalized by a common stock offering of a fixed number of shares, which are thereafter traded in one of the various securities markets. Shares are offered to the public through a securities dealer acting as an underwriter. They are registered with both the SEC and in all states in which shares are to be sold, unless falling under some provision where registration is not required (see Chapter Four, "Securities Regulations"). Shareholders have the right to vote on directors (or trustees), auditors, and on changes which would affect the form of the organization.

Closed-end, investment management companies are not business organizations in the classic sense of a *for-profit* corporation offering a product or service to the public. They are simply managed *investment money pools.* An investment manager is responsible for actively managing a portfolio of investment securities in accordance with the investment objectives stated in the prospectus. The investment manager is hired by the Board of Directors (or Trustees) of the fund, and the compensation is typically fixed as a percent of the fund's total assets (typically ½ % annually). A *custodian* (typically a commercial bank) is hired to hold all fund assets, and act as both registrar and transfer agent (see "Public Corporation" above for definitions).

Closed-end funds, as stated above, are initially capitalized with a common stock offering. However, additional capitalization can be achieved with a *rights offering* where additional shares are first offered to the shareholders, and then to the public if the existing shareholders do not participate fully in the rights offering. The fund can also offer a preferred stock issue where shareholders receive a promised dividend to be funded by the anticipated performance of the additional investment securities purchased with the proceeds.

The closed-end mutual fund is required to compute the *net asset value* (NAV) per share daily. The net asset value is the current total value of securities in the portfolio less a pro-rata share of daily expenses, including the investment manager's compensation. However, unlike open-end mutual funds whose shares are not traded in the securities markets, the market price for the closed-end fund shares is usually different from the NAV, and can be either higher or lower than the NAV.

Investment companies are not taxed as business entities providing they distribute at least 95% of the portfolio income, and 90% of capital gains to the shareholders. The shareholder is therefore responsible for tax on distributions received. A sale of closed-end shares will trigger a capital gains event (just as any other security sale). This will either be a gain or a loss, depending on the *cost basis* (the initial acquisition cost adjusted for any stock splits) of the shares.

Closed-End Fund Investment Objective

Closed-end, investment company shares are purchased by those who seek both incomes and capital appreciation. Investors invest into different funds by matching their individual investment objective with that of the particular mutual fund. Investment objectives are typically either for income, or for capital appreciation. Income objective funds typically invest in interest paying fixed-income securities, such as notes, bonds, and preferred stock. Capital appreciation funds, also called "growth" funds, invest in common stock of companies whose profits have the potential to increase significantly due to expected increases in business operations with a corresponding increase in the market price of the stock.

Income objective funds typically require very little management; therefore, total annual expenses are typically low, about ¾% of fund assets. However, growth funds typically require active management to follow continuously business and economic trends. The more effort that is expended to keep abreast of current market and financial conditions for each company security in which it is invested, the greater will be the expense.

The Real Estate Investment Trust

Real estate investment trusts (REITs) are closed-end investment management companies that are set up as a trust, and whose function is to provide real estate projects with capital for a fee. The trustees provide the investment management activity with advice given by a registered *Investment Advisor* hired under contract to provide recommendations on real estate investment opportunities. REITs are not tax-advantaged investments, and expenses and depreciation do reduce net taxable income.

Equity REITs invest in, and manage, a portfolio of commercial real estate holdings whose shareholders receive a share of the rental income and capital gains. Mortgage REITs lend money to real estate developers, with shareholders receiving the interest income generated by such lending activities.

REITs are capitalized by offering ownership units, by prospectus, to the public through sponsoring securities dealers (underwriters), as are public stock companies and closed-end investment management companies. Units are registered with the SEC, under the provisions of the Investment Company Act of 1940, and in the states in which units are to be sold, unless falling under some provision where registration is not required (see Chapter Four, "Securities Regulations"). These units are thereafter traded on one of the available securities markets providing liquidity to the investor.

The requirements for being classified as a REIT are:

1.   that a minimum of 75% of REIT assets be invested in real-estate holdings, or in mortgages on real property, or in other REITs with the remaining assets either held in cash or invested into U. S. government securities

2.   that a minimum of 75% of gross revenues be from real-estate activities

3. that a minimum of 95% of taxable revenues be distributed to shareholders

Therefore, REITs are of interest only to individuals seeking income, not to investors seeking capital appreciation.

The Unit Investment Trust

A unit investment trust (UIT) is typically a *limited life* investment company set up under a trust agreement, and administered by a trustee. UITs are capitalized by offering redeemable *units of beneficial interest* by prospectus to the public through sponsoring securities dealers (underwriters), in the same manner as public securities for corporations, investment management companies, and REITs. Units are registered with the SEC, and in all states in which units are to be sold unless falling under some provision where registration is not required (see Chapter Four, "Securities Regulations").

UIT units do not trade on any securities market, but they are not considered as an illiquid security. Investors can redeem units from the trustee who will liquidate a pro-rata share of trust assets. The unit value received, upon any redemption, will depend upon the current value of the investment portfolio, which can result in either a profit or loss at redemption. At maturity, all assets are liquidated and the cash assets are distributed to unit holders.

The investment portfolio is as described in the prospectus, and is fixed for the life of the trust. There is no active management of the trust assets, and the trustee cannot change the portfolio. However, the trustee can liquidate assets either to meet redemption demands, or to preserve trust capital by eliminating "at risk" securities. Since liquidated investment proceeds cannot be reinvested, capital from liquidated securities must be returned to investors as *return of capital*. Trust income from dividends and interest income must also be distributed to shareholders.

The Limited Partnership

A limited partnership (LP) is a business entity conducted by a *general partner,* which can be an individual, partnership, corporation, or another limited partnership. *Limited partners*—also called *subscribers* or simply *investors*—provide capital, to which profits (or losses) pass, and whose liability is theoretically limited to the amount invested. The general partner—also called the *sponsor* or *syndicator*—has all partnership liability. However, most limited partnerships have a clause within the partnership agreement that calls for limited partner indemnification to the general partner for any liabilities incurred.

LPs are chartered by a state with the filing of a Certificate of Limited Partnership. This document discloses:

1. both the purpose and location of the business organization

2. the names of the general partner and limited partners

3. the term of the partnership

4. the amount of the initial capital contributions of both the general and limited partners

5. the sharing arrangements between the general partner and limited partners for both profits and losses, and

6. the procedure for making changes in the general partner and also in limited partners

The majority of LPs are called "direct participation programs" (DPPs), offering tax advantages to investors. These are typically established for real estate, equipment leasing, and oil and gas programs. The tax advantages offered allow depreciation and resource depletion allowances (from oil and gas programs) to be deducted from LP income. In order not to be taxed as a corporation, investors are precluded from participating in management activities (therefore, they have limited voting rights), and the partnership is *required* to have both a limited life, and ownership units that are *not* transferable. Therefore, DPP LP units are illiquid securities, in which potential investors must be sure that they will not need the capital invested until the maturity date. However, LP partnership agreements frequently allow the maturity date to be extended at the discretion of the sponsor.

General Partnership Interests

General partnership interests, on occasion, are offered through securities dealers acting as sales agents, not as underwriters. These general partnership interests typically tout the advantages of passing through both business expenses and profits to the partners. The expenses are not subject to passive income restrictions for tax purposes (as are limited partnership interests). Therefore, startup oil or gas exploration limited partnerships typically offer what is called "working interests" to the public, which allows initial partnership expenses to offset other investor earned income in the early years when there may be little partnership income to offset expenses. A conversion provision may be offered in which partners may convert their status to limited partners after a specified period.

Theoretically, all partners manage the business and the Offering Circular usually states that all partners are encouraged to participate in management activities. However, it should be realized that every working interest partner has *joint and severable liability* for all partnership obligations, and solicited partners may incur liability that far exceeds the dollar amounts invested.

Sales distributors offer these interests only to persons that can meet financial suitability standards. To avoid being promptly rejected by risk-averse individuals, complete explanations of these interests as well as limitations and risks are usually not fully explained to investors by securities sales representatives. Solicitors seldom use the term *general partner,* and investors are typically left with an obscure assumption that they are purchasing limited partnerships. Consequently, the sales distributors' sales pitch may offer a *limited liability* option by suggesting that interests be purchased in an Individual Retirement Arrangement (IRA), for which a custodian typically will be provided. This tactic attempts to use a loophole in Federal law which limits liability of IRA accounts to the value of the account. However, this would be the worst possible type investment for an IRA because of the extremely high risk of a complete wipeout with these type investments.

CAPITALIZATION SECURITIES

The types of business organizations are all different, and so are the many types of new issue capitalization securities that are offered to the public. In order to able to achieve a security's explosive price appreciation, one must understand the characteristics of the different types of securities issued by business organizations. Therefore, the characteristics of new issue securities of interest to the risk-seeking investor are discussed below.

Common Stock

A new issue of common stock for companies with potentially explosive earnings is the investment of choice for the risk-seeking investor. When common stock is offered to the public for the first time, it is known as an *initial public offering,* or IPO. Shareholders are owners in common (thereby the term "common stock") and have the right to vote for directors, the auditor, and all matters requiring a vote as defined in the by-laws.

Liquidity (how readily the stock can be bought or sold) is perhaps the most important factor in any investment. Common stocks of publicly traded companies are considered liquid if they are traded either on the New York Stock Exchange, the American Stock Exchange or on the National Association of Securities Dealers Automated Quotation System called the "NASDAQ." Stocks listed on the Over-The-Counter Bulletin Board (commonly referred to as the "OTC-BB") and on the National Quotation Bureau's Pink Sheets should be considered as illiquid. There is little value in owning a security if it cannot be immediately sold, even at a loss, whenever the owner desires. These securities markets are discussed in Chapter Five, "Securities Markets."

Preferred stock and debt obligations are typically not offered to the public for startup or development stage companies (see Chapter Eight for business life cycles). No investor in their right mind would buy either preferred stock for dividend income, or debt obligations for interest income, from a company with uncertain earnings, from which dividend and interest payments are to be made. In fact, any security offering income must clearly show how the income is generated. (Note that fraudulent "Ponzi" schemes are still alive and well. These investment schemes continually solicit new investors, with a part of the invested sums being paid to previous investors as fictitious income, and the bulk of the money being confiscated by the promoter. There are no tangible investments made on behalf of the investors, and eventually the whole scheme collapses as the income payments to the previous investors gradually declines to zero as the pool of new investors dries up.)

If the company is considered to have an especially high financial risk, then the offering may include common stock bundled (combined) with warrants. These are offered as *units* consisting of a specified number of common stock and warrants per unit. Warrants are long-term rights to buy additional common stock at a particular price upon exercise (see the discussion on "Warrants" below). These are used as a sweetener (Street talk for inducement) to encourage risk-takers into subscribing to the offering.

The offering share (or unit) price includes the underwriter's compensation, called the "spread." The spread is the difference between the public offering price, and the price the issuer (company) receives after underwriting concessions. Spreads for stock offerings typically are between 8% and 10% of the offering price. A higher spread can be an indication of either a higher-than-normal risk by the underwriter, or as an additional incentive for securities dealers for distributing an offering in which there may be little public interest.

The securities are sold on the effective date (date of distribution of subscribed shares or bundled units to the public) to those that have previously indicated an interest to purchase various quantities at the offering price with distributing dealers. Shares, or bundled units, then start trading in the securities market on which they have been listed for trading. Thereafter, the transaction price quoted will be market prices: either the price of the last transaction during the trading day, or the last trade made before market close. Bundled units are separated—typically from 30 to 90 days—and both stock and warrants will start trading as independent securities in the same market.

Dealers that elect to make a market in the stock, provide continual firm quotes to the public during the trading day. The "bid" price is the price, which the market maker is willing to pay sellers, and the "offer" price is the price that the market maker is willing to sell shares, or units. The bid is always lower than the offer, with the difference (also called the price spread) representing either the market maker's *markup* or *markdown*. A minimum of two market makers is required for each publicly traded stock on the NASDAQ. However, exchange traded stocks use a single *specialist* as the market maker.

Common Stock Classification

The corporate Articles of Incorporation are required to define the type and amount of all capitalization securities to be eventually offered to the public. The total amount of common stock listed in the Articles of Incorporation is called "authorized stock." Initially, only a small quantity of common stock shares of the total authorized stock is offered to the public as an IPO. This provides capitalization needed for the first few years. Sufficient earnings should materialize by the end of this period to sustain business expansion, or else an additional security offering will be required.

Stock that is issued to the public is called "the float," or "floating supply," and is part of the *issued and outstanding stock* carried on the books. *Outstanding stock* includes stock that is distributed and held by the public, as well as by "insiders." Insiders (also called "control persons") include company officers and directors, their family members, as well as anyone owning 10%, or more, of the outstanding shares. (Control persons are subject to selling restrictions as described in Chapter Four, "Securities Regulations.") Outstanding stock that had been previously issued public stock but since reacquired is called *Treasury Stock* (see definition below), and is no longer considered as outstanding stock.

The difference between the amount of outstanding stock and floating supply represents the shares owned by *control persons,* and is called "control stock." The float represents the degree of liquidity that can be expected for the shares in the marketplace. A floating supply of less than 40% of the outstanding stock is apt to be *thinly traded.* Thinly traded stock typically has little public interest, and may not have any trade executed for days on end. However, it is technically considered as being liquid should it be listed on an exchange or on the NASDAQ.

Many corporations, with profits in excess of that needed for expansion, may repurchase an amount of its floating supply, either in the marketplace or in a formal stock buyback program. Such stock is called "Treasury Stock" that may later be resold, reissued to insiders exercising stock options, or it may be retired. Treasury stock is no longer considered as outstanding stock, and therefore no longer has the right to vote or to receive dividends. This is obvious, since officers and directors can only vote shares individually owned. Otherwise, the balance sheet for any such dividend payment amounts, would show a series of ridiculous transfers from retained earnings to accounts payable upon dividend declaration, then back to retained earnings on dividend payment (see Chapter Eight, "Business Life Cycles, Financial Statements and Analyses").

Voting Rights

Common stock owners, as mentioned previously, have the right to vote for members of the Board of Directors, the independent auditor, who is typically selected by management, and on all matters affecting the Articles of Incorporation. The usual method of voting is one vote per share on each issue and each director, which is called *statutory voting.*

In some instances, however, minority shareholders ban together and enact the *cumulative voting* method. Cumulative voting is an attempt to ensure that minority shareholders have some representation on the Board. In voting on directors, the allocated number of votes for each shareholder represents the product of the number of shares held times the number of directors standing for election. The shareholder can choose to vote any portion of the total number of allocated votes to as many, or as few, directors as is specified by the shareholder. For example, a shareholder owning 100 shares with eight directors to be elected would be allowed to cast 800 votes for one particular director instead of 100 for each director. This method is not popular with corporate executives, and is rarely used.

Voting takes place at the annual stockholders' meeting, typically in the city of the location of the corporate office. Since vast majorities of shareholders usually do not attend, voting by proxy is used. A *proxy statement* is sent to every shareholder, usually with the annual report, describing all items to be voted at the meeting. A *Power of Attorney Certificate* is also provided, which is typically a data processing voting card on which the shareholder can indicate how the shareholder's votes are to be cast. Alternatively, it may simply give the proxy holder the authority to vote at his or her discretion.

Subscription Rights

Shareholders typically have the right to retain their percent ownership (called preemptive right) whenever stock of the same class is later issued to raise additional capital. The new issue is offered to the shareholders of record with a *subscription rights offering*. Each shareholder receives one "right" per share owned, and the Board establishes the number of rights required to purchase each new share as well as the share price, which is called the subscription price. Rights offerings effectively dilutes the per share tangible asset value.

Subscription rights have monetary value; but, they have a limited life, typically between two to four weeks. They can be either transferable or nontransferable. Transferable rights can be traded, prior to expiration, in the same market on which the stock trades. If not sold or exercised, they will expire worthless. Nontransferable rights allow the holder to subscribe only to the new issue, and the rights will expire worthless if not exercised.

The Board sets the record date for the rights offering. Purchasers of the stock in the marketplace two business days before the record date receive stock "ex-rights" (Street talk for "without rights") because of the three-business day settlement period. Purchasers of stock three business days or more before the record date will receive stock "cum-rights" (Street talk for "with rights"). The value of the rights depends on the closing share price cum-rights, the preset subscription price, and number of rights required per share. It can be shown that:

Rights Value equals:

$$\frac{(\text{stock price cum-rights}-\text{subscription price})}{(\text{number of rights required}+1)}$$

For example, assume that subscription rights are issued offering shares at a price of $15 with five rights required to subscribe to each new issue share. (This indicates that for every five shares outstanding, one additional share is offered.) Also, assume the cum-rights, closing share price (set by market trading forces) is $33; therefore, the value of each right is determined to be $3, and the ex-rights, opening price would then be $30. Should the rights expire worthless because of investor inaction, the investor would have lost $3 per share (for this example).

Liquidation Rights

A corporation will occasionally cease operations and liquidate assets. Regardless of whether it is voluntary or by force of law, the common stock shareholders only have a *residual* claim on the corporation's tangible assets. They will receive a pro-rata share only after the claims of creditors, including bondholders, and lastly preferred stockholders have been satisfied.

Dividends

All shareholders of outstanding common stock are entitled to dividends only when declared by the Board of Directors. The declaration will specify the dividend amount, the *record date* (date on which all recorded owners will be entitled to the dividend), and the payment date. Dividends can be either a cash dividend, which is paid from retained earnings, or a stock dividend, which is obtained from the remaining unissued authorized stock.

Cash dividend payments represent distributions of earnings to the shareholders. They can be paid regularly, typically every quarter, or irregularly. Common stock of companies that pay consistent, quarterly cash dividends will have an investment value. The percent dividend yield will help prop up the stock price in order to maintain parity with yields paid by fixed-income securities during economic downturns. However, the market price for most common stocks that pay dividends is usually set by anticipated earnings growth, not the investment value.

Stock transactions take three business days to settle; therefore, a number of "ex" (meaning without) dates are important. For example, a buyer making a trade on a Monday will not be an owner of record until Thursday. Therefore, the "ex" date for each event is two days before the event. For example, should the record date for a dividend be on Thursday, the ex-dividend date for entitlement for a dividend would be on Tuesday. Anyone making a purchase on Tuesday, or thereafter, will not be entitled to the cash dividend that will eventually be distributed on the payment date (typically weeks later).

The cash dividend amount to be distributed switches from "retained earnings" to "accounts payable" on the Balance Sheet (see Chapter Eight, "Evaluation of Business Organizations") on the dividend declaration date. The stock price will reflect a lower stock price at the opening of trading on the ex-dividend date. The opening price will be reduced by the cash dividend amount. The dividend amount is deducted from both cash assets and accounts payable on the Balance Sheet on the payment date.

Stock dividends, or splits, are typically made when the share price becomes so high that the cost of buying the standard trading unit of 100 shares (called a "round lot") becomes too expensive for the average investor (typically above $100 per share). Directors feel that by offering a lower price stock, demand for the shares will increase, and thereby help to increase the market price with both continued investor interest and liquidity. A stock dividend of 25% or greater is called a "stock split." Stock dividends are paid from additional unissued shares from the authorized supply and distributed to existing shareholders based on a particular formula. Since the outstanding supply is increased without the balance sheet capitalization being affected, the share price is reduced at the opening of the market on the ex-dividend date.

The primary exception to stock-split theory is Warren Buffett's Berkshire Hathaway Corp., which has never had a stock split, and as a result supports a share price in the tens of thousands of dollars. However, Berkshire Hathaway has issued a Class B common stock with 1/30 the share price of the Class A common stock in order to be more attractive to the individual investor.

The opening share price on the ex-dividend date of a stock dividend will be affected by the inverse of the split expressed as a fraction times the previous closing price. For example, a 50% stock dividend (representing a 3 for 2 stock split) with a closing stock price of $90 per share the day before the ex-dividend date, will have an opening price of $60 (2/3 times $90) on the ex-dividend date. Of course, the price after market opening will be dependent on market action, the difference between buy and sell orders.

Table 2-1, "Stock Dividends," shown below, presents typical common stock dividend amounts expressed as a percent and fractional split.

Table 2-1
Stock Dividends

Stock Dividend	Split	New Shares Received Per Number of Shares Owned
5%	21/20	1 for 20
10%	11/10	1 for 10
20%	6/5	1 for 5
25%	5/4	1 for 4
33.3%	4/3	1 for 3
50%	3/2	1 for 2
100%	2/1	1 for 1
150%	5/2	3 for 2
200%	3/1	2 for 1
300%	4/1	3 for 1
400%	5/1	4 for 1
900%	10/1	9 for 1

Reverse stock splits are the exchange of a number of old shares for a lesser number of new shares. This technique is used for stocks whose market price has fallen so low that they have become penny stocks with little or no public interest. A reverse split attempts to provide the perception of a better quality, or a more financially stable corporation, but this should be considered as being comparable to a carnival "flimflam artist."

Stock splits, and reverse stock splits, do not alter the capital structure of the corporation. The dollar value of the balance sheet's common stockholder equity is unchanged. Only the number of outstanding shares issued is changed, which therefore results in a change in the share market price. Stock splits usually require a vote by the shareholders.

Common Stock Par Value

Par value is a value assigned to common stock prior to being issued and is meaningless for the investing shareholder. The total par value of all the outstanding stock is listed on the corporate balance sheet as *common shareholder equity*. The par value is purposely set low, often at one cent per share, because some states tax corporations on the value of the common stock upon incorporation.

The initial price for most shares offered to the public is typically set between $10 and $25 per share to allow it to be attractively priced. The value for the assigned par value for shares is typically set at a "nil" value, therefore, the amount of capitalization that company receives from the offering will be greater than the par value. The corporate balance sheet will then have an additional line item under shareholder equity called "Paid-In Capital," or "Paid-In Surplus," which is the difference between the amount received from the public offering, and the assigned par value (see "Balance Sheet" discussed in Chapter Eight, "Business Life Cycles, Financial Statements and Analyses").

For example, assume that a hypothetical corporation with 10 million shares outstanding at a ten cent per share par value was initially offered at $10 per share with an 8% underwriting compensation (see Chapter Seven, "New Issue Offerings"). The balance sheet will then indicate $1 million as common shareholder equity and $91 million as paid-in-capital (representing the balance remaining after the $8 million underwriter's take).

Preferred Stock

Preferred stock is an equity (ownership) security without voting rights. It is considered a fixed-income security because of the promise to pay a specific dividend amount from earnings, typically every quarter. These type securities are usually issued by corporations who have an established record of consistent earnings, and who want to raise additional capital with an equity security; but, without diluting the common stock value or giving additional shareholders voting rights (as would new issue achieve). Preferred stocks are of interest mainly to investors looking for income.

They are, however, of great interest to the risk-seeker looking for potential capital appreciation, when offered with a conversion feature: the right to convert to common stock at a specific price. Convertible preferred stocks are issued by corporations seeking additional capitalization that are not considered as *investment grade* quality. These companies may have an inconsistent history of earnings, thereby indicating some risk for future dividends. An explanation of preferred stock is presented here to provide an understanding of how the convertibility feature affects these securities when it is offered.

Each preferred stock offering issued by a company is separate and unique, since every issue will have different terms and conditions. Each subsequent preferred stock offering will be issued as a different class of preferred stock, and will carry a sequential "letter symbol" designation starting with the letter "A." The sequence sets priority on shareholder claim to dividends, and on company assets upon liquidation on a first-in, first-out basis.

Preferred Stock Par Value

Preferred stock shares are typically offered to the public as non-voting class equity securities, with par values of either $50 or $100 per share. These prices are considered attractive to the individual investor seeking income. Therefore, the standard round-lot trading unit would cost only $5,000 for a $50 par value, or $10,000 for a $100 par value.

Par value is the price the preferred stock shareholder would expect to receive, either upon being called (redeemed) by the company or upon the company's liquidation. Unlike common stock, the par value *is* important to the preferred shareholder. The market price, however, may be lower or higher than the par value. It will tend to be the *investment value*: a theoretical value based on the *dividend yield* being comparable with the dividend yield of equivalent quality securities (see the following discussion on "Preferred Stock Dividends").

Preferred Stock Dividends

The stated dividend per share at issue will represent a particular rate of return on the par value. This dividend yield will be comparable to long-term interest rates required by moneylenders for long-term, fixed-income securities of equivalent financial quality organizations. Therefore, should the annual current rate of return demanded for equivalent quality company securities be 12%, then the issuer of a preferred stock with a $100 par value would have to offer a $12 annual dividend at issue (typically paid quarterly) to be competitive.

The market price after issue will then depend upon changes in current equivalent interest rates. For example, should comparable interest rates for the above $100 par value issue example drop to 10%, the market price for the share will increase to $120 to maintain parity with the current the rate of return. The $12 dividend will represent a 10% yield on a $120 share price. Accordingly, market prices will decrease when equivalent interest rates increase. Therefore, current long-term interest rates, as well as the general perception about the company being able to continue to pay the dividend, typically affect the market prices of fixed-income securities. The price would be trading at its investment value when there is no such concern; however, the price will drop giving the new owners a higher yield for taking a higher risk when there is reason for concern.

Preferred stock dividend payments are promised, but not guaranteed. The Board of Directors must approve each payment. This underlying uncertainty for all preferred stock issues therefore requires serious consideration of the financial strength of the issuer, as well as the type of preferred stock being offered. The promised dividend amounts for preferred stock offerings are established by the financial health of the company. The yield demanded by the financial markets is typically based on a *premium* (stated as a percent rate) added to a particular interest rate, such as the *prime rate* (the rate charged by financial institutions for their most favored clients). The premium will be small for *investment grade* quality companies, and will be high (a multiple of the set rate) for companies whose debt-obligations are not classified as investment grade securities. Financial quality ratings as shown in Table 2-3, "Bond Quality Ratings."

The business cycle often will result in companies with periods of negative earnings, short-term. Since dividends are paid from earnings, during these periods, the dividends will then be paid from *retained earnings* (previous year's earnings that have not been used for business expansion or paid to common shareholders). Heavily capitalized, mature growth stage companies will have a significant amount of retained earnings on the balance sheet. However, lesser-capitalized *development stage* companies typically use most earnings for reinvestment in new business opportunities. Therefore, they will have little retained earnings from which to make dividend payments. Higher risk companies carry a higher degree of uncertainty for continued dividend payments; consequently, it is important to understand the difference between the several types of preferred stock that are offered.

The typical preferred stock offering is a *non-cumulative* issue. The holder of a non-cumulative preferred stock will lose dividends not paid when the Board fails to declare the dividend. Such securities should then be considered only when issued by an investment-grade quality company, since it would be unlikely that the Board of such a company would not declare dividend payments, even during periods of economic recession.

A *cumulative* preferred stock issue requires that any regularly scheduled dividend payments that are not voted by the Board, for whatever reason, be carried on the books as unpaid accumulated dividends. All such accumulated dividends must be paid before any common stock dividends are declared. As long as the company's fortunes do not lead to bankruptcy, the cumulative preferred shareholder will have some degree of certainty of eventually receiving dividends owed.

A *participating* preferred stock pays below market rate dividends, but dividend amounts will be increased should the common stock dividends exceed a particular amount. This type preferred stock should only be considered if the company has a history of consistent common stock dividend payments, as well as a history of dividend increases. It would not be attractive should the company have either a history of infrequent dividend payments or an absence of dividend increases. The inducement to accept a dividend yield below equivalent market rates for shareholders in a participating preferred stock offering is the potential for achieving a higher dividend amount in the future.

Call Provision

Companies that raise capital by issuing non-voting securities always consider the possibility of a lower cost for money in the future. Preferred stock offerings have to compete with current rates of return only at the time of issue. Interest rates in the future may well be lower, thus resulting in the stock dividend paid, as a percent of the par value, being more than that which may be demanded by the financial markets in the future, an unpleasant situation for company executives. Therefore, a "call" provision is typically included with a preferred stock offering. This gives the issuer the right to redeem the stock on a vote of the Board of Directors as a hedge to being able to take advantage of a potentially lower cost for money in the future.

In order to offset the uncertainty that the call proviso imposes on potential investors at issue, the issuing company typically offers a moratorium of a few years from the date of issue. It may also provide a premium of about 5% on the par value that will be paid if the issue is called within a specific period after the moratorium. The typical period for a premium paid on the par value is 10 years from issue. After year 10, if the issue were not previously called, the call price would be the par value.

The par value to be received upon redemption will typically be lower than the market price prior to issuing the call, because the typical reason for redemption is to refinance (offer a new issue) at a lower dividend rate. Therefore, a call for redemption will result in an immediate drop in market price to the redemption price. This can be illustrated with the previously stated example where the market price of a 10% dividend on a $100 par value issue increased to $120 when the equivalent quality securities rates dropped to 8%. On issuing a redemption notice, the market price would immediately drop to $100 (or $105 if a 5% call premium were valid). This would not represent any loss to the initial offering investors, but would represent a considerable loss for anyone that had purchased shares in the marketplace at the $120 price.

Convertible Preferred Stock

Convertible preferred stock is a hybrid between straight, preferred stock (as described above) and a warrant (see "Warrants" discussed below). When a convertible feature is included with a preferred stock offering, the stated dividend offered is typically lower than the dividend rate of return demanded on equivalent quality fixed-income securities. The issuer secures additional capitalization at lower than market rates, while subscribers have an opportunity for future capital gain by converting to common stock.

For example, a $100 par value, preferred stock issued by a lower quality rating company that would otherwise have to offer 12% dividend yield at issue (representing a 2% premium over higher financially rated companies that would only be required to offer 10%), may only have to offer 10%, or lower, by using a convertible issue. The convertible provision offers the opportunity for the owner to convert the preferred stock into common stock should the common stock price escalate sometime in the future. This would more than offset the disadvantage of the lower dividend rate offered at issue. Therefore, convertible preferred stock is the investment of choice for the low-risk tolerant type of risk-seeking investor.

The *conversion rate* is the number of common stock shares that can be exchanged for each share of preferred stock converted, and is expressed as a ratio such as 4 to 1 (4:1). The *common stock parity price* is the price for shares of common stock that are equivalent to the market value of the preferred stock. It is determined by dividing either the par value at issue, or the current market price of previously issued convertible preferred stock trading in the marketplace, by the conversion rate.

The conversion rate is established at the time of issue of the preferred stock, and is determined by the par value and the market price of the common stock at the time of issue of the convertible preferred stock. It is typically set such that the common stock parity value will be about 25% higher than the common stock's market price at the time of issue of the convertible preferred shares.

The market price of a convertible preferred stock, once issued, is thereafter established either by its investment value, or by the market price of the common stock into which it may be converted. For example, a 5:1 conversion rate for a $100 par value, convertible preferred stock with a 10% dividend yield (compared with 12% return for equivalent quality securities) would have been set, at issue, with the common stock price at about $16. This would then result in an initial common stock parity price of $20. A common stock price increase to $24 (a 50%

increase from $16), the value of the market price for convertible preferred stock would increase to the conversion value of $120.

If the common stock price drop to $8 (a 50% decrease from $16), the $10 annual preferred stock dividend would have to compete with equivalent quality security returns of 12%. Thus, the preferred stock market price would only drop to $80 compared to the current conversion value of $40 (5 times $8/share). This $80 preferred stock price would be its investment value since it is established by the dividend paid, and the current rate of return for like quality securities. For this example, a common stock decline below $16 would not affect the preferred stock market price, as long as there were expectations for the continued payment of preferred stock dividends.

Convertible Preferred Stock Redemption

Companies raising capital by issuing non-voting securities always consider the possibility for a lower cost for money in the future, and therefore will include a call provision in the preferred stock offering. The call price will be the par value, but it could include a call premium for an early redemption. Redemption of convertible preferred stock will force a conversion if the common stock market price is above the equivalent common stock parity price. This price is established by dividing the redemption price by the conversion ratio. For the cited example, the common stock parity price would be $20 with a $100 convertible par value. A common stock price above this price would force holders to convert to common and sell in the marketplace, before the redemption date.

Preemptive Rights

Owners of straight preferred stock have no preemptive rights either on future offerings of preferred stock, or of common stock. However, convertible preferred shareholders do have preemptive rights for subsequent common stock *rights offerings*. Chapter Seven, "New Issue Offerings," describes the mechanics of a rights offering.

Convertible Debentures

Corporations also issue long-term, debt obligations with greater than 10 years to maturity that are backed only by the "good faith and credit" of the corporation. The correct name for this type instrument is *debenture*, although they are commonly called bonds. The term *bond* has been used universally as a generic term for unsecured, long-term, debt obligations; however, it is correctly used only for corporate debt obligations backed by real property (a secured debt obligation). A debt obligation with 10 years or less to maturity at issue is called a *note*. All unsecured obligations less than 10 years are called *unsecured notes.*

Some interest paying debt obligations have a convertible feature in which the holder may convert the instrument into a fixed number of common stock shares, and thus the name *convertible debenture* (typically misquoted as a convertible bond). The convertible feature is also of interest to the more conservative risk-taker, as is convertible preferred stock, since it has the potential for significant capital appreciation depending on the fortunes of the company. Therefore, debentures (with emphasis on the convertibility feature) are discussed below for those interested in seeking potential capital appreciation over the longer term, meanwhile receiving investment income as a corporate obligation, not as a promise as is dividend income from preferred stock.

Typical Bond Characteristics

Most debt obligations are classified as fixed-income securities because they make semi-annual interest payments, and are of interest to the individual seeking income. The annual payment is specified as a rate of return on the face value at issue, and is called the "coupon." Unlike preferred stock, interest payments are a legal obligation, and therefore the term "debt obligation" is used. However, some debt obligations are issued at a discount to the face value at maturity. These are referred to as "original issue discount" obligations (OIDs), or more simply, "zero-coupon bonds." OIDs make no interest payments, and the maturity date and the amount of the discount at issue determine the annual rate of return to be received at maturity. Therefore, OIDs are of interest to conservative investors seeking capital appreciation to fund a particular financial need in the future.

The typical corporate debt obligation face value is $1000 per security. Some obligations are issues with a face value of $100, and are called "baby bonds." These lower face value securities compete with preferred stock, but are more secure because the annual payment to the investor is an obligation, whereas preferred stock dividends are not.

Debt obligations for companies whose stock is listed on an exchange may also trade in the bond room of the exchange. However, bonds mostly trade in the OTC securities markets with bond dealers quoting *bid* and *offer* prices. Like all fixed-income securities, market prices for bonds will vary to maintain parity with the current rate of return demanded by the financial markets for equivalent quality and maturity debt obligations.

Long-term corporate debt obligations are not quoted in dollars and cents, but are quoted in percent and fractions of percent of face value. The reason for quoting price as a percent of face value is that debt obligation certificates are issued in various dollar increments, the smallest of which is $1000. Therefore, an offer price quoted "97 3/8" would cost the buyer of a $1000 face value bond $973.75 (97 and 3/8 percent of $1000), while a $25,000 face value bond could be bought at $24,343.75 (97 and 3/8 percent of $25,000).

The move toward decimalization has yet to be extended to the bond market. Until such time, investors will have to continue to memorize decimal equivalents of current fractions used in bond trading (it should be noted that long-term U. S. Treasury obligations are traded in 1/32% increments).

Yield Definitions

There are different terms used for the "yield" from debt obligations. The term *nominal yield* is another term for *coupon rate,* and is the annual rate of return of the annual interest payment based on the face value of the obligation. Debt obligations trade in the marketplace after they are issued, at prices that reflect current rates of return of equivalent quality and maturity obligations. Obligations purchased in the marketplace receive the defined coupon dollar payment, but the yield is defined by the purchase price. *Current yield* is the annual rate of return that the buyer of the bond in the marketplace would receive annually for the coupon payment based on the *current offer* (also called *asked)* price quote. This is a better representation for yield from annual income received, for the purchaser of a debt obligation in the marketplace, than would be the nominal yield.

Market prices for non-OID, debt obligations typically are either above or below the face value. *A premium* price is greater than the face value, and a *discount* price is below the face value. Premiums and discounts must be factored into the rate of return computation because the buyer will receive both the face value at maturity as well as semi-annual coupon payments.

The *yield-to-maturity* (YTM) represents the annualized total return that a buyer of a bond, purchased in the marketplace, would receive if held to maturity. Bonds bought at a premium will result in the YTM being lower than the nominal yield, while those bought at a discount will result in a YTM being higher than the nominal yield.

The YTM is actually determined by a "present value" computation of all future coupon payments, as well as the face value payment at maturity, discounted by a specific interest rate. This discount interest rate is considered the YTM. Since the actual computation can be a tedious trial and error computation without a financial calculator or an appropriate computer program, an approximate value (also called a "rule of thumb value") can be estimated by dividing the expected average annual return to maturity by the average bond price. The computation for YTM can be performed from the expression given in Table 2-2, "Bond Yield to Maturity Approximation."

Table 2-2
Bond Yield to Maturity Approximation

Yield to Maturity =

$$\text{Annual Interest} + \frac{(\text{Face Value} - \text{Market Price})/ \text{Years to Maturity}}{(\text{Face Value} + \text{Market Price})/2}$$

The "years to maturity" term in the above table is the number of years to maturity. It should be expressed as a mixed, decimal number (the number of months that are less than a year being expressed as a decimal). For example, a hypothetical $1000 face value bond with a $100 annual coupon payment, purchased in the marketplace for $900, and having a maturity of 10 years, 9 months (10.75 years) would have a YTM, determined by the approximate value computation, as:

$$\text{YTM} = \frac{\$100 + (\$1000 - \$900)/ 10.75}{(\$1000 + \$900)/2}$$

or,

$$\text{YTM} = 0.1059, \text{ or } 10.59\%$$

Call Feature

Most long-term, debt obligations have a call feature that allows the issuer to *call-in* the obligation before maturity. Like preferred stock, bonds with an early call date (typically 10 years or less from issue) are usually redeemed at a premium of about 5% on the face value. Therefore, the YTM for callable bonds will actually be expressed as the *yield-to-call* (YTC) if it is less than the YTM, and will be quoted under the "Yield to Maturity" heading in financial periodicals. The YTC can be easily computed from the expression shown above in Table 2-2, by using the number of years to the closest possible call date, with the call premium price (if applicable) used instead of the face value amount.

Debt-Obligation Quality Rating

Debentures and unsecured notes are rated based on the financial strength of the issuer. The lower the financial rating, the higher is the risk, therefore, a higher coupon is demanded. The more common organizations providing such services are Moody's, Standard & Poor's, and Fitch.

Table 2-3
Debt Obligation Quality Ratings

Investment Grades	Moody's	Fitch and Standard & Poor's
Highest investment quality	Aaa	AAA
High quality	Aa	AA
Medium grade,		
Principal & interest safe	A	A
Fundamental weakness	Baa	BBB
Speculative (Junk) Grades		
Low-medium grade,		
moderate risk	Ba	BB
Low grade, concern for		
principal & interest	B	B
Poor, possibility of default	Caa	CCC
Weak, often in default	Ca	CC
Lowest quality, interest in default	C	C
Principal in arrears or in default,		
no value	-	DDD, DD, D

Typical bond ratings are shown above in Table 2-3, "Debt-Obligation Quality Ratings," which presents ratings of quality ranging from highest to lowest. Both Fitch and Standard & Poor's may also grade issues within a rating grade with a "+" or "-" symbol. Moody's uses numerical modifiers from "1" (highest) to "3" (lowest) for grades listed from Aa to Ca.

Rating service organizations operate on a fee basis; therefore, some debt obligations are listed as being *unrated*. Most unrated obligations take place when the underwriters feel that they would have no trouble distributing the new debt issue to the public. This is frequently true with municipal bond issues that are purchased almost entirely by an individual mutual fund for its portfolio. Therefore, an unrated obligation does not necessarily imply poor quality.

Characteristics of Convertible Debentures

Convertible debentures, like convertible preferred stock, are hybrid instruments having features of both a bond and a warrant (see "Warrants" discussed below). Companies with a history of consistent earnings that desire additional capitalization from debt obligations will use a convertible feature to ensure a successful offering. In addition, the potential for capital appreciation allows a coupon rate that is lower than the rates of return demanded by the financial markets for equivalent quality and maturity debt issues. Eventually, the issuer will exercise the call feature that will force the conversion to common stock. The issuer will no longer be obligated to make coupon payments when bondholders become stockholders.

The conversion rate (or conversion ratio) is the number of shares of common stock into which each single denomination bond can be converted. Therefore, a 50:1 (fifty-to-one) conversion rate means that 50 shares of stock can be obtained for each debenture converted. The conversion rate is set, as it is for convertible preferred stock, such that the face value of the convertible is at a premium of approximately 25% greater than the value of the equivalent number of converted shares at issue. For example, a $1000 face value convertible bond with a 10% coupon rate and a 50:1 (50 to 1) conversion rate may be offered when the common stock market price would be at about $16, thereby resulting in a common stock parity price of $20. A straight bond issue would probably have required paying a 12% coupon rate as an inducement.

The market price for convertible debentures after being issued, like convertible preferred stock, is determined either by the investment value or by the common stock price. The investment value is determined by the YTM of equivalent quality and maturity bond issues. The price of the convertible, should there be little change in interest rates and very little interest shown in the market for the common stock, will fall to seek parity with the YTM for straight bond issues (because of the lower coupon being paid by the convertible). For the above-cited example, the investment value of the convertible would be $800, not the $1000 face value. The price of the bond will decrease to the investment value should the common stock price actually decrease, or be perceived to be able not to increase. In addition, an increase in long-term interest rates after issue will force the bond price downward to maintain parity with equivalent YTMs for straight bonds. Like convertible preferred stock, the market price for convertible debentures will also be supported by its investment value.

However, an increasing common stock price will allow the convertible to be priced at the conversion value, instead of the investment value. The conversion value is computed by multiplying the conversion rate by the current common stock price. For the above-cited example, assume that the common stock price increased to $24 per share. The conversion rate of 50:1 would result in a conversion value of $1200 per bond, compared to an $800 investment value set by the coupon and current YTM rates. This represents a 20% increase over the face value!

It should be noted that the investor could have purchased $1000 worth of stock at a price of $16, instead of subscribing to the convertible debenture. A price of $24 would have achieved a 50% return for this hypothetical example instead of 20% return for the convertible. A decrease in stock price from $16 to $8, would have resulted in a 50% loss; whereas, the convertible price would have only decreased to the investment value of $800, resulting in a loss of only 20%. This characteristic of limited downside risk for both convertible debentures and convertible preferred stock is what attracts the conservative, low-risk tolerant, risk-taking investor.

Warrants

Warrants are securities entitling the holder to buy authorized, unissued common stock at a fixed price, called the "subscription price," often called the "exercise price." The subscription price is usually set about 25% higher than the common stock price at issue (similar to convertible securities). Most warrants are issued with a definite maturity, or expiration date, typically from 4 to 10 years after issue, which is oftentimes extended. *Perpetual warrants*, although not commonly issued, have an indefinite lifetime with no expiration date.

Warrants are typically issued as a *sweetener* in conjunction with a common stock offering by development stage companies, for which there may otherwise be little investor interest (perhaps because of a lack of either renowned management, or a unique product or service). They appeal to risk-seekers looking for potentially enormous returns to subscribe to an offering, for which they would otherwise have no interest, by allowing the holder to purchase one share of common stock at the subscription price with each warrant in the future.

Warrants are issued bundled with common stock in a new issue offering. The offering security is then called a "unit." The unit can include one or more common stock shares, and one or more warrants. After the effective date of the public offering, the units are traded in the listed securities market for a period of from 25 to 90 days, which is called the *quiet period* (see Chapter Seven, "New Issue Offerings"). Thereafter, the units are *unbundled* (separated) and then trade individually as common stocks and warrants in the same securities market.

Warrants can be exercised at any time up to expiration, and are similar to exchange traded (listed) Put and Call options on stock. However, it makes no sense to exercise warrants unless the market price of the stock is greater than the subscription price. Each warrant typically permits the holder to purchase one share of common stock, unless so stated otherwise (for example, two warrants per common share). Warrant trading is a little more conservative strategy than trading listed stock Call options because they can be held for longer periods without an excessive decrease in its time value. (The time value component of warrant and option prices decreases with time.)

Risk-seekers holding warrants typically *do not* exercise them; they will trade them in the marketplace. They can make a greater profit by trading warrants, instead of exercising the warrant, buying the stock, then selling it in the marketplace. Both the purchase and sale of stock generates a securities dealer's commission that can be significantly higher for trades of stock than for warrants.

The same market forces that govern stock option prices also determine warrant prices in the marketplace. Eventually, as the time to expiration nears, *scalpers* appear on the scene. These investors will buy warrants at a discount to the intrinsic value near expiration, from those not desiring to exercise the warrant, and typically require a fractional profit of 15% to 20% for their trouble.

Warrant Value

Warrants have little initial value when bundled with an IPO offering. The uncertainty of the success of the offering and the future stock price requires that warrants be essentially distributed as a *freebie*. For example, assume a hypothetical unit consists of two shares of common stock and one warrant with an offering priced of $24 per unit; each common share having an assigned a value of about $11.625 with a $0.75 value assigned for the warrant.

Warrants are a *derivative* security because value in the marketplace is determined by the current price of the common stock relative to the exercise price, and the time remaining to the warrant expiration. The theoretical value for the warrant is established by the Black-Scholes Pricing Model (a discussion of this mathematical model is well beyond the scope of this work), which is the basis for computing all derivative security values. The value in the marketplace will be determined after the unbundling of the unit, and is established by both the theoretical value as well as by market forces, such as liquidity and trading volume. In the marketplace, warrant value commonly consists of two components, the *intrinsic value* and the *time value*.

A warrant has intrinsic value when the common stock price is greater than the defined subscription price (called being "above water"). The intrinsic value is equal to the dollar amount by which the stock price is above the exercise price. However, warrants in which the underlying common stock price is below the exercise price (called being "below water") have zero intrinsic value, only time value. For example, should the common stock of the previously cited unit offering, having a subscription price of $15, trade up to $20 after being unbundled, the warrant's intrinsic value would then be $5. However, the market value would be greater than the intrinsic value because of the time value component. For this hypothetical example, the warrant value would then be about $8, with an intrinsic value of $5 and a time value of $3.

Time value is the term given for the dollar amount for any derivative security value amount that is in excess of the intrinsic value. It has several components that define its value; of which stock price volatility and time to expiration are the most predominant. Time value is greatest when the stock price is the same as the exercise price, and decreases toward zero with either increasing or decreasing stock price. A very low stock price would result in a warrant being worthless, while a very high stock price would result in a warrant value being essentially all intrinsic value.

Hypothetical Warrant Example

Typical warrant values, for the above-cited example, are shown below for a range of stock prices in Figure 2-1, "Hypothetical Warrant Value." The reader should note that this example is for illustrative purposes only, and the values given should only be construed as being illustrated for the hypothetical example.

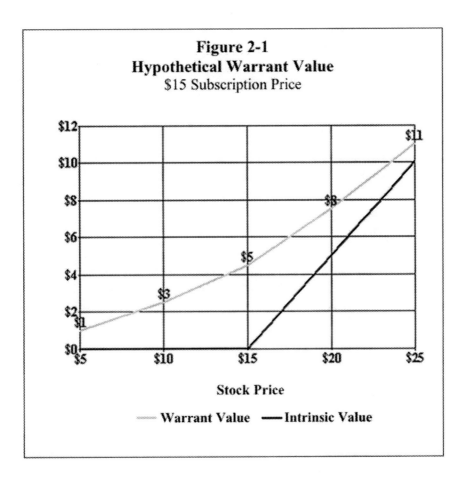

Figure 2-1
Hypothetical Warrant Value
$15 Subscription Price

Figure 2-1 shows, for the example cited above, that should the market price for the common stock trade at $15 (the subscription price), the price for the warrant would be about $5. This amount would be all time value because the intrinsic value would be zero at the common stock price of $15 (and lower). The time value amount decreases with the stock price either increasing above the exercise price or falling below it. If the stock price, for the above cited warrant example, increases to $25, the warrant would have a value of about $11, with $10 as intrinsic value and $1 as time value. Likewise, should this stock fall to $5, the warrant value would only have a time value of about $1 (with zero intrinsic value).

Time value also decreases with time to expiration. Therefore, all derivative securities are called "wasting assets" (especially listed stock options). At expiration, all time values go to zero. Theoretically, in the absence of scalpers mentioned previously, the warrant will only be worth the intrinsic value on the day of expiration. It will be worthless if it is under water. An approximation of the time value remaining, everything else remaining constant, can be estimated by taking the square root of the ratio of time remaining to the warrant expiration date. Therefore, the decrease in time value accelerates as expiration nears.

For example, after the first year of a four-year life, the time value remaining would be 87% of its initial value (the square root of 3 years/4 years), assuming no change in the stock price. The estimated time value after two years would be 70% ($\sqrt{2/4}$), and after three years, it would be 50% ($\sqrt{1/4}$). Thus, for this example, the decrease in initial time value (called time value erosion) would be 13% in the first year, 17% in the second year, 20% in the third year, and the final 50% in the last year, all other factors remaining constant.

Forced Redemption

Most warrants are *conditionally redeemable*. This is a provision that allows the issuer to redeem warrants before expiration, typically when the stock price reaches a value well above exercise price. A redemption notice essentially forces the exercising of the warrants, which increases the capitalization of the company.

Announcement of redemption will cause the warrant market price to drop to a value about 15% *below* the intrinsic value due to scalpers. Most warrant investors do not wish to exercise the warrant and buy the stock. They have purchased warrants in the marketplace, as a long-term substitute for listed Call stock options, with the potential of achieving a spectacular capital gain by selling the warrant with a substantial intrinsic value. Redemption attracts scalpers, who will initiate warrant bid prices at a discount to the intrinsic value so that warrant holders not desiring to exercise can unload their warrants. The scalpers make a quick profit by exercising warrants purchased at a discount to the intrinsic value. They then immediately sell the stock in the marketplace on the same day to insure that their profits are not eroded by a drop in the stock price. Inaction by the warrant holder results in the warrant being worthless after the redemption date.

For the above cited example, should the warrants be called when the stock price reaches $25, the warrant's market price of $11 just prior to the call (with a $10 intrinsic value), will drop in price to about $8.50 immediately upon a call announcement that forces a redemption. Sellers will try to get as high a price as possible, but scalpers who intend to exercise them need at least a 15% profit (which is represented by the bid price being below the intrinsic value).

American Depository Receipts

Many foreign corporations (corporations incorporated in foreign countries) desiring access to U.S. investors often offer shares to be traded on any of the U. S. securities markets. This is accomplished with a public offering of shares for foreign companies that meet all of the financial reporting requirements of the SEC. Thereafter, these securities will trade in both a securities market in the foreign country of residence, and the selected U. S. market. The U. S. shareholders are entitled to dividends and have voting rights, unless shares are issued as a non-voting class security.

However, another way for foreign companies to have access to U. S. investors is to offer American Depository Receipts (ADRs), which are issued by the U. S. branch of an international commercial bank. The ADRs are backed by the foreign corporation shares held on deposit in the international bank branch located in the country of issue. ADRs trading in the public U. S. markets must comply, as do foreign shares offered in a public offering and trading in U.S. markets (as mentioned above), with all SEC reporting requirements. Dividends, if any, are passed on to the ADR holders. However, these securities typically do not offer voting rights.

Each ADR issued can represent a different number of the company's shares. This will typically occur when the foreign country's currency rate would represent a price that would make the security a penny stock for U.S. owners. For example, ten million ADRs could be offered at $15 each, which would be backed by 100 million foreign shares on deposit having a dollar value of $1.50 per foreign common share (10 million ADRs at $15 would be equal to 100 million company shares at $1.50).

Listed ADRs are popular securities, but they carry additional risk to the normal, ever-present market risk. There is the currency rate risk, which would result in a lower ADR price when the dollar gains strength against the foreign country currency. There is also a dual trading market with the ADR trading in a U.S. market, and the foreign shares trading in the foreign country's stock market, thereby permitting international arbitrage trading that can cause volatility in both markets. Arbitrage occurs when astute speculators recognize that a difference in equivalent share prices (even fractional dollar differences) exists between the two markets. They will sell massive quantities of stock in one market while purchasing an equivalent number of shares at a cheaper price in the other market, thereby effecting a riskless transaction for the arbitrageur.

Many ADRs represent foreign company stocks which do not choose to file financial statements with the SEC. Typical financial statements and other material information, such as executive compensation and perquisites, as well as insider trading, are not disclosed. Consequently, these ADRs cannot be publicly traded, but are listed as over-the-counter securities on the "Pink Sheets" (see "Other OTC Markets" discussed in Chapter Five, "Securities Markets"). Aggressive sales representatives of the sponsoring securities dealers may tout such ADR securities. However, the lack of liquidity of these ADRs renders them as ineligible as an investment for the average individual investor.

Limited Partnership Units

Limited partnership (LP) interests are called *units,* and are offered to the public with a public offering through a securities dealer acting either as an underwriter making a firm commitment, or as a sales agent with a *best efforts only* type of underwriting agreement (see Chapter Seven, "New Issue Offerings"). Units are registered with the SEC and in all states in which the units are to be sold, unless falling under some provision where registration is not required (see Chapter Four, "Securities Regulations"). The underwriting compensation for *managed* LP offerings (firm commitments by the underwriters) is limited to 10% of the offering price. Sales compensation for *non-managed* offerings (best efforts only) can be much higher providing an incentive to sales personnel engaged in the distribution. The NASD guideline for non-managed offerings is 15%, but many such offerings are substantially higher. This writer has seen one such offering where the sales charge was 50%, a truly onerous charge.

Tradable Limited Partnership Units

Some businesses and sports franchises are organized as a LP where units are indeed liquid securities and are traded on one of the securities markets after the public offering. However, the Internal Revenue Service (IRS) considers these organizations to be acting as corporations and they are therefore taxed as such. The liquidity benefit that the investor receives is offset by the typical claim of *double taxation,* with income tax imposed both on the LP profits as an organization, as well as on the residual distributions made to the investors.

CHAPTER SUMMARY

There are a number of different types of business organizations offering different kinds of capitalization securities. Not all securities are suitable for the average investing public. Therefore, the individual investor must be completely aware of all of these different organizations and the securities offered for capitalization. Summaries of these are presented as follows by Table 2-4, "Summary of Business Organizations," and Table 2-5, "Summary of Investment Securities."

Table 2-4

Summary of Business Organizations

Organization Form	Securities Typically Issued	Investor	Securities Market
Public corporation:	Common stock	Public	Exchanges, or OTC on NASDAQ
	Preferred stock	Public	Exchanges, or OTC on NASDAQ
	Convertible preferred stock	Public	Exchanges, or OTC on NASDAQ
	Debt obligations	Public	Exchanges, or OTC with NASD dealers
	Convertible debt obligations	Public	Exchanges, or OTC with NASD dealers
	Warrants	Public	Exchanges, or OTC on NASDAQ
Private corporation:	Common stock	Private individuals	No public market (1)
Closely held corporation:	Common stock	Public	OTC Bulletin Board, or NQB Pink Sheets
Closed-end mutual fund:	Common stock	Public	Exchanges, or OTC on NASDAQ
	Preferred stock	Public	Exchanges, or OTC on NASDAQ
Real estate investment trust:	Common stock	Public	Exchanges, or OTC on NASDAQ
Unit investment trust:	Units	Public	No public market (2)
Limited partnership			
Publicly traded LP:	Units	Public	Exchanges, or OTC on NASDAQ
Direct participation program LP:	Units	Public	No public market (3)

Notes: (1), Isolated sale made to private individual who has had a prior business or personal relationship with seller.
(2), Units redeemable from trustee.
(3), Sales of units prohibited.

Table 2-5
Summary of Investment Securities

Security	Voting Right	Income	Other
Common stock:	Yes (1)	Dividends when declared	Dividends policy set by Board of Directors Shareholders have preemptive rights
Preferred stock:	No	Quarterly dividends	Dividends backed by anticipated earnings Promised dividends may be suspended by Board No preemptive rights (2) Risk of being called by issuer
Convertible preferred stock	No	Quarterly dividends	Dividends backed by anticipated earnings Promised dividends may be suspended by Board Preemptive rights (3) Risk of being called by issuer Right to convert to common stock at a fixed price Market price set as either the investment value, or by the common stock price
Convertible debenture:	No	Semi-annual interest	Fixed interest payments a legal obligation Preemptive rights (3) Risk of being called by issuer before maturity Right to convert to common stock at a fixed price Market price set as either the investment value, or by the common stock price
Warrant	No	No	Issued as a sweetener to common stock offering Redemption into common stock at a fixed price Considered as a derivative security (4)

Notes: (1), Stock other than single class stock, may not be issued with voting rights.
 (2), Preferred stockholders have no preemptive rights to additional common stock offerings. Additional preferred stock
  offerings made as different class preferred stock.
 (3), Convertible securities have preemptive rights on additional common stock offerings.
 (4), Market price dependent upon price of common stock relative to redemption price

Three
Securities Dealers and Investors

◆

Meeting the Players!

Business organizations that pursue public capitalization for starting or expanding business operations must depend upon securities dealers and investors. Securities dealers both underwrite new issue securities, and offer capitalization securities to the investing public. They also promote these securities in the marketplace, once issued, to suitable clients. Investors provide the capital needed by business, and are motivated by either hopes of capital appreciation from equity securities, or the desire for income from fixed-income securities.

The role performed by securities dealers in underwriting and distributing new issue securities to the public is called "wholesale" securities sales, and is explained in Chapter Seven, "New Issue Offerings." The other role performed by securities dealers to promote suitable investments to clients, and effecting securities transactions of all kinds for various types of public investors is called "retail" securities sales. This role is discussed in this chapter.

SECURITIES DEALERS

Securities dealers are firms that effect securities transactions, either for their own account, or for the public. Therefore, they are officially called "broker-dealers," but are referred herein as simply *securities dealers*. As stated above, when executing securities transactions for public investors, securities dealers engage in retail securities sales (as opposed to wholesale activities represented by the underwriting of new issue securities). All securities dealers are registered with, and are regulated by, a self-regulating organization called the National Association of Securities Dealers (NASD). They are also registered by the individual states in which they do business. The larger, national firms typically have memberships ("seats") on the New York and American stock exchanges, as well as being market makers in many stocks in the over-the-counter market listed on the National Association of Securities Dealers Automatic Quotation trading system (NASDAQ). The smaller, regional firms contract with the national firms to use their information services, as well as for both transacting and clearing securities transactions, and for holding the regional firm's clients' securities. The national firms that engage in the business of providing these services are called *correspondent* securities dealers.

Since the industry's deregulation in the 1970s, retail securities dealers have been classified as either *full service* or *discount* securities dealers. These describe the cost acquisition policy for transaction fees charged. The different types of full-service dealers and the traditional services provided, as well as the different types of discount dealers are both discussed herein. However, the information-age explosion of the 1990s resulted in the public becoming financially sophisticated with instant access to information on the securities, and market trading offered by Internet service providers through the personal computer. Therefore, both full service and discount dealers have adopted online computer trading services at discounted rates to compete for these hands-on investors. Where once the differences between dealers were clear, these differences are now gradually becoming indistinguishable.

Full Service Securities Dealers

Full service firms once represented the majority of the investing public. They are the traditional, old-line security dealers, which offer a full line of investment products and services, and typically hold seats on the major stock exchanges. Services include individual buy and sell stock recommendations backed by investment research reports. Investment products include common and preferred stocks, corporate and government bonds, mortgage-backed securities, variable annuities, and mutual funds. The national, full service securities dealers also offer accounts for the commodities trader, which permits trading in futures contracts that are regulated by the Commodities Futures Trading Commission.

Each full service securities dealer account is serviced by an individual Registered General Securities Representative who may also be called a *registered representative, investment executive, financial consultant,* or more simply a "stockbroker." They provide both securities suggestions and incidental investment advice to investors, either for securities held or those that are under consideration. A research department continuously analyzes most of the available traded stocks and typically classifies them into one of three main categories; buy, hold, and sell. Other variations consist of such categories as; strong buy, accumulate, or strong sell. It should be noted that because of their investment banking activities, securities dealers rarely would place a sell classification, especially a *strong* sell, on any stock since it would possibly preclude future underwriting deals.

Dealers are required to supervise brokers from becoming *loose cannons* and therefore violating securities regulations. Every firm is required to have a *compliance officer* who is responsible for insuring compliance with all securities laws, especially those concerning fraud and fair trade practices. However, the manager for each branch office is the supervising authority for compliance within the branch. He or she is required to report all compliance issues to the firm's compliance officer. The individual broker and employing securities dealer assume legal liability for soliciting only securities that are consistent with both the clients' stated investment objectives and financial status. The broker must also clearly explain investment risk prior to any securities purchases. The most frequent complaints about broker misconduct are securities recommendations that are unsuitable to the individual investor, and not explaining investment risk.

Brokers for the national full service firms tend to be closely supervised and are not allowed to make securities recommendations that are not authorized by the firm. They are permitted to make any suitable transaction requested by a client, which is called a "non-solicited order"; however, they are not permitted to solicit orders on individual securities that are different from their firm's classification. For example, a broker would not be authorized to recommend that a client buy stock that the firm classifies as sell. Nor could they recommend that shares held be sold to take a profit if the firm had a *buy* classification on that stock.

However, brokers of regional, full service securities dealers have more flexibility in dealings with clients. They are typically free to solicit securities transactions from clients that they feel may be in the best interest of the individual client, as long as the recommendations are suitable. Nonetheless, all brokers are required to comply with securities regulations prohibiting engaging in fraud and unfair trade practices.

Full-Service Dealer Commissions

Commission rates vary between full-service dealers. Each firm has its own fee schedule, and the commission formulas all include a fixed dollar charge, a percentage rate on the transaction dollar amount, and a fixed dollar charge for each round lot (100 shares) or fractional round lot. The commission charged tends to be much greater for a large quantity of a low priced stock, than for an equivalent dollar amount trade consisting of a lesser quantity, higher price stock. Most all the full-service dealers consider their commission schedule to be proprietary, and therefore not for public disclosure. Brokers must quote what the charge will be for any potential transaction upon request, but the formulae for such is rarely, if ever, publicly disclosed.

The typical commission charges for full-service dealers are shown in Figure 3-1, "Typical Full Service Dealer Commission, 101 to 5000 Shares." This table illustrates typical dollar sales charges for transactions of more than a round lot (100 shares) for various dollar amount trades.

For example, Figure 3-1 indicates that a $25,000 transaction amount for 500 shares at $50 per share will generate a commission charge of about $400. However, the charge for a transaction for the same dollar amount consisting of 5000 shares at $5 per share would be about $680. Thus, for any given dollar amount, a higher full-service dealer commission will result for purchasing a larger quantity of shares at a lower price.

Clients of full service securities dealers that make frequent transactions (called "traders") typically can receive a commission discount upon request, providing that the trading histories indicate that annual commissions generated in the account have reached a particular level. Should the securities dealer allow a client to receive a discount, the minimum that one should expect is 20%.

Minimum and Maximum Commissions

Each transaction (buy or sell) is subject to overriding minimum and maximum charges. Typical overriding commissions are $40 minimum per transaction, and $100 maximum per round lot (100 shares). Every full service securities dealer not only has its unique commission schedule, but also overriding minimum and maximum ticket charges. Any transaction, in which the applicable commission schedule would indicate a lower dollar value than the overriding minimum, will generate the higher minimum charge amount. Any transaction in which the applicable commission schedule would indicate a higher dollar commission than the overriding maximum dollar amount per round lot will result in being charged the overriding maximum round lot limit amount for round lot (or fractional round lot).

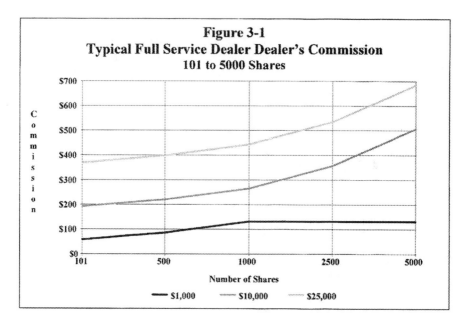

Figure 3-1
Typical Full Service Dealer Dealer's Commission
101 to 5000 Shares

For example, a transaction for 200 shares (two round lots) at a price of $125 per share, totaling $25,000, would be charged only $200 in commissions (assuming a $100 per round lot maximum charge) instead of an approximate $375 commission as indicated by Figure 3-1. However, the charge for a transaction for the same dollar amount for 500 shares at $50 per share would be about $400 (from Figure 5-1), which would be less than the overriding maximum dollar amount of $500 ($100 times 5 round lots).

Odd-Lot Trading Commissions

An *odd-lot* transaction refers to any order to buy or sell a quantity of stock, which is less than the standard, 100-share round-lot. Odd-lot orders are executed differently than orders for one or more round lots. Therefore, the commission schedule charged for odd lots are different from what the typical commission schedule would indicate.

The full-service dealer commission for odd-lot transactions typically depends solely upon the transaction dollar amount for the order. A typical example odd-lot commission schedule amount is shown below in Figure 3-2, "Typical Full Service Dealer Commission, 100 Shares or Less." This figure illustrates the typical full service broker's sales charge for transactions involving quantities less than the standard round lot. However, odd-lot orders are also subject to the overriding minimum and maximum transaction charges.

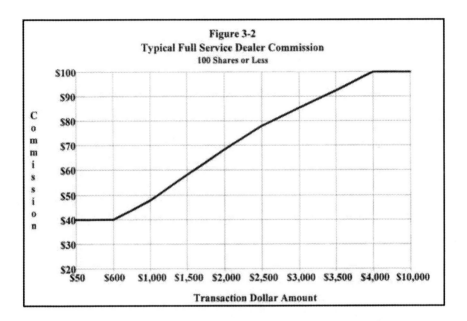

The reader should note that the typical $40 minimum commission would be charged for an odd-lot transaction of about $600 or less, and the typical $100 maximum commission would be charged for odd-lot transactions of about $4000 or more. Therefore, for this example, the charge for a transaction of 10 shares at $12 per share, totaling $120, would be the $40 minimum ticket charge, which would represent a 25% commission rate. In contrast, the charge for two shares of a $50,000 per share stock (such as Berkshire Hathaway, Class A stock) would only be the $100 overriding maximum ticket charge. (As an aside, the NYSE has sanctioned a 10-share round lot for Berkshire Hathaway's Class A stock.)

Penny Stock Commissions

Penny stock is the term used for stocks whose market price is less than $5 per share (real penny stocks have market prices less than $1 per share). These stocks are particularly risky; therefore, brokers have the responsibility to disclose risks for penny stock offerings by issuing a SEC published *Penny Stock Risk Disclosure* pamphlet. They also have the responsibility for determining that the penny stock speculation is consistent with the investor's financial status, and the ability to withstand a complete loss.

Commissions on penny stock transactions usually are a percentage of the transaction dollar amount. The percent rate charge is illustrated by the flat portion on the curve for the $1000 transaction, in Figure 3-1, for quantities greater than 1000 shares (which represent share prices less than $1). However, penny stock commissions for some securities dealers may also include a substantial fixed charge per share in addition to the fixed percent rate fee on the transaction dollar amount.

Asset-Based Accounts

Most of the national, full service firms also offer individual, asset-based accounts, where the client receives investment advice from a registered *investment advisor,* who is also a registered broker. The client is charged an annual asset based fee and a nominal flat-charge transaction fee to cover the dealer's cost for each transaction. This type account would appeal to investors having substantial investment assets that they plan to actively trade in the account; as well as for either buy and hold type investors, semi-active traders (about one trade a month), or investors seeking income from fixed-income securities with a substantial lump sum investment. For example, one national firm advertises an asset-based account that is available for a minimum deposit of $100,000 with an annual, asset-based fee of 1.5% plus a $24.95 flat-charge per transaction. The annual fee rate for this dealer is gradually reduced, with greater asset values, to 0.4% for assets over $75 million.

Regional Securities Dealers

Many full service securities dealers are local firms that do business in a particular geographical area. They are registered broker-dealers that comply with all securities regulations, but who usually do not have seats on the major exchanges, and also do not make a market in over-the-counter stocks traded on the NASDAQ.

Therefore, regional firms usually contract with one of the national securities dealers to place client accounts with the national dealer acting as a "correspondent" securities dealer. Client orders are wired directly to the correspondent firm who then executes the transaction either in the over-the-counter market, or on an exchange floor at either of the national exchanges or on any of the regional stock exchanges.

Investment research reports from the correspondent firms are also made available to clients of the regional securities dealers. Payments for purchases are typically made by check payable to the correspondent firm. The firm clears all trades, keeps and maintains all securities in street name accounts, and distributes periodic account balance and confirmation statements (usually in the name of the regional securities dealer). The regional dealers maintain client files and transaction records for up to three years, as is required by law for all securities firms.

Full-Service Dealers' Advantages

A full service securities dealer offer the widest range of investment security products, and includes open-end mutual funds that can be held in street name in the client's brokerage account. Individual sales representatives provide investment advice, and recommendations based on investor suitability. This personal relationship can be a stabilizing influence to nervous investors during volatile market conditions. Most securities dealers have agreements with various dealer distributed, open-end mutual fund companies. These fund shares are also available to clients of regional firms that have a correspondent relationship with a clearing member securities dealer.

Many of the national firms also engage in the wholesale securities business by providing capitalization for governments and businesses. Therefore, retail clients of these firms have an opportunity to participate in purchasing these securities as a new issue. Some regional securities dealers will also underwrite new issue securities for smaller, local firms attempting to go public. They may also participate in a new issue distribution as a member of an underwriting syndicate, or selling group. (These functions are explained in Chapter Seven, "New Issue Offerings.")

Retail clients of the national firms will not incur a commission on trades that the dealer executes as a market maker in the over-the-counter market. Confirmation statements will indicate, "Trade made as a market maker in this security." They also have access to extensive, in-house, investment staff recommendations, which are also available as a correspondent to clients of regional firms. However, the most widely reported advantage is that they tend to get better execution on limit orders than clients of some discount dealers. *Poor* execution, as used here, refers to the illegal practice of *front running*, the practice of making a transaction in the marketplace prior to executing the trade as a market maker with the client, typically to the detriment of the client.

All brokers are under pressure to generate the firm's minimum required commission dollars, and national full-service brokers are "encouraged" to promote in-house products. The long-time brokers of the national securities dealers will have large client books. They have demonstrated investment success for their many clients. These brokers will generate much more than the minimum commissions required by the employing firm. Therefore, they tend to be shielded from pressure to promote dubious in-house investment products. Other than the lucrative financial incentives that are typically offered on these products, brokers of regional securities dealers tend to be free from any pressure to promote the in-house products of the correspondent firm.

Full-Service Dealers' Disadvantages

The obvious disadvantage of the full-service dealer is the high commission fees imposed on broker-serviced accounts. In addition, clients of regional full-service dealers will incur a commission on trades in which the correspondent firm makes as a market maker in the over-the-counter market. Therefore, active traders in over-the-counter stocks are seriously disadvantaged if they use a regional, full-service, securities dealer linked to a national firm as a correspondent market maker. They pay commissions to the regional securities dealer on trades that would otherwise generate no commissions if they were made as a client of the national, market-making, correspondent securities dealer.

Brokers of the full service securities dealers have pressure applied to promote in-house sponsored investment products, in addition to generating minimum required sales commission dollars. New securities representatives are added to increase the retail securities sales force during periods of economic expansion. These not-yet-productive, new brokers typically will have a small *client book* (a book containing the record of securities investments of assigned investors). Therefore, most of the new broker sales are typically generated by cold calling prospective clients with whom the broker has no prior knowledge.

To generate interest with cold calls, sales pitches to strangers typically puff up the potential benefits of a suggested security, and ignore both the broker's obligation for investment suitability, as well as for providing risk disclosure. Despite the close supervision that newer brokers receive, it is difficult to adhere fully to the spirit of the law, let alone the letter of the law, when one is working diligently to generate commissions in order to keep his or her job.

Discount Securities Dealers

Discount securities dealers offer reduced charges for securities transactions. They first appeared in the 1970s following the deregulation of securities trading commission rates. The discount dealers at first represented a small fraction of public securities accounts, and offered stock trading at discount rates without providing clients with investment information and advice. Over the years, there has been an increase in the number of individuals trading securities through discount securities dealers, especially those offering online trading services. The explosion in the personal computer market, online information services, and electronic communications networks, enabled the bull market explosion of the 1990s. In fact, this type trading has become so popular, that the national full service securities dealers, as well as established discount dealers, now offer online trading at discounted rates.

Sales representatives for the discount securities dealers usually do not solicit transactions from clients, and are usually paid a salary for executing trades. They typically do not share in the commissions because of the low commission rates charged. Discount dealers make money with a high-volume transaction business.

Discount Dealer Commission Categories

Discount securities dealers, as well as full-service dealers with online trading accounts, offer retail securities services that can be classified into one of four following categories:

1. the *value* dealer
2. the *flat-charge* dealer
3. the *cut-rate* dealer
4. the *commissionless* dealer

The value dealer charges either a fixed percent rate on the transaction amount, or a fixed dollar charge per share subject to a minimum dollar ticket charge (referring to *buy* and *sell* tickets written for each transaction), which is typically about $35 minimum per trade. This type of discount dealer would be more suitable to the individual trading moderate quantities (500 to 1000 shares) of lower priced stocks ($5 to $20 per share).

The flat-charge dealer charges a fixed dollar amount per transaction regardless of the share price, and typically imposes a share limitation such as offering "$39 per transaction for up to 1000 shares." Frequency of trading is encouraged, and the flat-charge rates decrease with an increasing number of trades made in a calendar quarter.

For example, E*Trade advertises a $4.95 transaction charge for "active traders" with an online account. However, for this particular discount dealer, reading the fine print reveals that this charge applies only to transactions made for market orders on exchange-listed stocks on trades exceeding more than 75 in a calendar quarter. Transactions which number less than 29 in a quarter will incur a flat-charge of $14.95 for up to 5000 shares of any listed stock, and $19.95 for both NASDAQ stock and all limit orders. In addition, broker assisted transactions will add an additional $15 per trade. Each flat-charge dealer has a different fee schedule, which is frequently changed; nevertheless, this E*Trade example is typical of what is available. Therefore, the flat-charge dealer is the dealer of choice for active stock traders, especially day-trading investors.

The cut-rate dealer typically has a commission schedule similar to that described previously for the full-service dealer except the rates and fixed charges are lower. They compete with the full service firms for clients desiring broker assistance, but at a discounted price. Charles Schwab, one of the oldest and largest of the discount dealers, uses a cut-rate commission schedule for broker-assisted transactions; however, a flat-charge fee is used with online accounts. Schwab's cut-rate schedule uses a percent of the trade amount plus a fixed dollar charge. The rate decreases from 1.4% for a $2500 trade, down to 0.068% for trades over $500,000. The corresponding fixed charge is $22 for a $2500 trade, increasing to $205 for a $500,000 or greater trade. The minimum commission is the greater of either $37.50 per trade or 6 cents a share up to 1000 shares and 3 cents a share over 1000. The maximum charge is $49 for the first 100 shares plus $0.50 a share thereafter.

Cut-rate discount dealers are of interest to investors that have moderate amounts of capital (from $10,000 up to $100,000) with a growth investment objective from stock purchases. They are best for either the buy and hold type investor, the semi-active trader who makes about one trade a month, and investors seeking income from particular fixed-income securities, but not for fixed-income, open-end mutual funds.

The commissionless dealers advertise *zero commission* per transaction. These are similar to the full-service dealers offering asset based fee accounts. However, the required minimum deposit for this dealer is lower, typically about $10,000, and the annual charge may either be an asset based fee or a fixed fee. Some may also charge a flat-charge fee per transaction, and others put a limit on the number of transactions allowed. This type dealer is attractive to the investor with the minimum dollar amount required for such an account, who intends to achieve capital gains by actively trading lower priced stocks. A buy and hold type investor should avoid this type of dealer.

Benefits and Difficulties with Discount Securities Dealers

The main advantage of the discount dealer is the low commission fees charged. Therefore, they are the securities dealers of choice for the active, financially sophisticated investor.

Most discount dealers do not offer the full range of investment products that are offered by full-service dealers, and limit the number of open-end mutual funds to a few no-load mutual fund families. They should not be considered by unsophisticated investors that need handholding by a broker, as well as investors that only desire to invest in open-end mutual funds.

Common complaints include unfavorable executions of client orders, and the most frequent (but less serious) complaint is *harvesting*. Harvesting is the practice of charging fees for a variety of common services, such as: delivering stock certificates; redeeming bonds at maturity; issuing copies of past account statements; making copies of investment research reports; and executing Power of Attorney and Stock Power (assigning ownership) certificates. The deep discount dealers have even more services on which charges are levied and greater dollar amount charges. In all fairness, it must be recognized that reduced dealer income associated with discounted commissions requires that harvesting be practiced as an economic necessity.

Another disadvantage is that an individual representative does not usually service the investor's account. Orders are made either online, or by toll-free telephone numbers typically answered by the first available broker. Online accounts process orders electronically without the assistance of a broker. Investors must make their investment decisions without benefit of incidental investment advice from a broker, who should be acquainted with the client. Brokers that assist in client transactions do not have the time to advise clients because of the discounted transaction charges. Therefore, many discount dealers advertise for financially sophisticated investors and typically screen their clients. In spite of established screening criteria, they are still legally responsible for allowing suitable investment transactions, and giving advice on investment risk.

Most discount securities dealers cannot afford to have a research department providing in-house investment research reports. However, they do provide commercially available subscription research reports issued by investment analyst firms, such as the Dow Jones Financial News Service. Research reports can be downloaded into clients' computers for those having online accounts, and must make sense and be understood fully. Every investor is fully responsible for accepting the outcome of any investment; therefore, transactions should be made only after careful consideration of both the potential reward and the risk.

However, the biggest disadvantage of online securities dealers, for those who are interested in new issue securities, are that these dealers typically do not participate in the investment banking function of underwriting legitimate new issue securities. Any new issues that may be offered are distributed as an unmanaged offering on a *best effort* sales basis, in which the dealer gets a high percentage of the offering price for distributing such issues. The NASD guideline for such offerings is 15%; however, most unmanaged offering sales charges run higher at about 20%.

INVESTORS

The function of the securities industry is to facilitate the capitalization of both businesses and governments, and to provide a marketplace for the exchange of publicly issued securities. Investors are those persons sought by the securities industry to provide resources for the capitalization function. Investors are not all financially astute equals; therefore, securities laws attempt to provide fair investment opportunity when dealing with the public. This has been accomplished by regulating both the issuing of public securities and everyone associated with their distribution and exchange. In addition, persons giving investment advice to the public for a fee (called *investment advisors)* are required to be registered, and are regulated by both the Federal government and individual state governments, which is discussed in Chapter Four, "Securities Regulations."

Though the antifraud provisions of the securities laws cover every investor, the fair practices and full disclosure provisions do not protect every investor. These include high net worth individual investors, and financial institutions, both of whom are called "accredited investors." Investor classifications are described in the sections that follow.

Accredited Investors

Securities dealers often offer securities to only *accredited investors.* This category consists of both institutional investors (defined below), and high-income individuals having a high net worth Accredited investors are generally not protected by securities laws, which are mainly designed to protect the public from fraud. Therefore, accredited investors are prime targets for securities brokers distributing high-risk securities, such as private placements and both limited and general partnerships.

Securities offerings to accredited investors must comply with all the anti-fraud regulations established by law but they are not registered with the SEC. The SEC does not review the offering circulars; therefore, the information disclosure provided is typically limited requiring the accredited investor to determine whether the financial information contained in the offering circular is complete. The theory behind the lack of SEC regulation for accredited investors is that they should have the financial sophistication to understand potential risks for these investment offerings, and if not, they have sufficient resources to retain professional advice.

Institutional Investors

Institutions are defined as pension funds, banks, insurance companies, labor union funds, corporate profit-sharing plans, college endowment funds, and investment companies (mutual funds). Collectively, institutional assets represent over two years of spending by the U.S. government, half of which are in equities (corporate stock), and the balance split between fixed income (debt securities) funds and hybrid funds consisting of both fixed income and equity securities. Therefore, the great numbers of securities traded daily by institutional investors literally drives the financial markets.

Institutional investors, as well as professional investors, often use "arbitrage" to achieve a higher, short-term return with little risk when conditions seem appropriate. Arbitrage is the simultaneous buying and selling of securities that are traded in different marketplaces, whenever the price difference between the marketplaces is greater than the anticipated yield that can be obtained from typically available short-term securities, such as T-bills.

The most common use of arbitrage in the securities markets is called *program trading*. A portfolio of specific quantities of various common stocks, which represents a model portfolio of a stock market index that is also traded in the futures market, is constructed for a given dollar amount. The most common index used is the Standard and Poor's 500 Stock Index. A properly modeled stock portfolio will change value, over time, consistent with the change in the stock index. The real time value of the S&P 500 Index (called the "cash value") is then continually compared with the current price for any future settlement month for an S&P 500 Index futures contract.

A futures contract is a binding agreement for the future delivery of a specific quantity of a given commodity by a seller to a buyer at a pre-established contract price. The seller is called "being short" and is obligated to make the delivery. The buyer is called "being long" and is obligated to receive the delivery and pay the contract price. Commodities futures contracts can be made for delivery of various natural resources, agricultural products, livestock products, and financial instruments. A cash payment upon delivery is made on the settlement date.

However, stock index futures contracts use a cash settlement (instead of a basket of stock making up the index) which is made at the contracted price, and represents the value of the stock index value in the future. Futures traders speculate on what they think the value of the S&P 500 Index will be in the future. A settlement date is set for each calendar quarter, up to two years in advance. Therefore, the current S&P 500 Index price for any future contract month represents the collective wisdom of futures traders, and can be higher or lower than the current index's cash value.

The settlement value for each S&P 500 Index contract is 500 times the index value at settlement. (One contract would be valued at $600,000 at a S&P Index value of 1200.) Long positions represent contract purchasers with bullish opinions, while short positions represent contract sellers with bearish opinions. (Bulls expect stock prices to increase and bears expect stock prices to decline.) If the bullish opinion proves to be correct and the index increases in value, the long position's account would be credited with the difference between the contract's cash index, dollar value and the contract's dollar value established when making the commitment. The short position's account would be debited the net amount. The opposite would result should the bearish opinion have been correct.

There is little risk with arbitrage. Preprinted buy or sell order tickets are maintained for stocks that model the index. These orders are executed simultaneously with opposite orders for S&P 500 futures contracts of equal dollar value, when the difference between the cash index and the futures price is greater than the "cost-to-carry" the portfolio dollar value. (The cost-to-carry is the rate of return of an equivalent duration T-bill or T-bond to the particular futures contract settlement month of interest.) Futures contracts are sold and the stocks making up the modeled portfolio are purchased when the future's price for the index exceeds the cost-to-carry. Futures index contracts are bought and the stocks making up the modeled portfolio are then sold short when the future's contract price is lower than the cash index by more than the cost-to-carry.

The values of both the S&P 500 Index modeled portfolio and the futures contracts converge as the future's contract settlement date nears. Both futures contracts and stock positions are closed with offsetting transactions (selling long stock or covering short stock, and buying short futures contracts or selling long futures contracts). The result is to realize a gain of the initial difference between the modeled index stock portfolio and the index future's contract. This riskless spread strategy can achieve yields greater than that available with short-term money rates, and requires only that the executions for the index modeled stock portfolio and the corresponding index futures contracts be nearly simultaneous.

Accredited Individual Investors

Securities dealers often offer securities only to accredited individual investors. This category consists of individuals having a net worth of over $ 1 million, with an annual income of at least $200,000 per year or $300,000 if married with joint income (and with every expectation that this income level will continue in the future). Securities laws protect against fraud, and require full disclosure for securities offered to the public. Full disclosure of restricted securities are not required for accredited investors; therefore, accredited investors are prime targets for securities brokers distributing high-risk, exempt securities such as private placements, exempt limited partnerships, and general partnership working interests (typically masquerading as limited partnerships units).

The information disclosure contained in offering circulars is typically limited because the SEC does not review exempt and restricted securities offerings. It is up to the accredited investor to determine whether the financial information contained in the offering circular is complete. The assumption behind the lack of SEC regulation for accredited investors is that they have the financial sophistication to understand potential risks for these securities offerings. If not, they have sufficient resources to retain professional advice. However, sales reps of many not-so-scrupulous securities firms peddle such high-risk securities through cold calling the public. Although this practice is illegal, the amount of money involved is too great to pass up (especially with a fraudulent securities offering).

Smart Money

The term "Smart Money" refers to investors that make use of defined investment rules. Charles Dow is credited as the first person to deduce a series of tenets for market investments. He combined the stock prices for a select number and types of companies, and created a price average for the two different groups. The invention of the market averages in the late 1800's allowed the stock market to be an indication of the overall economy. The supposition was simple. The economy should be strong when most manufacturers were producing at near capacity, and the manufactured goods were all being transported to market. Therefore, Dow focused on an Industrial Average and a Transportation Average (which consisted of railroad companies at that time).

Dow was also the first to report on the wavelike price behavior of the newly established market averages, and set down investment rules based on the relative movements between the Industrial Average and the Transportation Average. These so-called, "technical" guidelines, as well as other indicators generated over the years by a host of other technical analysts, are not absolute, as are the laws of physics. However, they are based on observations of reactions of the investing public, which are correct most of the time.

Smart Money investors, who include professional money managers, realize that markets do not go up forever, nor do they fall to zero. They understand that stock market downturns of about 20% are frequent events, while market declines in excess of 30% occur several times a decade. They also are aware that a 60%, or greater, market downturn occurs about every 6 decades, as for example the downturns following both the late 1920's market bubble as well as the one following the late 1990's market bubble. Smart Money investors also stay aware of the financial conditions, called "fundamentals," of various sectors of business, and use the stock market wavelike price movement to full advantage by using select technical indicators as tools to help determine when to buy securities, and when to take profits. They have preset limits for both taking profits, and limiting losses. In essence, Smart Money approaches investing as an art. They use various investment guidelines, and have the discipline to adhere to the selected strategy. They also have the "smarts" to decide when the time may be appropriate to abandon their previously established strategies.

Nostradamus' "black mirror" aside, no one has yet invented a crystal ball that can foresee the exact future as far as the stock market is concerned. Therefore, Smart Money are never completely out of the market with 100% cash, nor are they ever 100% invested, which is called leaving some "powder dry." Smart Money includes not only managers hired by investment companies and other institutions, such as pension funds, but also private individuals that have studied the markets, and have become self-educated in investment strategy and tactics while managing their own account. These private individuals have come to realize that the only persons that have the most interest in managing their money are themselves.

Day Traders

Online trading has also become very popular with the individual "day trader" (also referred to as a "scalper"). Day trading should be considered as the opposite of Smart Money. Day traders make hundreds of trades each day, attempting to "scalp" a fraction of a dollar profit per share from each trade, and then closing out all positions by the end of the trading day. Many day traders operate out of a day trading salon, which are offered by a number of specialty, day-trading, securities dealers having real-time quotation services. However, online securities dealers also encourage the day trader with super-low, flat charge rates for active traders.

Day trading was once the domain of the sophisticated professional. It has become popular with risk-seeking individuals in the last 10 years, but with universally poor results. What many do not realize is that day trading is pure gambling. Unless there is a buying or selling panic in the markets, an individual stock price change over any given 30 to 60 minute period during the trading day, is as likely to increase as it is to decrease (random walk theory). Therefore, attempting to scalp a fractional point gain is just as likely to result in a fractional point loss.

Decimal pricing was fully implemented in 2001, and the average spread (difference between the bid and asked prices) runs about six cents (1/16 dollar). Market orders to buy are executed at the asked price while market orders to sell are executed at the bid price. Consequently, the spread range would need to move about 1/8 dollar for the trader to make a 1/16-dollar profit. Assuming a nominal $15 charge on both the buy and sell transactions for a 1000 share order (larger quantities are not likely to get immediate execution), a 12¢ per share market price gain move will result in a 6¢ per share gain because of the spread. The result will be a net profit of $32.50 after nominal sales charges. However, a 12¢ per share market price decline results in 18¢ share price loss, with the total loss (including commissions) of $217.50. The trader must make a profit on seven of eight trades in order to break even. However, over any given period during the trading day, odds of four out of eight trades going the scalpers' way would be more realistic. Therefore, one could expect to lose $740 on every eight trades of 1000 shares.

It becomes even more improbable to make money if the transaction charge is greater, such as $30 per trade, which appears to be the fee of choice for the majority of day trading dealers. Here, the trader needs to be correct 100 out of 101 trades just to break even (one loss trade negates 100 win trades). Therefore, it is inevitable that within a very short time (typically weeks), most day trading individuals will completely lose their typical $50,000 minimum initial deposit required for day trading accounts.

Public Investors

Greed causes many investors to be enticed into high-risk securities touted by high-pressure salespersons. One high-risk security that attracts the greedy is the *penny stock* offering—stock offered at less than $5 per share. These have such high risk that the SEC requires giving a penny stock, risk disclosure document as well as a prospectus to penny stock investors. Investors in high-risk securities must demonstrate that such securities are suitable by providing a financial statement.

Therefore, individuals not included in the accredited investor category should never engage in conversation with cold calling telephone solicitors touting new issue penny stocks, as well as other high-risk securities, such as private placements, and both limited and general partnerships. Email solicitations of such securities should be immediately deleted. Even though email and cold-call solicitations to the public for such securities are illegal, such practices are commonplace, using loopholes in the law. Anyone indicating an interest will quickly be declared qualified to participate in such offerings by these rogue brokers. Once these dealers have a check in hand, virtually little can be done to get money returned to those who may later have a change-of-heart.

All individual, public investors require the services of registered securities dealers to make investments into publicly held securities. Investors considering initial public offerings have little choice but to maintain accounts with several of the major underwriting securities dealers in order to have an opportunity to be able to participate in such offerings. These firms typically will make firm commitments for the issue of such securities, and provide adequate "due diligence" on the companies offering such new issues. The investor can never be assured that the investment will be a success. However, underwriters making a firm-commitment in bringing securities public, and maintaining support for them in the marketplace, are key factors in whether the securities may eventually be a success.

Successful IPO investing is not solely the result of the selection of a superior performing new issue security. Only a few, so-called "hot" issues, increase in market price to a multiple of the price at which they are offered to the public. New issue investment success is largely dependent upon understanding new issue behavior and adopting a new issue investment strategy, as well as having the discipline to maintain this strategy. The key to making money, once a new issue is obtained, is to use appropriate trading tactics in the days or months after the effective date (see Chapter Ten, "New Issue Investment Tactics"). Since most legitimate new issues can only be obtained from established full service underwriters, the investor is generally required to maintain accounts with several of these firms in order to have the opportunity to participate in the new issue market. Purchasing recent new issue securities in the marketplace with non-underwriting dealers severely limits any chance of making money with new issues (see Chapter One, "Getting Rich Quickly").

The conventional wisdom for a risk-seeking investor having little knowledge of securities and the financial markets, is to use a broker associated with a full-service securities dealer, in which a comfortable relationship has been developed, so that the client can receive all the benefits cited previously. Risk-seeking investors, who demonstrate that they have sufficient income and net worth to engage in high-risk securities purchases, should ask the broker to notify the client whenever new issue securities are available. The dealer always assumes legal responsibility for investment suitability and risk disclosure; therefore, the risk-seeking investor should feel assured that all new issues offered by the securities broker will be suitable.

However, investors who look only for capital appreciation opportunities by trading previously issued stock in the marketplace should then consider the full range of securities dealers available. As stated previously, the two basic types of securities dealers are the full service firm and the discount dealer (which were discussed in detail earlier in this chapter under "Securities Dealers"). Their different commission rate schedules make them suitable for different individual investors. Therefore, individual investors should consider which type of securities firm is best suited for them.

Four
Securities Industry Regulations

✦

The Rules of the Game!

Everyone considering marketable securities as investment vehicles should have knowledge about the business organization and the type of security being offered (as were discussed in Chapter Two, "Business Capitalization Securities"). Investors should also be acquainted with the different functions of the securities industry, and its laws and regulations. Existing securities laws and regulations evolved out of necessity; therefore, all public investors should realize what these are, why they exist, and how important they for individual investors.

The financial prosperity in the last decade of the 20th century placed many of the existing financial and securities regulations—the bulk of which are over 60 years old—in jeopardy. The common argument given was that they are too ancient for the present economic environment and need reform. The individuals pushing for drastic reform either were serving special interest groups, or apparently have never even tried to understand the environment that precipitated the Stock Market Crash of 1929 and the necessity for securities regulations. Perhaps both reasons were valid. The assault on these regulations has quieted in recent years, but one wonders for how much longer. The corporate governance and accounting scandals that were disclosed in the first few years of this third millennium strongly indicate that fraud is alive and well. The adage that *"Those who ignore history are condemned to relive It."* is as valid now as whenever it was first stated.

THE SECURITIES INDUSTRY

The securities industry is represented by a great number of individuals and firms who are all registered by the federal government, or its authorized agencies, in one or more specific functions. Regulation of securities that provide capitalization for business organizations, and the exchange of these securities in the public securities markets, is the responsibility of the Securities and Exchange Commission (SEC). However, these do not cover activities of those engaged in trading commercial futures contracts for commodities. Regulation for commodities futures (the industry effecting contracts between buyers and sellers of various goods at some future date) is the responsibility of the Commodities Futures Trading Commission (CFTC). A discussion of futures contracts is beyond the scope of this work and therefore is not covered herein.

Individuals entering the securities industry are required to have sponsorship by a member organization, pass an appropriate qualifying examination, and pursue annual continuing educational requirements. Individuals that solicit buy and sell transactions for securities investments with the public must be a *Registered General Securities Representative.* These individuals typically are labeled by various titles, such as "financial consultant," "investment executive," or "registered representative"; but they are simply called a "stockbroker." A firm registered as a *Securities Broker-Dealer*—that is simplified herein to *securities dealer*—must employ only registered individuals, whatever title they elect to put on business cards. Other individuals, who solicit only specific securities, such as mutual funds or municipal bonds, are allowed to pass less inclusive qualifying examinations that are tailored strictly for either of these types of securities.

Supervision of sales representatives is the responsibility of the branch manager, who is registered as a *General Securities Sales Supervisor/Branch Office Manager.* Individuals managing persons engaged in investment banking—offering new issue securities to the public—must be registered as a *General Securities Principal.* The chief financial officer, as well as any person involved in the financial and operational management, must be registered as a *Financial and Operations Principal.*

Every securities dealer must be a member of the National Association of Securities Dealers (NASD), a self-regulating organization over which the SEC has oversight responsibility. They must also be a member of the Securities Investor Protection Corporation (SIPC). This nonprofit organization protects client accounts from being affected by any securities dealer's failure, but not from losses due to fraud, high-risk securities, or market downturns.

The securities industry, as mentioned previously, facilitates the capitalization of business organizations and governments, by promoting the distribution of new issue equity securities (stocks) and debt obligations (bonds, debentures and notes) to the public—subject to both SEC and NASD regulations. Public offerings are made by the issuing organization through a securities dealer underwriting the new issue, acting as what is called an "investment banker." There may be multiple underwriting firms involved as well as a number of other securities dealers acting only as selling agents (see Chapter Seven, "New Issue Offerings"), but there is only one *managing* underwriter.

The industry also provides for, and maintains, a fair and orderly marketplace for the exchange of securities that are not listed for trading on registered stock exchanges. U.S. stock exchanges consist of the two national exchanges, the New York Stock Exchange (NYSE) and the American Stock Exchange (AMEX), and a number of regional stock exchanges. The exchange of U. S. Treasury securities, as well as municipal debt obligations are subject to the SEC, NASD, and Municipal Securities Rulemaking Board (MSRB) regulations, as applicable, even though they are both exempt from registration with the SEC.

PRE-REGULATION TRADING ENVIRONMENT

The economic transition of the developed countries from agrarian to industrial began in the 18th century with the invention of the steam engine by James Watt. Industries were then freed from being located adjacent to flowing rivers and streams to use water as their power source. The 19th century saw this new technology expand with its adoption to the steam locomotive, which provided easy access to faraway places by land routes. Electric power was developed at the turn of the 20th century with the invention of the electric light bulb and electrical power generators, and quickly surpassed steam power.

By 1919, Europe's economy labored under the burden of five years of poison gas warfare, and a generation of young men were killed or permanently injured. However, the United States emerged from World War I as the strongest economic nation in the world. The 1920's were dominated by the loosening of moral principles, the so-called "flapper era." This euphoria was also experienced in the stock market with an unprecedented amount of leverage being used to purchase securities investments. One could buy securities for 10 cents on the dollar. The Dow Jones Industrial Average (DJIA) increased by a then phenomenal 25% per year, year after year, from 1921 to a high in 1929. A 500% increase over 8 years! It was inevitable that the average working individual would be attracted to the stock market as the investment of choice in the 1920's.

Previously the domain of the wealthy, the average working person could become rich by purchasing securities using credit extended by dealers in securities. The market bubble allowed stocks to be bought at a tiny fraction of the price and additional stock purchases could be made without depositing any additional money as stock prices increased. Investors became convinced that *new financial times* had been discovered. (Note, the exact same words were uttered in the late 1990s during the dot-com bubble). A speculator could have achieved a rate of return of over 60% per year totaling more than 4000% over this 8-year period by borrowing 90% of the price for the thirty common stocks making up the Dow Jones Industrial Average. Little wonder that the public should become attracted to a bull stock market, especially in its later stages.

In the midst of this runaway market, securities abuses became rampant. Fraudulent stock certificates were issued for nonexistent businesses, because there was no authority to insure full and fair disclosure. Stock price manipulation became a prevailing practice with some securities dealers, who were not satisfied with just earning commissions on securities trades and obtaining capital appreciation of securities held in their own account. Unscrupulous dealers collaborated in stimulating the public's interest in selected securities by first engaging in *wash sale* activities that artificially increased trading volume and stock prices. After over-leveraged public investors had jumped on these apparently hot investments and increased prices even higher, the syndicate would then drive down the market prices with an avalanche of short sell orders. This forced margined investors to sell therefore causing a waterfall decline. The syndicate members thereby made huge profits by covering their short positions at depressed prices; making money by first selling borrowed shares high and then buying back low. The prevailing attitude of government toward the securities industry up to and during this period had been to "let the buyer beware."

Wall Street (location of the New York Stock Exchange in New York City), by the fall of 1929, was the investment choice for almost everyone regardless of the extent of his or her financial sophistication. Despite these abuses, the public would still made money in this runaway market by owning shares in American companies. Ignored, however, was the fact that the Gross National Product during this period increased at the rate of only 5% per year, which was overshadowed by the explosion in stock prices. This anomaly, for those few who wished to observe it, signaled that the stock market was fueled by pure speculative buying that could not be expected to be continued, and would eventually have a brutal end as does a bursting balloon when over inflated.

The inevitable economic collapse started in October of 1929 with a breakdown in the stock market. As with all bubbles, all the possible buyers finally had bought all they could and eventually no buyers were left to continue bidding up share prices. The bottom of the economic and stock market depression occurred in 1932. The securities markets had declined nearly 90%, as represented by the Dow Jones Industrial Average, from its 1929 high. Fortunes lost! Careers shattered! Moreover, in the era of the one wage earner family, about one third of the employable work force was out of work! Workers without jobs had no unemployment compensation available. Those who were lucky to have kept their jobs simply had to accept huge pay cuts resulting in incomes that barely covered food and shelter costs. New clothing was a luxury that only a few people could afford.

SECURITIES REGULATIONS

In the depths of the Great Depression, a public who urgently needed change elected Franklin Roosevelt President in 1932. He promised a *New Deal* for the American public, and Congress enacted a series of financial and securities regulations. This drastic change in policy resulted in securities industry regulations being evolved over the ensuing years with a series of laws that started in 1933. It transformed an industry from what was an unregulated, freewheeling, let-the-buyer-beware industry, into a highly regulated industry where "full disclosure" is required. The Congress, ever since 1933, has taken an activist role by passing laws whenever new areas of regulation appear to be required, the era of "big government." The major regulations are discussed herein so that every person engaged in purchasing new issue securities can understand their effect.

Glass-Steagle Act of 1933

One of the first actions was the Glass-Steagle Act of 1933, which separated the functions of the banking, insurance, and securities industries in order to avoid the risk to the other two industries in case of a financial collapse of any one industry. However, during the bull market of the 1990s, persistent attacks were made on Federal regulations in general as being too archaic for these "modern times." One Congressman unsuccessfully lobbied to discard *all* securities regulations. In 1999, an ebullient Congress and President did repeal this Act at the peak of the stock market bubble. They seemed to have forgotten both the insurance industry crisis of the late 1980s, and the savings and loan crisis of the early 1990s, as well as the manic market conditions leading up to the 1929 Crash. This is mentioned as an example of the frequent, and sometimes successful, attacks on securities laws. Only the passage of time will determine whether this repeal will be detrimental to the public.

Securities Act of 1933

The Securities Act of 1933 is referred to as the "paper act," because it established regulations to prevent fraud in issuing securities. It requires all *interstate* public offerings to be sold by "prospectus" only. The prospectus must make full and fair disclosure of all material facts about the offering, and it must contain financial statements that are audited by an independent, certified public accountant.

The prospectus is registered with, and reviewed for completeness by, the Securities Exchange Commission (SEC), which was created in 1934 (see "The Securities Act of 1934" as follows). New issue investors must realize that the SEC *does not vouch for the accuracy* of the enclosed information, only that the information disclosed is complete. The prospectus must stand on its own merits, and securities dealers and representatives cannot make glowing performance projections, nor tout the benefits of the offering to interested clients. Essentially, the broker should give the preliminary prospectus to *suitable* clients and comment words to the effect that "You may find an interest in this offering."

Each security offering must be a *bona fide* public offering; therefore, no underwriters, selling dealer agents and their representatives can withhold "hot" issues for their own account. A hot issue is determined during the registration period when the number of solicited *indications of interest* demonstrates that the public demand for the securities will be much greater than the quantity that is being offered. On the other hand, this prohibition does not apply to "turkeys" (see Chapter Seven, "New Issue Offerings").

The 1933 act exempts a number of securities from SEC registration. These are securities issued by:

1.   the U. S. Government and U. S. Government agencies

2.   state, municipal, and Native American tribal governments

3.   insurance companies offering fixed annuities and insurance contracts

4.   non-profit organizations

Other exemptions from registration are allowed for public offerings of:

1. commercial paper with less than 270 days to maturity

2. *intrastate* offerings

3. *small capitalization* offerings

4. private placements (see Chapter Seven, "New Issue Offerings"), which are intended for "accredited" investors and not the public

The deficiency of the 1933 securities act was that it gave no authority for its enforcement, and did not provide for needed reform of the securities industry participants.

The Securities Exchange Act of 1934

The Securities Exchange Act of 1934 created the Securities and Exchange Commission (SEC) making it the primary enforcement authority for the securities industry. It is called the "people act" because the SEC became responsible for regulating the securities trading markets and all securities industry participants, in addition to registering nonexempt, public, interstate securities offerings.

The Act also requires that full and complete financial disclosure for public corporations be continued annually after the public offering. SEC registered corporations are required to submit annual, audited financial reports to stockholders as well as for allowing proxy vote solicitation on all matters requiring a vote by shareholders. The Act also gives the Federal Reserve Board (FRB) authority for the control over the amount of credit extended both by commercial banks to securities dealers, and by securities dealers to their clients.

All stock exchanges are registered with the SEC and they must be self-regulating-organizations (SROs). A Compliance Officer must ensure compliance with all securities regulations for every organization member and participant. Every securities dealer must also be registered with the SEC, and maintain a Compliance Department. Securities dealers must be members of the National Association of Securities Dealers (NASD), established in 1938, which is the regulating authority for the securities dealers and their employees.

Securities dealers are required to maintain sufficient capital to ensure that they remain solvent. They must pay client cash balances, free of credit restrictions, on demand. Client cash balances cannot be used for business operations unless the client is so notified. They must keep physical control over fully paid, *street-name* securities (securities of clients held by the securities dealer instead of taking possession of stock certificates), and must not commingle these with street-name securities which have been pledged for credit purchases (called "hypothecated" securities). Failures to police activities of employees that ignore investment suitability and rules of fair practice can make the securities dealer liable for triple damages.

Individuals are considered "insiders" if they are corporate officers or directors, family members of officers and directors, owners of 10%, or more, of the outstanding common stock, and anyone having non-public information about the company. This last category is the "I gotcha" for non-insiders. It has been used to try in court and convict any outside investor of illegal trading activity when they act on tips touted by friends or even strangers having *inside information*. No one is allowed to profit from any trading activity initiated because their knowledge of non-public information. Insiders holding stock are required to file a personal statement with the SEC pledging not to use non-public information for financial gain. This filing becomes an "I gotcha" document for any insider who is found to have profited from inside information.

A 13D Statement must be submitted to the SEC within 10 days by anyone acquiring 5%, or more, of the outstanding stock of any public corporation. The statement must include both the purpose for such acquisition, and whether there is any intention for further acquisition. This public information gives notice to shareholders about potential takeover action. Such individuals must also file 13D amendments for each 1% of the shares outstanding that are additionally acquired.

The manipulative and deceptive trading practices, which give false impressions of public trading activity in a stock, are prohibited. Some individuals and their coconspirators engage in illegal *wash sale* activities by transacting alternate buy and sell orders continuously throughout the trading day. A transaction is classified as a wash sale when the same security is purchased 30 days either before, or after, the sale date. Most wash sales transactions are legal. They can occur daily with day traders and other active investors. However, they become illegal when there is no net beneficial ownership change, and the intent is to induce others to buy the stock based on the deceptive trading volume created.

Other prohibitive practices include securities dealers, and their representatives that create deceptive trading activity by entering illegal offsetting buy and sell orders to induce public interest in a stock. This is similar to illegal wash sales and consists of matching of orders for their own account and for client accounts. They are also prohibited from soliciting securities sales based on either false information, or information that has no factual basis.

National Association of Securities Dealers

It had become evident, by 1938, that the SEC was unable to enforce the existing securities regulations on all the securities industry participants. This was especially true for those engaged in securities transactions in the dealers markets (called "over-the-counter" (OTC) market). Therefore, the Maloney Act of 1938 established the National Association of Securities Dealers (NASD) to regulate the conduct of both securities representatives and dealers effecting interstate transactions in the over-the-counter dealer market.

The NASD is a self-regulating organization (SRO), as are registered exchanges, and reviews all complaints and allegations of misconduct against all registered participants in the over-the-counter market. It registers all participants (securities dealers and sales representatives) by administering qualifying examinations for every member of the securities industry. Every person must be sponsored by a registered dealer to be able to take the sales representative examination. However, membership is excluded for anyone that has ever been:

1. expelled or suspended from any SRO

2. convicted of a felony

3. convicted of a securities misdemeanor in the last 10 years

4. forced to discharge debts by filing personal bankruptcy

NASD Rules of Fair Practice

The NASD's Rules of Fair Practice ensures fair dealing by securities dealers and market makers with their clients. It prohibits many practices, which were once widespread and common before these securities regulations were enacted. The principal rules are summarized as follows:

1. securities dealers, and their personnel, are limited to $100 per year for gifts made to, or received by, any person in the industry

2. market makers must not mislead the public on prices of over-the-counter (OTC) market securities by either delaying the reporting of large transactions until after the market close (called "painting the tape"), or trying to influence securities prices with public advertisements (See explanations of market makers and the OTC securities markets in Chapter Five, "Securities Markets")

3. underwriters engaged in distributing "hot" new issue securities (issues in which indications of interest far exceed the number of shares to be distributed) cannot withhold shares any for their own account, nor for those of the firm's personnel, or their families

4. market makers' quotations for OTC securities must be firm, and cannot back away from making trades at quoted prices

5. market makers cannot charge a fee on securities bought or sold to clients when trading from market makers' inventories, because their compensation is the spread between bid and offer price quotes

6. market makers are prohibited from involving another market maker as a third party in a transaction unless it results in a better price for the client, which would occur when the "inside market" quote (see Chapter Five, "Securities Markets") is better than the market maker's quote representing the client, the market maker then acting as an agent for the client and therefore is entitled to an agent's fee (commission)

7. market makers cannot trade through, which is the practice of ignoring more favorable inside market quotes and making trades with clients at their quoted price

8. market makers must sell from inventory at, or near, the current market price and not their acquisition price. The risk taken is compensated by the amount that the market maker sets as the markup, the difference between the market maker's bid and asked quotes (also called the spread)

9. market makers are prohibited from front running (otherwise called "trading ahead"), which is the illegal practice of trading in the market to obtain a better price before executing a client's limit order at a less favorable price to the client

10. registered representatives (stockbrokers) are precluded from making excessive trades in a client's account simply to generate commissions (Each transaction must be made with the approval of the client, unless the client has signed a discretionary trading agreement. Discretionary accounts are a source of frequent client complaints: the signing of such an agreement by a client would be foolish, unless the compensation is based on an annual asset based fee, not on sales commissions.)

Members found in violation of the Rules of Fair Practice can be fined, suspended, or expelled from industry membership. Written or telephone complaints made to the stockbroker can never be ignored. Brokers must promptly inform the branch manager of any complaints. All complaints involving Rules of Fair Practice must be reported to the firm's compliance officer. The firm's compliance officer can adjudicate minor infractions and then report the action taken to the NASD. However, serious complaints will be referred to the NASD District Business Conduct Committee.

NASD Compensation Guidelines

All securities dealers have commission schedules for transactions that they make when acting as an agent. Many publish these schedules; but, for obvious reasons, some of the larger firms consider their schedules as being proprietary and not for public dissemination. These fees are charged for all exchange listed securities transactions, and OTC transactions in which the dealer acts as an agent and not as a market maker.

Dealers that are market makers are allowed to impose a *markup* amount for offer quotes *(markdown* for bid quotes) which would represent fair compensation for the risk of maintaining an inventory of securities in which it elects to make a market. Market makers in "thinly" traded stocks (low daily volume or infrequently traded stocks) will impose a high markup compared with the markup on a heavily traded stock. The markup/markdown amount is given as a percent of the per share price quoted. Therefore, market makers cannot charge clients a commission when selling from, or buying for, their inventory.

The NASD gives a markup guideline of 5% for various types of transactions. These include market maker inventory trades made with a high volume traded stock (which is considered a *riskless* trade), or when acting as an agent for open market transactions. The 5% guideline is also imposed for making both a *simultaneous trade* (one made between offsetting client open market trade orders), and a *proceeds transaction* (an order to buy one security made simultaneously with an order to sell the same dollar amount for another security).

All securities account agreements have an arbitration agreement clause included. Disputes between clients and NASD members are settled by arbitration, providing the client signs an arbitration agreement. However, no account will be opened unless the client signs the agreement.

Securities Investor Protection

Enacted in 1970, the Securities Investor Protection Corporation (SIPC) is a non-profit organization consisting of all registered securities dealers, which protects client accounts against the financial failure of the securities dealer. Securities and cash are protected for amounts up to $500,000 with a maximum of $100,000 allowed in cash. The protection is limited by Social Security identification for all account registration forms such as individual, joint, or custodial. SIPC membership is mandatory for all NASD securities dealers.

Cold-Call Telephone Solicitation

The Telephone Consumer Protection Act of 1991 defines the rules for "cold-call" solicitations. Cold-calls are telephone contacts to prospective clients that have had no prior business relationship to the sales representative initiating the call, or to existing or former clients that have had no business dealings for more than 12 months. Cold-calls must be made only between the hours of 8 A.M. and 9 P.M. The caller must clearly state his or her name, the name and phone number of the securities dealer employer. The caller must disclose that the purpose of the call is for soliciting the sale of securities. Persons receiving cold calls can request that they receive no such further calls. The securities dealer must honor this and maintain a *do-not-call list* separate from the National Do-Not-Call List.

Sarbanes-Oxley Act of 2002

The manic market of the late 1990s somehow enticed the senior management of more than a few companies to commit accounting fraud. Enron, WorldCom, and Tyco, are some of the companies whose senior management felt compelled to "feed" at the company "trough" by enriching themselves at shareholder expense. They constructed schemes involving massive accounting irregularities to hide debt and siphoning cash for personal use through various devices. And, they had help from auditors who weren't exactly "independent," as well as Board Members, who never required management to give an accounting of these questionable practices. It appears that despite all the regulations enacted over 70 years, managements intent on committing massive fraud developed ways to circumvent the established safeguards. These companies were assisted by securities dealers that, because of being engaged in the investment banking business, "encouraged" financial analysts of these firms to give glowing analytical reports to maintain warm relations in anticipation of future investment banking business.

One of the abuses consisted of hiding debt, which would normally appear on the balance sheet, in "off-balance sheet arrangements" with "unconsolidated entities." These complicated schemes can be explained simplistically by a hypothetical situation in which a corporation sets up an entity like a limited partnership, transfers long-term debt and some fixed assets to the partnership, and in turn receives ownership units in the partnership equal to the amount of the fixed assets. The corporation then leases the fixed-assets from the partnership to cover debt service interest and repayment; meanwhile it retains all income generated by the fixed-assets. The net result is that the new balance sheet assets column contained ownership units in place of the value of the fixed-assets (no gain or loss here). Lease payment expenses were substituted for servicing the debt (again no net change), but the debt nicely disappears from the corporate balance sheet because the partnership is not consolidated with the corporation's financial statements. (This is explained further with the discussion of Balance Sheets in Chapter Eight, "Business Life Cycles, Financial Statements and Analyses.")

Other abuses consisted of making and then forgiving massive interest-free loans to executive officers, and contracting with accounting firms to perform non-audit services (who were initially hired for auditing services). The most egregious offense was corporate officers who sold stock prior to public disclosure of adverse financial facts, while at the same time publicly encouraging employees to purchase company stock in their pension accounts, and employee stock purchase plans.

Sarbanes-Oxley was enacted to provide "transparency" and "accountability" in financial reporting of corporations to eliminate the above abuses. It established the "Public Corporation Accounting Oversight Board" under the SEC to regulate accounting firms who are prohibited from providing various non-audit services to corporations that are audit clients. It also requires public corporations to establish Audit Committees headed by an independent member of the Board of Directors to appoint an accounting firm, as well as requiring the corporation CEO and CFO to certify the accuracy of the financial statements. The audit committee has authority to engage an independent counsel, if required. Other provisions include prohibiting corporate loans to officers and directors, as well as prohibiting officers and directors from either selling stock, or exercising stock options and selling these shares during "blackout periods" that preclude employees from selling company stock held in employee retirement plans and employee stock purchase plans. Public companies are required to disclose all off-balance sheet transactions and unconsolidated entities. Lastly the Act requires securities dealers to adopt conflict of interest rules for research analyst employees.

Uniform Security Act of 1956 (State Registration)

Federal securities laws allow new issue stocks that are listed on a national exchange (NYSE or AMEX), or on the NASDAQ National Market (see Chapter Five, "Securities Markets") to be traded interstate without individual state registration. However, OTC stocks that are not traded on the NASDAQ National Market cannot be issued, nor traded by residents of a state without first being registered with the state. In addition, sales representatives and the employing securities dealers soliciting securities transactions also are to be registered in each state in which they solicit clients.

Prior to 1956, issuing new securities required separate filing documents for each state, and securities dealers and brokers were required to take separate examinations for each state in which brokers of the firm would be soliciting clients for OTC stock transactions. The Uniform Securities Act of 1956, also known as the Blue Sky Law, provided for a single, uniform securities registration and a single securities representative examination. The term "blue sky" refers to previous fraudulent real-estate promotions, where buyers of unseen property later found the property to be unusable—swampland—therefore, having the value of only a "patch of blue sky" (meaning worthless). Since its passage, most states (but not all) have adopted the Uniform Securities Act. Registration with these states is a matter of filing the appropriate application and submitting the required state fee after passing the Uniform Securities qualification examination.

The Uniform Securities Act also requires *Investment Advisors* to be registered. An Investment Advisor is any person engaged in the business of providing investment advice to public clients for compensation. Although they cannot charge fees relative to investment performance, annual asset-based fees are allowed. They also cannot take possession of client securities and cash moneys. Licensed professionals, such as CPAs and securities brokers and dealers, whose advice is considered incidental to the practice of their profession, are not considered investment advisors. Also exempt from registration are persons giving investment advice for compensation to private individuals under contract, who have become clients because of having a prior business or personal relationship with the advisor, and not from public advertising.

The designated state Administrator of the Blue Sky Law may require the posting of a guaranty bond of up to $10,000 for security dealers, brokers, and investment advisors, as well as requiring the passing of all appropriate NASD qualification exams. Dealers and investment advisors are also required to file financial statements and an immediate notice for material changes in their financial condition. Registrations are valid for one year, and are effective on the 30th day after the filing.

All OTC securities that are not defined as *exempt securities* (see "Exempt Offerings" presented in Chapter Seven, "New Issue Offerings") are required to be registered with each state in which it will be offered to the public. Registration consists of filing a registration statement, which must include consent for the state Administrator to act as *power-of-attorney* for non-criminal action, submitting an appropriate registration fee, and filing for registration with one of three types of possible securities registrations. The different types of securities registration are for companies that:

1. have previously issued securities in the state, and have been doing business for the previous five years

2. are issuing securities for the first time in the state with registration pending with the SEC

3. are issuing securities that are either not required to be registered with the SEC, or SEC registration has already become effective

The registration for securities does not require annual filing, and is effective for as long as a public market exists for such securities. However, quarterly financial reporting to the state Administrator is required.

Most of the securities that are exempt from SEC registration (small cap offerings, intrastate offerings, and private placements) are also exempt from Blue-Sky registration. However, *intrastate offerings* greater than five million dollars, and *private placements,* which are offered to more than 10 persons, must be registered with the state. As mentioned previously, SEC registered securities that are traded on the national stock exchanges or the NASDAQ National Market (see Chapter Five, "Securities Markets") are also exempt from state registration requirements. Finally, securities listed on the regional exchanges are exempt from Blue Sky registration for the states in the region covered by the exchange.

Rule 144: Restricted Securities

Some publicly issued securities, and all securities not publicly issued, are called "restricted securities." These consist of all publicly issued corporate securities held by *control persons,* as well as any securities of public companies that are acquired by anyone outside of a public offering, and therefore, have not been registered with the SEC.

A control person (also called an "insider") includes corporate officers and directors, along with their immediate family members. It also includes any persons, that acquire 10%, or more, of the outstanding stock, who are also classified as *affiliated persons* if they are not a corporate officer or director. A *non-affiliated person* is anyone who holds unregistered securities, and who is not a control person. Unregistered, restricted securities include private placements, unregistered authorized stock acquired by exercising stock options (but not Treasury Stock), and unregistered securities acquired by merger or acquisition.

Affiliated and Control Person Trading Restrictions

There is no holding period requirement for affiliated and control persons holding registered stock (either acquired in the open market, distributed to insiders as part of a public offering or as an exercised stock option purchase of Treasury Stock) before selling. However, the quantity sold, in any 3-month period, is limited to the greater of either 1% of the outstanding shares, or an amount equal to the weekly trading volume averaged over the past four weeks, whichever is greater. They are only required to file a Form 144, Intention to Sell on, or up to 90 days before, the sale date. A notice of sale, Form 4, must be filed by the 10th of the month following the month of sale.

A holding period of two years is required by SEC Rule 144 for unregistered securities held by control and affiliated persons before restricted securities can be sold. After this holding period, these securities can then be sold subject to the same filing and quantity restrictions, as stated above, for selling registered securities.

Non-Affiliated Person Trading Restrictions

Non-affiliated persons holding unregistered, restricted securities are required to hold the stock for a minimum of two years, and then file a Form 144, Intention to Sell on, or up to 90 days before, the sale date. There is no limit on quantities sold by non-affiliated persons. However, if the holding period, before sale, is three years, the non-affiliated person is exempt from filing Form 144.

Restricted Securities Trading Restriction Summary

The regulations governing restricted securities are summarized below in Table 4-1, "Rule 144 Sales Restrictions, Control Persons and Restricted Securities."

Table 4-1
Rule 144 Sales Restrictions:
Control Persons and Restricted Securities

Securities	Type Person	Holding Period	Filing Requirements	Sales Restrictions
Registered Securities Held By:				
Control Persons	Control	None	File Form 144 --> File Form 4 -->	Sales in any 3 month period limited to greater of either: (1) 1% outstanding shares, or (2) Average weekly volume for previous 4 weeks.
Restricted Securities Unregistered Stock Including: Reg. D Issues, or Exercised Stock Options, or Rule 145 Stock	Control	2 Years	File Form 144 --> File Form 4 -->	Sales in any 3 month period limited to greater of either: (1) 1% outstanding shares, or (2) Average weekly volume for previous 4 weeks.
	Non-Affiliated	2 Years	File Form 144 -->	None
	Non-Affiliated	3 Years	Exempt -->	None

Note:

Control Person: .... Officers, directors, and family members, or any person, including family members holding more than 10% any class stock, who are also called "Affiliated Persons."

Non-Affiliated Person: .. Any person, not a control person, who holds unregistered stock

Reg. D Issues: .... Unregistered private placement securities

Rule 145 Stock: .... Unregistered stock acquired by merger or acquisition

Form 144: .... Intention to Sell filed on, or up to 90 days before, the anticipated sale date

Form 4: .... Notice of Sale filed by 10th of month following sale month

Five
Securities Markets

✦

The Investment Arenas!

One factor that can indicate the potential success of an IPO is the securities market on which it is to be traded. Markets represent the arena, or playing field, for equity securities after they are distributed to the public. The type of playing field in any sporting contest can ultimately influence the outcome of the event. Therefore, every potential IPO investor should understand the securities market on which the stock of interest will trade once issued. They should know all the idiosyncrasies of that market, which are different with each of the different securities markets available. Accordingly, this chapter explains how different securities markets operate, and the ways that securities are currently traded within each market.

The different types of securities markets on which stocks are traded that are of interest to the IPO investor are the auction markets and the dealer markets. Auction markets consist of buyers and sellers, meeting at a centralized location, trading securities in an open, continuous, bid-and-offer exchange environment. Dealer markets consist of securities being exchanged between securities dealers from their individual offices using electronic communications systems. However, the recent rapid changes within the securities industry, which have been brought about by technology advances in electronic communications over the last 20 years, are transforming both of these different markets into connected markets, as well as evolving toward being linked with global securities markets.

THE STOCK EXCHANGE

Stock exchanges traditionally are auction markets wherein members of the exchange come together at a particular location (called a trading post) to exchange securities that have been listed for trading with the exchange. The technique used for centuries has been the double auction process with open outcry of share prices. Those offering shares for sale shout out "offer" (otherwise called "asked") price quotes, representing the price at which they are willing to sell. Those seeking to purchase shares shout out "bid" price quotes, representing the price the buyers are willing to pay. The exchange appoints a person to facilitate the trading for each individual listed security, who is called a "specialist." The difference between the bid and offer prices is called the "spread." The smallest theoretical spread that can exist is the minimum price trading increment allowed. Stocks traded on stock exchanges are referred to as "listed securities" by virtue of being *listed* on an exchange.

For nearly two centuries, the principal U.S. auction market has been the New York Stock Exchange (NYSE), the oldest U. S. stock exchange, and is commonly referred to as the "primary market." This should not be confused with the terms "primary offering" or "primary distribution" (as explained in Chapter Seven, "New Issue Offerings"). The NYSE has the most stringent financial requirements of all U.S. stock markets for listing common stock. Traditionally, securities of companies having the greatest financial strength, and highest per share market prices, have been traded there. Until year 2000, the NYSE has historically exchanged more shares annually than any other type of stock market. However, the explosion in electronic trading in the dealer markets has caused the dealer's market, trading volume to eclipse the primary market's trading volume.

The other national stock exchange is the American Stock Exchange (AMEX) that adopted this name in 1953. It was formed in 1921 as an organization called the Curb Market, coming indoors from curbside trading on Wall Street where gongs were sounded by "banging on swill buckets." Listing requirements are less strict than the NYSE, and therefore these companies are less capitalized and have lower share prices.

There are also a number of regional stock exchanges. Securities listed on the regional exchanges typically are from companies domiciled within the region that are not nationally recognized. All regional exchanges have electronic links to the national exchanges; therefore, they also make trades on stocks listed on the national exchanges. Regional stock exchanges are located in Boston, Cincinnati, Philadelphia, Chicago, Arizona, San Diego, and the Pacific Stock Exchange located in both San Francisco and Los Angeles (option contracts on the Pacific Stock Exchange are traded only at the Los Angeles exchange location).

The regional exchanges that list regional securities have less stringent requirements than the national exchanges, and list regional stocks that are offered to the public to residents of the states covered within the region. The regional exchanges also trade selected stocks listed on either the NYSE or AMEX, and a few offer the trading of *listed options* on stocks, stock indices, and on foreign currencies. Option contracts are traded in an options exchange, and every contract is guaranteed by the Options Clearing Corp. Some regional exchanges still maintain a trading floor; however, the Pacific Stock Exchange (which closed its trading floor in 2001) and exchanges located in Arizona, Cincinnati, San Diego, and the Pacific now trade securities using electronic communication systems only.

Exchange Listing Requirements

All U.S. stock exchanges are registered with the SEC as self-regulating entities. Public securities listed on the exchange are traded between individual exchange members, who acquire "seats," with approval with the exchange, mainly by buying their seat from a previous member. Therefore, IPOs that are listed on an exchange will tend to be more heavily capitalized, and have a higher financial rating than most of those that trade in the Secondary Market (see "The Over-The-Counter Market" presented below).

A listing on one of the national exchanges would imply that the corporation is a viable business with earnings. A NYSE listing requires meeting the most stringent financial requirements for being listed. A listing on the AMEX, or on one or more of the regional exchanges, would indicate that the issue would not be able to meet all of the requirements for listing on the NYSE. In general, exchange listings have more visibility and potentially greater liquidity (more active trading) than a great number of unlisted stocks trading in the over-the-counter market. There are, however, many exceptions, such as Microsoft and Intel, who still choose to be listed on the NASDAQ National Market.

Stocks will be removed (called delisting) from trading on the exchange upon bankruptcy or liquidation; or for a lack of public interest in the stock; or if, in the opinion of the exchange, it ceases to be a viable business entity. Delisting will also occur when a listed company merges with another company thereby creating a new entity. Delisted exchange stocks may trade on NASDAQ if they are able to meet the requirements for such listing. If not, they may usually be found on the OTC Bulletin Board or the NQB Pink Sheets (explained herein under "Other OTC Markets").

NYSE and AMEX Listing Comparisons

Typical requirements for companies that seek listing their common stock on either of the two national U.S. exchanges are shown below in Table 5-1, "Exchange Listing Minimum Requirements." Alternative listing guidelines, however, are available for financially sound companies that, for reasons that may be unique to that company, may not be able to meet all of the typical listing requirements.

Table 5-1
Exchange Listing Minimum Requirements (1)

	NYSE	AMEX
Corporate Financial Requirements		
Market value (2):	$100 million (3)	$3 million
Operating history:	3 years	3 years
Earnings before taxes:	$6.5 million (4)	$750,000 (5)
Stockholder equity (6):	$1 trillion	$4 million
Share Distribution Requirements		
No. of shareholders:	2200	400
No. of publicly held shares:	1.1 million	500,000
Avg. daily share volume:	5000	2000
Minimum stock price:	-	$3

Notes:

(1) Alternative requirement guidelines are also available. More stringent criteria may be imposed if warranted in opinion of the exchange executives.

(2) Current market value of public shares excludes value of shares held by control persons (insiders).

(3) IPOs and REITs with less than 3 years operating history require $60 million shareholder equity. Closed-end funds with less than 3 years operating history requires $60   million net assets.

(4) Over the past three fiscal years.

(5) For 2 of previous 3 fiscal years.

(6) Includes:

   par value of equities, paid-in surplus, and retained earnings.

The New York Stock Exchange

The NYSE is the oldest U.S. exchange. It started in 1792 when members met under the Buttonwood Tree on Wall Street to exchange stock. It had traditionally been a non-public, membership only, organization governed by a 33 member Board of Governors; however, in 1971, it became a non-profit, private corporation. Currently, there are 27 members on the Board of Directors: 12 members from the securities industry, 12 public directors, a Chairman and CEO, and two Presidents who function as co-COOs and Executive Vice Chairmen. The scandal, in 2003, over former Chairman Grasso's excessive compensation has resulted in a number of changes to improve its corporate governance in an attempt to restore public confidence in the NYSE.

Most of the other exchanges have patterned themselves after the NYSE, with minor differences. NYSE listed stocks are traded on the "trading floor" at a number of specific locations called "trading posts." Over 3000 companies are listed on the NYSE, including nearly 400 non-U.S. corporations, which account for nearly 80% of the value of all publicly, traded companies.

Listed stocks are assigned to trade at one of the 17 trading posts, each of which is monitored by a specialist at the center, and all transactions for assigned stocks occur at these locations. Computer monitors located above the trading post indicate the stocks that trade at that location, as well as a variety of trading data including the last transaction price for each stock. Transactions are made by *open outcry* in a double auction process between selling floor brokers shouting out "offer" prices and buying floor brokers shouting out "bid" prices.

The NYSE has approximately 1500 trading booths along the perimeter of the trading floor where member firms receive market orders from across the country electronically, and submit these to the floor brokers for execution. Once a floor broker receives an order, the broker becomes an agent of the member firm for that stock order.

Most all exchange-listed securities represent companies that have significant financial assets. Therefore, they are *marginable,* meaning that they may be purchased on credit extended by the securities dealer member, by depositing a specific dollar amount—called buying on margin. Marginable stock shares can also be sold by borrowing shares from the securities dealer (called "selling short") after tendering a specific dollar deposit. Eventually, these borrowed shares will be required to be *covered* (given back to the owner from which borrowed), which is accomplished by purchasing the stock in the marketplace and delivering them to the securities dealer. The Federal Reserve Board (FRB) sets the deposit requirement for such *leveraged* trading activities, and SEC regulations require that a securities account holding margined securities be separate from an account holding fully paid securities. The different forms of security ownership and types of accounts are described in Chapter Six, "Securities Accounts."

There are concerns that a continuation of the explosion in stock trading will soon make the NYSE antiquated. Therefore, tentative plans are eventually to become a public corporation to raise the capital needed to install the latest in electronic communication systems to enable it to handle an even greater volume of securities transactions, mostly through electronic communications. In addition, it is also working on developing links with the major European exchanges that would allow U. S. investors to trade foreign securities.

NYSE Membership

The current NYSE membership is fixed at 1366, which are individuals, typically, partners or officers of securities dealers. Only exchange members, and specific exchange employees whose duties involve assisting stock transactions and reporting every stock transaction made during the trading day are allowed on the trading floor. The membership is classified into four basic types:

1. Registered Traders, which act for their firm's account or on their own

2. Floor Brokers, which act on the floor for other members for a small fee and are therefore referred to as "two dollar brokers"

3. Commission House Brokers, who act for their own firm's account, or for nonmembers for a commission, and typically represent large clearing house, securities dealers

4. Specialists, representing firms whose employees are authorized by the Exchange to be market makers in specific stocks listed for trading

Other NYSE Trading Systems

Over the years, daily stock trading volume has ballooned. Where 40 years ago one million shares traded on the NYSE would have represented an active trading day, today a one billion-share trade day is now considered a fairly low-volume trading day. Several electronic systems have been implemented in order to make life bearable for the exchange floor members and employees handling the ever-increasing trading volumes.

The Intermarket Trading System was installed at each trading post in 1978. This allows every NYSE specialist and floor broker to be linked to regional exchanges in order to compare prices for NYSE listed stocks quoted on the exchange floor with prices for those same stocks quoted on regional exchanges. The executing floor broker can therefore direct trades to other exchanges for a better execution if possible.

The SuperDot is an electronic order-routing system through which member firms transmit both market and limit orders for quantities over 2000 shares. These are sent directly to the trading post where they are automatically exposed to the "crowd," thus eliminating the floor broker intermediary. However, any transaction for 10,000 shares or more, or a transaction of $200,000, whichever is smaller, is considered a "block" trade, and NYSE rules require a different procedure for their execution. Block trades are discussed below under "Exchange Transaction Orders."

NYSE Trading Curbs

The NYSE has adopted circuit breakers, which limits or halts all trading in periods of extraordinary trading volume. The first circuit breaker (Rule 80A) is triggered when the Dow Jones Industrial Average (DJIA) moves 50 points from the previous close. At this point, program traders are limited to trading on ticks—individual changes in stock transaction price—that are opposite the general direction of the market. A plus tick indicates a higher transaction price, while a minus tick indicates a lower transaction. Program traders engage in computerized arbitrage trading with 15 or more stocks modeled after a stock index when the price between the modeled stock index and the stock index futures contracts differs by a defined amount. Although this activity is generally riskless to the arbitrageur, it tends to destabilize the markets in times of rapid price movements. Therefore, this rule attempts to prevent program trading from destabilizing the market by feeding a buying frenzy or intensifying a market decline.

Another circuit breaker, Rule 80B, halts all exchange trading for various periods when the DJIA moves from 10% to 30% from the average DJIA price for the last month of the previous quarter. If a 10% decline occurs before 2 P.M. E.T., the trading halt would be one hour. A 20% decline before 1 P.M. halts trading for two hours. A 30% decline anytime closes the NYSE for the balance of the day. The value of the Rule 80B circuit breaker has been disputed, since many maintain that halting trading tends to destabilize the market. However, it has rarely been invoked since being established after the October 1987 market dislocation.

Minimum Share Price

For years, the standard fractional increment for any listed NYSE stock order traditionally was $1/8 (12 ½ cents), with the average spread between bid and asked quotes being about 16 cents. In an attempt to reduce the cost for trading securities, the SEC in 1997 changed to a $1/16 increment (6 ¼ cents), but this was found to have no significant effect on spreads. Eventually, the goal for decimal (one-cent) price increments was achieved in 2001 on most listed stocks. The result on spread price has been to reduce the average spread to about six cents.

Exchange Transaction Orders

There are three types of basic trade orders available for trading listed stocks, each having a different purpose. These basic orders are the "market," "limit," and "stop-loss" orders. A number of other orders are used by experienced stock traders that request specific types of executions. These are directives to the floor broker or specialist to:

1.   execute orders only at market open or market close

2.   keep limit orders open until execution or cancellation

3.   execute the entire order amount in one transaction, or else not at all

Explanations of exchange transaction orders and how they are used are discussed below. Every common stock investor should understand these orders.

Market Order

A market order ("at-the-market") is an order given to the exchange floor broker to sell, or buy, a given quantity of stock immediately, and at the best possible current price. Therefore, a market sell order is most likely to be executed at the current open outcry bid quote, and a market buy order will most likely be executed at the current open outcry offer (or asked) quote. As mentioned previously, the difference between the bid (lower price) and offer (higher price) quotes is called the spread. The dollar amount of the spread depends upon the amount and volume of activity in a particular stock. With decimalization, the average spread has evolved to about 6-cents for NYSE stocks. The opening bid and offer quotes are established by the specialist upon reviewing both existing *good-until-canceled* (GTC) limit orders (see explanation below under "Limit Orders"), and limit orders received overnight prior to the start of trading.

Since market orders require the entire quantity to be made immediately at the best possible price, large quantities are not likely to find an immediate floor broker with a matching order to complete the trade. This will tend to distort the price as the broker raises the offer price to attract sellers, or lowers the bid price to attract buyers. The exchange, therefore, has special rules for all orders that are considered block trades, which are for quantities of 10,000 shares or a dollar value of $200,000, and greater. Block trade transactions are explained below.

Limit Order

Limit orders are orders to either sell, or buy, a given quantity of stock at a particular price. The prices on these orders are higher than the current market offer price for sell limit orders, or lower than the current market bid price for buy limit orders. These orders have no immediacy. They are activated once the market-trading price moves to, or beyond the limit price specified and are to be executed at the limit price, or a price that is more favorable. Limit orders are considered as "day orders," and will be canceled at the close of the trading day if they are not executed. However, a limit order can be made into a non-cancelable order by adding a "good-until-canceled" (GTC) modifier to the order.

Limit orders are directed to the specialist of the particular stock, and is entered in what is called the "specialist's book." The execution of a limit order is not guaranteed. Orders at each price increment are entered in the specialist's book in order of receipt and are executed as first received, first executed. If the market moves against the limit order price before all orders have had a chance of being executed, the orders remaining in the book then become unfilled.

Limit orders for large quantities of stock—typically over 1000 shares—may not be filled at the same time. Execution of limit orders depends upon the quantities being quoted by floor brokers on the other side of the transaction. The order may have to be transacted with several orders to execute the complete order quantity at the stated price. Piecemeal executions, besides being annoying, will also incur separate securities dealer commissions, and may result in paying much more than anticipated in total transaction costs. Most limit orders for 1000 shares, or less, will most likely be executed in entirety. To prevent incremental executions for a large quantity limit order, the initial order should include adding an "all-or-none" (AON) modifier to the order (this is explained below). However, it may take some time before a matching quantity can be found at the stated price.

Stop-Loss Order

Stop-loss orders, also called "stops" or "stop orders," are used to minimize losses should a potential adverse price move be more than the investor desires to absorb. They are used when is not possible to keep an eye on the trade quotation ticker minute-by-minute. All "sell stops" are set at a price lower than the current market price for stocks held in a portfolio on which the individual would wish to minimize the loss from a potential decline in market prices.

"Buy stops" are used for short positions, a position established by a transaction in which stock is first borrowed and then sold with the proceeds credited to the borrowers account. The borrower then is obligated to replace the borrowed shares (called "covering") by buying shares in the market and delivering them to the lender, sometime in the future. Buy stops are set at a price above the current market price to minimize the loss from an increasing stock price by having to replace borrowed shares with shares purchased at a much higher price.

Stop orders are also directed to the specialist to enter in the specialist's book. When the market trades at the stated stop price, the order automatically becomes a "market order," and immediacy of execution is then required. However, the price is not guaranteed. In a fast moving market, the execution may occur at a more unfavorable price than the stated stop price.

Order Qualifiers

Limit and stop orders are always considered as *day orders* (only valid for that trading day), unless modified by a "good-until-canceled" qualifier using the symbol "GTC." These orders remain indefinitely in the specialists' books as "open orders." The NYSE, however, will cancel all existing open orders both in April and in October to clear out forgotten orders from the specialists' books.

The *all-or-none* (AON) qualifier is a directive to execute the entire quantity of a market or limit order. If used with a GTC modifier to a limit order, the order will remain open indefinitely until a matching order occurs at the specified price.

The *fill-or-kill* (FOK) qualifier directs the floor broker to execute a market or limit order immediately and completely, or else it is to be canceled.

The *immediate-or-cancel* (OC) qualifier directs the immediate execution of at least a portion (called a partial fill) of either a market order or limit order at the specified price, the unfilled balance of the order is to be canceled.

The *market-at-open* or *market-at-close* qualifiers to a market order are provisional orders directing the floor broker to execute the market order either within the first minute of trading, or within the last minute of trading, as applicable.

However, the floor broker is not held responsible for a lack of execution because of the time constraint imposed. Trade reports for provisional orders in which executions are not filled will indicate "nothing done."

When companies pay cash dividends, the stock price at the opening on the ex-dividend date is automatically reduced by the amount of the dividend. The stated prices on open buy limit and sell stop orders will also be reduced by the same share price amount to prevent executions from being inadvertently triggered by the automatic price reduction. Price reductions on the buy limit order prevent purchasing a dividend, and price reductions on sell stops maintains parity for the potential loss limit because of the dividend received. (Note that sell limit and buy stop order prices are not automatically reduced since they are entered above the market price.) These automatic price reductions on open orders can be prevented by adding a "do-not-reduce" (DNR) qualifier on all GTC buy limit and sell stop orders. This instructs the specialist not to reduce the stated price on ex-dividend dates.

Odd-Lot Orders

Odd-lot orders are orders for a quantity less than the standard, 100 share round lot, and are directed to the specialist or an odd-lot dealer member for execution. The price for an odd-lot market order is executed immediately at the last round-lot trade price upon receipt of the order. A differential fee, which is typically a fractional dollar amount per share, is added to the purchase price for buy orders, and subtracted from the selling price for sell orders as compensation to the odd-lot dealer. Odd-lot, limit orders are executed by the specialist on the first round lot transaction that is at the least smallest trading increment from the stated limit price (below the stated price for buy limit, and above the limit price for a sell limit). The differential fee is also applied, as is described above.

Stop-loss orders for odd lots are also executed with the specialist. It is triggered on the first round lot transaction at or below the stated price for a sell stop order, and at or above the stated price for a buy stop order. The trade is made by the specialist who executes the trade at the price of the next round lot transaction No differential fee is applied on odd-lot stop transactions.

Block Trades

A block trade is any order that is expected to distort the market by creating a major imbalance between buy and sell orders. Orders for 10,000 shares or more, or an order representing a transaction amount of $200,000 is typically considered a block trade.

Block trade orders are transacted with permission of the exchange through special procedures that do not affect the ordinary market action at the trading post. However, these transactions are reported on the ticker tape. The exception to such reporting is with block trades in thinly traded stocks, which are made as a private transaction with the specialist.

The Specialist

Specialists are located at each trading post on the NYSE. They are individuals representing firms selected by the exchange to be responsible to make, and maintain, a fair and orderly market in one or more listed stocks. Each specialist is a "market maker" in a specific number of stocks acting both as a principal and as an agent, thereby providing both liquidity and an orderly market.

Specialists are responsible for setting a fair opening price for each stock traded at the exchange. The price is determined after reviewing orders coming in overnight to the trading post, prior to the start of trading. A gross imbalance between buy and sell orders may result in delaying the opening of trading for the stock while offsetting orders are sought to mitigate the imbalance.

They also serve as auctioneers, which ensure orderly executions for marketable trades at the trading post with accurate and timely reporting of all bids and offers. In addition, they also act as catalysts to maintain a stable market by seeking investors when bid or ask quotes are not sufficiently matched.

Specialist Role as an Agent

The role as an agent consists of executing both limit and stop-loss orders. For this purpose, the specialist keeps a "specialist's book" listing all limit and stop-loss orders received from exchange members on each authorized stock. Until the SEC changed the order handling rules in 1996, this book was not public and only exchange executives, or the SEC, were authorized to view it. However, specialists, as well as are NASDAQ market makers, are required to publicly report limit orders within 30 seconds upon receipt.

An example of the specialist's book for a hypothetical stock symbol of QRX is shown below in Table 5-2, "Hypothetical Specialist's Book." It shows examples of both buy and sell limit orders, as well as several buy and sell stop-loss orders. (Note that for clarity, the minimum price increment for this stock has been shown as five cents per share for this example.)

Table 5-2
Hypothetical Specialist's Book
QRX

BUY	Price	SELL
2 Schwab 3 ML 5 Prud.	55.10	5 ML (STP)
3 DWSB 4 ML	55.15	
		8 PW (STP)
	55.20	
	55.25	5 Schwab 3 DLJ 5 ML
3 DLJ (STP)	55.30	5 DWSB 1 ML 2 Prud
10 DLJ (STP)	55.35	

The prices in the book define the bid and offer price quotes for the stock, unless floor broker quotes are more favorable. Each order is listed in sequence (first in, first out) for both buy and sell orders, with the member recording the orders in the book.

The quote for the hypothetical QRX stock shown in Table 5-2 would be reported as 55.15 bid 55.25 asked, unless floor brokers were quoting higher bid prices or lower asking prices. The "size" (quantity available) would be quoted as 700 by 1300 (700 shares ready to be purchased at the bid, and 1300 ready for sale at the offer).

The specialists also act as auctioneers by setting the opening bell bid and asked price quotes for each listed stock based on orders received overnight before the start of trading, as well as current day orders during the trading day. It is easy to understand why the spread between bid and asked quotes for thinly traded stocks will tend to have a wide spread.

Specialist Role as a Principal

The role of the specialist as a principal is to stabilize the market for stocks when severe order imbalances exist. Specialists maintain an inventory for each stock in which they are authorized to be market makers. They will sell from their inventory when there is a lack of sellers and an overwhelming number of buyers to keep the price from moving up too rapidly. Likewise, they will buy for their own inventory when there are a lack of buyers and an overwhelming number of sellers to attempt to keep share prices from falling precipitously. In some instances, when the order imbalance of a particular stock is greater than the specialist can accommodate, the specialist will halt all trading in the stock, with concurrence of the exchange officers.

Maintaining an orderly market forces specialists to buy low and sell high, which is the widely touted magic formula to wealth. However, they can and do suffer losses in a protracted falling market where sell orders persist and continue to outweigh buy orders. Market prices and sentiment can vary widely, and principal trades made to stabilize the market are likely to include trades made both at a profit and at a loss within any given 30-day period. Therefore, the specialist is exempt from the Internal Revenue Service (IRS) Wash Sale Rule, which limits deducting capital losses from gains if the same security is purchased 30 days either before or after the loss sale date.

Another principal transaction is the execution of odd-lot orders with the specialist. As mentioned previously, odd-lot orders are orders for a quantity less than the standard round lot of 100 shares. (These transactions were explained previously under "Exchange Transaction Orders.")

Regional Exchanges

Stocks can be listed for trading on a number of regional stock exchanges. Such stocks require registration with the SEC, as does any public security, but does not require Blue-Sky Registration (see Chapter Four, "Securities Regulations") for distribution to investors in states covered by the regional exchange. For example, regional stocks listed on the Chicago Stock Exchange can be traded by residents in the Midwestern states without requiring Blue-Sky registration for each of the individual states. However, should it be offered as a new issue in states outside the Midwest area, registration would be required in each of the other states, or it could be listed on either the AMEX or NYSE—if the issue could meet the listing requirements—or on another regional exchange. (As stated previously, many actively traded stocks listed on the both the NYSE and AMEX will also trade on regional stock exchanges.)

The regional exchanges have less stringent requirements than the major exchanges for publicly issued stocks that are offered as new issue securities to residents of the states covered within the region. The regional exchanges also trade selected stocks listed on either the NYSE or AMEX, and a few offer the trading of *listed options* (option contracts traded at an options exchange and guaranteed by the Options Clearing Corp.) on stocks, stock indices, and on foreign currency. The regional stock exchanges are located in Boston, Cincinnati, Philadelphia, Chicago, Arizona, San Diego, and the Pacific Exchange located in both San Francisco and Los Angeles.

Most all exchanges are patterned after the NYSE; however, they all have individual membership and listing requirements. Some of these still act as regional exchanges listing regional company securities and maintaining a trading floor. However, the exchanges located in Arizona, Cincinnati, San Diego, and the Pacific (which closed its stock trading floors in 2001) now trade securities strictly using electronic communication systems. Trading hours may also differ. For example, the Pacific Stock Exchange closes at 1:30 P.M. Pacific time (4:30 P.M. Eastern Time) which allows executions for nationally listed, active stock to be made for an additional half hour after the national exchange market close at 4:00 P.M. Eastern Time.

The Pacific Stock Exchange (PSE) is another example of the changes occurring within securities industry. This 118-year-old exchange closed its trading floors, and merged with the Archipelago electronic communication network ("ECN," which is explained below in "The Fourth Market") in 2001. Therefore, PSE members have direct access to dealer traded NASDAQ listed securities, and subscribers to Archipelago ECN will have access to the Intermarket Trading System, which connects the NYSE traded stocks to the regional exchanges.

Consolidated Ticker Tape

All exchange stock transactions are reported on an electronic, moving display of letters and numbers called the *ticker tape*. All trades made on the exchanges—the AMEX, NYSE, and regional exchanges—or in the "Third Market" (described below) are shown, and is called the "Consolidated Tape System" quotation. It is supplied under contract by the firm, Securities Industry Automation Corporation (SIAC). The ticker tape indicates the stock defined by an assigned letter stock symbol, followed by both the round lot volume and price listed on a lower line.

It should be noted that exchange listed stocks are identified by letter symbols ranging from one up to three letters. OTC stocks are identified by four or more letter symbols, and are displayed separately from listed stocks.

An example sample of a tape transaction display for hypothetical exchange transactions is shown below in Table 5-3, "Ticker Tape Quotation Example." The quotation example indicates that volume is reported in the number of round lot shares up to 1000 shares. At 1000 shares, the volume is reported in thousands and represented by the symbol "k."

Table 5-3
Ticker Tape Quotation Example

IBM	GE&M	MMM	XON&P	T
3k @85.12	200 @61.20	500 @86.57	5k @22.71	3k @41.11

In the above hypothetical example, the quote for "IBM" shows 3000 shares traded at a price of $85.12, the quote for "MMM" reports 500 shares exchanged for $86.57 per share, and the quote for "T" shows 3000 shares traded at $41.11. (Prior to 2001, trades were reported by the number of round lot trades when followed by the letter "s," with the per share price shown as dollars and fractions following the volume. Ten thousand share trades were reported with a decimal between the thousands place and hundreds place. A single round lot transaction was reported as just the stock symbol and the share price.)

An ampersand and the additional letter following the stock symbol indicates that the trade was made on one of the regional exchanges. In this example, the 200 share trade reported for "GE" at $61.20 was made on the Midwest Exchange in Chicago (code symbol "M") while the trade for 5000 shares of "XON" at was made at $22.71 on the Pacific Exchange (code symbol "P").

THE OVER-THE-COUNTER MARKET

The dealer securities market is commonly called the Secondary Market, which is not to be confused with the terms "secondary offering," or "secondary distribution," as is explained in Chapter Seven, "New Issue Offerings." This market represents trading of securities not listed for trading on the stock exchanges between clients of securities dealers. The market for securities not listed on exchanges is commonly called the Over-the-Counter Market (or simply, OTC). Historically, individuals would make OTC stock transactions directly with securities dealers, with certificates and payment being exchanged *over-the-counter* in the dealer's office (thereby obtaining its name).

NASDAQ

Congress created the National Association of Securities Dealers (NASD) in 1938. Its role is that of a self-regulating organization to provide the enforcement of fair and orderly trading in the OTC market. Up until 1971, every OTC transaction was essentially a private trade, with the securities dealer acting as principal, or as an agent arranging a trade with another dealer. Surveillance of fair trade practices were essentially nil under these procedures; as a result, complaints about OTC transactions were widespread.

In 1971, the NASD established an electronic quotation system called the National Association of Securities Dealers Automated Quotation System, or simply "NASDAQ." The NASD became an association of securities dealers linked together by electronic communication systems and computers. It also set financial requirements for stocks to be listed on the NASDAQ. Trading transparency permitted individual investors to feel secure enough to participate actively in OTC public securities investments. In 2000, the AMEX and NASDAQ merged as an organization that is called the AMEX-NASDAQ. However, the AMEX and NASDAQ stock markets remain distinct and separate—at least for the time being.

All registered securities firms are members of the NASD, and about 500 are market makers in NASDAQ listed securities. Market makers are required to submit firm price quotes for which they are willing to both buy, and sell, at least 100 shares of stock in which they are registered. The minimum number of market makers required by NASDAQ for continued listing is only two (less would mean there is no market). The more heavily traded stocks attract a large number of market makers; therefore, the quotes for these issues are likely to be as fair as the quotes for stocks traded on an exchange with the double auction market. Daily NASDAQ stock transactions are reported in all financial publications, and in most large daily newspapers, as well as in real time on the Consolidated Tape System (explained previously under "Consolidated Ticker Tape").

NASDAQ Listing Requirements

The great majority of new businesses issuing stock to the public for the first time typically cannot meet exchange-listing requirements, and typically trade on the NASDAQ. Over 6200 individual securities are listed on the NASDAQ, with over 5000 actively traded public stock companies, including over 400 foreign companies. These are reported under two different tiers: the "NASDAQ National Market" (NM), which lists over 4400 stocks; and the "NASDAQ Small Cap," which lists about 1800 stocks.

The NASDAQ listing requirements are shown on the next page in Table 5-4, "NASDAQ Listing Minimum Requirements." The table indicates the initial listing requirements for both NASDAQ tiers, as well as the requirements on companies for continued listing (shown in the table under the heading "Continual").

The strict listing requirements for NASDAQ NM stocks allow them to be "marginable," as are most all exchange listed stocks. Marginable means the ability to be bought on credit extended by the securities dealer or to be sold short (see "Margin Securities Accounts" in Chapter Six, "Securities Accounts"). Thus, investors can trade NASDAQ NM stocks in a margin account. All NASDAQ Small Cap stocks, as well as stocks whose share price falls below $5, must be fully owned and essentially cannot be sold short. In addition, NASDAQ NM listings do not require Blue-Sky registration at issue (see Chapter Four, "Securities Regulations"); whereas, NASDAQ Small Cap listings do require Blue-Sky registration.

A listing on the NASDAQ Small Cap would be the minimum acceptable listing guideline for the investor, with a NASDAQ National Market listing being the preferable, but mot a mandatory, criterion. As mentioned previously, delisted exchange stocks may trade on NASDAQ if they can meet the requirements for such listing. If not, they may be found on the OTC Bulletin Board or the NQB Pink Sheets

Table 5-4
NASDAQ Listing Minimum Requirements

	NASDAQ Small Cap.		NASDAQ National Market	
	Initial (1)	Continual	Initial (1)	Continual
Financial				
Tangible Assets:	$4 million	$2 million	$18 million	$2 million
Capitalization (6):	(2)	(5)	--	--
Total revenues:	(2)	(5)	--	--
Pretax income:	--	--	--	--
Operating history:	1 year (4)	--	2 years	--
Distribution				
Public shares (3):	1 million	500,000	1.1 million	750,000
Market value:	$4	$1	$5	$5
Min. Shareholders:	300	300	400	400
Min. Market makers:	3	2	3	2

Notes:
 (1), Typical minimum initial listing requirements.
 (2), If $4 million net tangible assets not met, require either $50 million market capitalization, or $750,000 revenues in two of previous three fiscal years.
 (3), Held by the public. Control persons shares are excluded.
 (4), If less than 1 year operating history, $50 million market capitalization required.
 (5), If $2 million net tangible assets not met, require either $35 million market capitalization, or $500,000 in revenues in 2 of last 3 previous fiscal years.
 (6), Market capitalization includes balance sheet shareholder equity, plus "paid-in surplus."

NASDAQ Trading Hours

Regular hours for trading on NASDAQ are the same as for the NYSE and AMEX: 9:30 A.M. to 4:00 P.M. Eastern Time, five days a week from Monday to Friday, except for holidays. Pre-market and after-hours trading were initiated in

1999. Pre-market trades can be made through ECNs from 8 A.M. to 9:30 A.M. and after-hours trades can be made from 4:00 P.M. to 6:30 P.M. However, "closing prices," which define the price computed for stocks, the various stock indices, as well as the share value for mutual funds and unit investment trusts, are stated at the last trade price as of 4:00 P.M.

NASDAQ Quotation Levels

NASD members are connected to each other through communication systems that display quotations for the NASDAQ stocks. Most securities dealers will make Level I, "inside market," quotations readily available to clients. Inside market quotations show the highest, single market maker's bid price and quantity available (called the "size") at which the market maker is willing to buy, and the lowest, single market maker's offer price and size at which that market maker is willing to sell. Therefore, Level I quotes will likely display bid and offer quotations from different market makers. The price difference between a Level I, bid quote and a Level I, offer quote is called the "spread" (which most likely will be less than any single market maker's markup).

Market makers cannot quote a bid or offer price that would result in the absence of an inside market spread. There must be a spread of at least the minimum trading increment. Quoting a price that would result in an overlap with the current inside market quote is incomprehensible. No market maker (or investor) would offer to buy stock with a bid price at a higher price than that which another market maker (or investor) is willing to sell.

A Level II system displays the firm quotes from each market maker in a particular stock. It also displays the market makers' "limit order book." Level II systems were traditionally only found in the trading departments of securities dealers. However, the 1997 change in order flow rules and the creation of the "electronic order book" for limit orders in 1999 has given public access to these quotes, especially through a number of ECNs that advertise Level II access for their clients. The electronic order book therefore results in merging the secondary OTC market with the Fourth Market (as is explained below).

Level III systems are used only by market makers themselves. It allows market makers to update their quotes continually throughout the trading day on all stocks in which they make a market.

NASDAQ Price Quote Increments

OTC stocks traditionally had been quoted in fractional dollar increments. The most common price quotation increment was $1/16 on stocks over $10 per share. The average spread between bid and asked quotes was about 30 cents (compared to 16 cents for the NYSE). The inside market spread for heavily traded stocks with multiple market makers was typically small with transactions in fractional dollar increments of either $1/32 ($0.03125) and $1/64 ($0.015625), The smaller fractional increments were also common for lower priced stocks (under $10 per share).

The mandated change to decimals in 2000 at first created a problem with the electronic trading for many OTC market makers using older systems. Therefore, the trading increment was at first reduced to five cents, with many market makers and ECNs having newer systems quoting prices in both decimal and decimal equivalents of fractional dollar increments (therefore accommodating $1/64 increments). Finally, true decimal price increments ($0.01) in the OTC market were mandated in April 2001 on all NASDAQ stocks. The result was spread prices being reduced to an average spread of about four cents for NASDAQ (compared with six cents for decimal priced NYSE stock spreads).

NASDAQ Transaction Orders

OTC stock transaction orders are the same as those presented previously for exchange-listed stocks. All trading between market makers and securities dealers are for round lot quantities. Therefore, all odd-lot orders (orders for less than 100 shares) are handled by procedures defined by the individual securities dealer involved. Mixed quantity orders (orders for one, or more round lots, plus a fractional lot amount) are reported as the lowest, complete round lot size. However, it is important to understand both how OTC transactions are made and the requirements of the market makers, because the trading process for OTC stocks is different from that of the auction process for exchange listed stocks.

Inside market quotations continually change during the trading day indicating the imbalance, if any, between buy and sell orders. Many, but not all, market makers indicate a typical size of 1000 shares available for both bid and offer quotes, but the required minimum size is 100 shares (a round lot). Best current price and immediacy are mandatory for market orders; therefore, an order for a large quantity (but less than block size) can be executed at more than one price, in multiple trades, which eventually fulfills the total number of shares indicated in the order. This occurs when the order size is greater than the inside market quote size, and the transacting securities dealer is required to go to a second, or even a third, market maker to fill the order. Trade prices then become whatever the stated price quotes are for the different market makers.

Electronic Trading Network Transaction Orders

Prior to the 1997, OTC trades were best made with market orders to effect an immediate execution at a firm price quote. Without a central marketplace, and a single specialist as the market maker, both limit orders and stop orders were recorded in the market maker's order book.

NASDAQ changes in order handling rules in 1997, allowing the incorporation of ECN limit orders (see the "Fourth Market" presented below) on NASDAQ National Market stocks with Level II quotes by NASD market makers, thus resulting in a hybrid system. Individual client limit orders became visible on the quotation system for the first time. An order from an ECN client is electronically matched against other orders, and if there is no match, it is posted on NASDAQ as an ECN quote. It can be executed on NASDAQ, or with a subsequent matching order on the ECN. The system can be explained with the following example.

Assume, for a particular stock, that the Level I inside market quote is $17.50 bid, $18.35 offered, both with a 1000 share size. Also, assume that a client of an ECN (or a securities dealer) that wishes to sell 500 shares is not satisfied with the quoted bid price that would be received if the holder were to place a market order to sell. Therefore, a limit order to sell 500 shares at $18.00 is then issued. This immediately gets posted as a new inside market offer price of $18.00 with a size of 500 shares as a firm quote on the quotation system.

The most frequently quoted ECNs for after-hours trading by the media are "Instinet," "Archipelago," "The Island ECN Inc.," and "Redibook." However, these ECNs are by no means the only ECNs available to the individual investor. As of spring of 2000, nine ECNs were registered with the NASD for trading NASDAQ listed securities.

Small Order Execution System

The major complaint from individual investors, after the October 1987 market-dislocation, was that OTC market makers were unavailable to execute orders. It appears that many market makers, after making the then obligatory 100-share trade, just closed down for the day. As a result, the NASD now requires market makers to provide continuous quotes during trading hours (unless trading is halted), and has installed an automatic execution system called the "Small Order Execution System" (SOES). Market orders of 1000 shares or less on the NASDAQ NM, and 500 shares or less on NASDAQ Small Cap are directed to a registered SOES market maker who is obligated to execute the trade at the current inside market price. Securities dealers are not permitted to split larger market quantity orders to gain access to the system.

SOES attempts to provide the small shareholder direct access to market makers; however, it has been abused with the explosion of "day trade" investors. Day traders do not hold positions overnight. They make scores of trades each day attempting to make a fraction of a point on each trade. Day trading is touted and encouraged by many newly formed ECNs. However, few traders last more than the several months that it takes to reduce their typical $50,000 minimum required initial investment to zero despite the low commission rates available.

Large Quantity Orders

"Block trades," orders for 10,000 shares or $200,000, whichever is the greater, are made using "SelectNet" in order to not disrupt trading in a particular stock. SelectNet broadcasts the order to all market makers, any one of which can accept, reject, or make a counter offer. These trades are then reported after execution. Trading hours are extended for SelectNet to 5:15 P.M. Eastern Time.

Orders for NASDAQ quoted stocks that exceed 1000 shares can be also directed to the "OptiMark Trading System," which allows quotations made at any price and size, with orders being matched and executed anonymously. This system is beneficial to institutional investors desiring to make large order trades without visible market exposure. (Since institutions make up the bulk of daily trading, being visible can be a detriment to the institution.)

The Third Market

Another type of dealer market is the Third Market. This market consists of trading of popular, exchange listed stocks between securities dealers in the OTC market, typically with financial institutions trading large blocks of 10,000 shares or more. Third Market transactions during exchange trading hours are to be reported to the market on which the stock is listed within 90 seconds. Trading on this market can affect market prices of recent IPOs after the *quiet period* if they are listed on one of the national exchanges, and have drawn a lot of institutional investor interest.

The Fourth Market

The most rapidly expanding form of stock trading in the dealer market is the Fourth Market. This is the exchange between subscribing members of an "electronic communication network," or ECN, for both exchange and NASDAQ listed stock. Prior to 1997, these transactions were private trades made typically between institutions with the Instinet Corporation. Instinet was founded in 1969, to act as a global agency broker effecting private transactions of domestic and foreign securities between institutional members. Trading in a private marketplace between subscribing members did not require following secondary market trading rules. Any member could make any price bid, or offer, on any security. However, in 1997, changes in NASDAQ order handling rules allowed incorporation of ECN orders with NASDAQ market maker quotations, creating a hybrid system, and thus merging both the Third Market and Fourth Market into the Secondary Market.

The explosion of the personal computer, computer software, and telecommunications industries in the 1990s provided easy access for public, online trading in both exchange listed and OTC stocks through a number of public ECN securities firms. There are currently eight registered ECNs providing such services, beside Instinet. ECN clients can effect transactions by entering buy and sell limit orders (explained above under "Exchange Transaction Orders") online. Transactions are made between fund managers, securities dealers, market makers (see definition below), and exchange specialists around the world. The greatest benefit of online trading for individuals is the expansion of ECN trading activity for exchange and OTC stocks in the *off-hours,* before and after normal market trading hours. ECNs expand trading hours beyond the typical 9:30 A.M to 4:00 P.M trading day, and allows trading to occur between the hours of 8 A.M. to 8 P.M. Eastern Time.

OTC Market Makers

Market makers are securities dealers authorized to make a market in specific NASDAQ stocks. They are required to have only a $2,500 cash position for each stock in which they are registered to make a market. Details of all market maker transactions are to be reported within 90 seconds. Market makers remain open from 8:30 A.M. to 4:30 P.M. Eastern Time (unless they participate in pre-market or after-hours trading), and continuously quote bid and offer prices, as well as the quantity, at which they are willing to effect a transaction.

Market makers can act either as a principal in a transaction, or as an agent. The role as principal is fulfilled when a sale (or purchase) is made from the market maker's inventory. Principal transactions will be made for their clients when the market maker's bid, or offer, quote is the current inside market quote of all market makers for that stock.

The market maker acts as an agent when a client of the firm inputs an order for a stock in which the firm makes a market, but another market maker is quoting a more favorable price. Market makers are required to execute client orders with another market maker when the quote from the other market maker is more favorable.

Market Maker Compensation Acting as Principal

The market maker's compensation, when acting as a "principal" in an OTC stock, is the amount of "markup" per share imposed on stock sold from inventory, or the amount of "markdown" imposed on stock purchased for inventory. This spread, the difference between the prices that the market maker is willing to buy and sell, is the amount of compensation that the market maker receives for making a market in the stock on each transaction made as a principal.

Market maker quotes are largely dependent upon the price established by market action, not the actual cost basis of the shares maintained in inventory. The markup/markdown guideline set by the NASD is 5%, but market makers can set spreads that vary widely from this guideline, depending upon the amount of risk the market maker feels is at stake.

The stock price and activity indicate the degree of risk. A market maker in a high price stock with hundreds of thousands of shares traded daily (indicating multiple market makers) would have relatively little risk as market maker in this OTC stock. The high price ($80/share or more) would indicate a heavily capitalized balance sheet, and a large, daily transaction volume would indicate that more than adequate liquidity exists. Consequently, the market maker's spread on this type stock most likely would be less than 1%, at about $0.75, because of the relatively low risk.

On the other hand, stock that is "thinly traded" with only few thousand shares traded daily, would result in having only a few market makers. (OTC thinly traded stocks are considered as having less than 5000 shares traded daily.) This type stock can have volatile price swings because of the lack of liquidity, which can result in a high-risk situation for market makers. A thinly traded, low-priced stock is especially vulnerable to volatility. Therefore, the market maker's markup would probably exceed the 5% NASD guideline.

For example, the NASD guideline would suggest that the market maker's markup for a $10 per share bid price stock would be $0.50 (half-dollar). However, the market maker may decide that a $1½ markup is necessary resulting in an offer price of $11½ (a 15%, markup). This is especially true for "penny stocks," where the market maker's offer quote may be more than double the bid.

When the market maker makes a trade for one of its clients as a principal, it cannot also charge a commission. The confirmation receipt will be marked "trade made as a principal" with no commission amount shown. However, clients of smaller, regional securities firms that are associated with a national securities dealer as a "correspondent" securities dealer can be extremely disadvantaged with OTC transactions. These clients will be charged an agent's commission from the regional securities dealer on top of the correspondent market maker's markup/markdown when it acts as a principal in the transaction; a double whammy!

Market Maker Compensation Acting as Agent

In most OTC transactions, the securities dealer acts as an agent, arranging a trade between a registered market maker and the client. For this service, the agent's compensation is a fee (called a commission) that is added to the cost for a purchase, or subtracted from the proceeds of a sale. The NASD agent's commission guideline for this riskless transaction is 5%, but securities dealers have different commission formulae depending upon the type of security dealer used.

Most all securities dealers, regardless of type, will impose inordinately high commission fees on penny stocks to discourage activity in such issues. For example, the commission for a purchase of 10,000 shares of stock bid at $0.50 and offered at $1.00 (100% markup by the market maker) typically will include a flat charge of about $15, plus a charge of about 2 cents a share. Therefore, the total cost for the purchase would be $10,215 ($10,000 asked price, plus a $215 agent's commission). The stock would need to increase to a bid price of $1.19, from the current $0.50, a 109% increase, just to break even.

Other OTC Markets

With over 18,000 public stock corporations in existence, about 3000 are listed for trading on exchanges and about 6000 are actively traded in the NASDAQ OTC dealer market. However, with only about half of publicly traded stocks meeting financial requirements for listing either on an exchange or on the NAS-DAQ, the other non-NASDAQ half (about 9000) are reported under the heading of "Other OTC Stocks," which includes companies listed on either:

1.   the National Association of Securities Dealers Bulletin Board, commonly called the Over-the-Counter Bulletin Board, or OTCBB

2.   the National Quotation Bureau's (NQB) Pink Sheets, which is a private quotation service that assists investors to effect exchanges of non-tradable securities

The OTC Bulletin Board

The OTC Bulletin Board (OTCBB) is a regulated, electronic quotation service that displays real-time quotes, last trade prices, and volume information on OTC equity securities that are listed neither on NASDAQ, nor on any stock exchange. OTCBB stocks typically meet all SEC regulations for financial reporting; however, they may not be able to meet NASDAQ listing requirements because of too low a share price, a lack of sufficient market makers, or an insufficient number of public shareholders. Many of these stocks may have been previously listed on the NASDAQ, the NYSE or AMEX, but have since been delisted. Others may be thinly traded stocks that may have only a few public shareholders (called a "closely held company"), companies which may not have any market makers, or companies which may have less than the minimum number of outside shareholders. Any of which would preclude listing on the NASDAQ or on either of the national exchanges.

OTCBB stocks meet SEC financial reporting requirements having current "10-k" financial statements filed with the SEC available to the public. These statements can be viewed online on the SEC's database called "EDGAR." Stocks quoted on the OTCBB are sponsored by participating market makers who have filed a "Form 211" registration statement with the NASD OTC Compliance Unit. The only requirement for eligibility is that the companies, as well as limited partnerships considered as direct participation programs, must report, and continue to report, current financial statements with the SEC, or with other appropriate reporting agencies for exempt securities.

Bulletin Board stocks are *thinly traded,* meaning that daily trading volume may be a few thousand shares at best, with periods of many days in which no trades at all are made. Bid and offer quotes for Bulletin Board stocks are updated twice daily. Transactions are reported at the close of trading in some periodicals under "Other OTC Stocks", which will report only the total volume and the last trade price.

Many of these issues come under the heading of *penny stocks* (low priced stocks). True "penny stocks" are those with a price of less than $1 per share. However, most stocks under $5 per share are considered penny stocks because securities dealers will not allow them to be margined (bought on credit or sold short) even if they are listed on NASDAQ. Most legitimate securities dealers discourage client trading in penny stocks. They may restrict the number of shares traded on each penny stock order, or impose a substantial per share charge, in addition to the normal commission fee, that results in an abnormally high transaction charge. Despite these detriments, however, there is still interest in penny stocks by extreme, risk takers (gamblers) looking for a "big score."

A new issue that will be listed on the OTC Bulletin Board should be a warning that the issue will likely have no active trading market for exchange of shares, and thus is very likely to be an illiquid security. Moreover, not all Bulletin Board stocks are penny stocks. Many support share price bids well above the minimum requirement for listing on NASDAQ. However, because of the limited liquidity of these stocks, all Bulletin Board stocks should be considered as risky as penny stocks.

Pink Sheet Stocks

Many companies do not meet, or purposely choose not to meet, the financial reporting required for public securities. Other companies, called "shell companies," have no meaningful financial assets. However, owners of these securities still need a vehicle on which to buy or sell shares. Therefore, these stocks are listed on the National Quotation Bureau's (NQB) Pink Sheets. The NQB is a private organization established in 1913, and was the sole source of information on all securities not listed with the two national exchanges until the establishment of the NASDAQ in 1971. Information on stocks listed on the Pink Sheets are obtained by subscription, which up to 1997 had been printed weekly as a hard copy on pink paper (hence the name). In 1997, the Pink Sheets went online with real-time quotes.

Stocks listed on the Pink Sheets include:

1. *closely held* company stock where insiders own most of the stock with only a few public shareholders

2. *penny stock* companies who have a market share price less than a few dollars and typically a few cents

3. *shell company* stock that have neither assets nor any business operations

4. securities sold as *private placements,* which are unregistered stock in both non-public and public companies, or limited partnership (as explained in Chapter Two, "Business Capitalization Securities")

Currently, over 700 securities dealers and financial institutions subscribe to the Pink Sheets. Only financial institutions and SEC registered securities brokers and dealers may subscribe. Likewise, only registered market makers may sponsor securities and give quotes on the Pink Sheets. Market makers are charged by the NQB for each security in which they make a market, and must have filed a Form 211 registration statements with the NASD OTC Compliance Unit (as does the OTCBB market maker).

Unlike the OTCBB stocks, Pink Sheet stocks do not require SEC mandated financial reporting. Transactions for stock listed in the Pink Sheets are essentially private transactions, which do not require adherence to securities regulations imposed on public stock. The Pink Sheets list the names and phone numbers of all market makers It also provides either the market maker's "subject quote" (a non-firm workup quote for information purposes only), or "offer wanted" and "bid wanted" solicitations. Public reporting of transactions made on Pink Sheet stocks is virtually non-existent.

Pink Sheet stocks include many domestic and foreign country companies that either may not provide any financial reporting, or whose financial statements do not conform to American accounting standards and formats. Therefore, many financial swindlers use the Pink Sheets as the domain for their stock fraud schemes.

The Better Business Bureau for the State of Massachusetts reports that 90% of penny stock investors lose most, or all, of their investment. Without any fraud, this number would drop to 70%. This clearly indicates clearly that even in the absence of fraud, most investors in penny stocks lose money anyway. However, in an attempt to minimize fraudulent incidents, the SEC has instituted Rule 15c2-11, in 1999, holding the market maker responsible for "due diligence" (an earnest evaluation of the investment potential) on sponsored securities, which is currently very controversial with market makers.

New issue offerings that are to be listed on the Pink Sheets should be considered as if sending a warning with both red flags and bursting rockets. Owners of these company shares need a place to be able to make trades, but new issue offerings touted to individual investors that are to be listed on the Pink Sheets should be especially avoided. Unfortunately, these non-NASDAQ markets are the realm for many stock swindlers and should be avoided completely.

Six
Securities Accounts

✦

The Mechanism for Securities Investments!

Shareholders of public securities have a choice of a number of different forms of ownership. Many think that owning stock is simply the possession of stock certificates; however, holding stock certificates represents the least common form of ownership. The most popular form is "street-name" ownership. With this form, the securities dealer holds ownership in the name of the dealer, who then records the name of the stockholder on the dealer's book.

Securities can be held in different types of securities accounts. Account ownership can be registered as an individual, or "joint ownership with right of survivorship" for a married couple, or "joint ownership as tenants in common" for several individuals, or a "custodial account" for the benefit of a minor, or a trust account (which is also called a fiduciary account), or for a number of different forms of business accounts. Individuals can also have a retirement account, such as an Individual Retirement Arrangement (IRA) or one of a number of small business retirement plans. The securities representative (stockbroker) is responsible for obtaining the financial status and all investment objectives for each client to establish a basis for future securities transactions being in compliance with the investor's suitability, and financial status.

Most registered ownership account forms can have securities held in the account in either of two types. Fully paid securities are held in a "cash account;" and, both credit purchases and short sales are made in a "margin account." Even though initial public offerings initially can only be purchased as fully paid securities, after a specific number of days, the shares of the more heavily capitalized issues usually can be transferred into a margin account. This tactic provides equity for using "leverage" for credit purchases of additional securities in the marketplace. However, the ownership form of the account may preclude certain leveraged investments. For example, margined securities, as well as Put and Call option activities are not permitted in either custodial or retirement accounts.

Many individuals establish an IRA with "rollovers" from 401(k), or other pension plans. Security account IRAs with a security dealer are called "self-directed" accounts, because the owner assumes complete responsibility for "growing" these assets with judicious securities investments. Therefore, it is very important that owners of such accounts be fully aware of all the rules for IRAs. For example, a prohibited transaction may result in the IRA being declared null and void, and the owner will then being taxed on the entire IRA asset value plus penalties.

TYPES OF SHAREHOLDER OWNERSHIP

Any purchase of publicly issued securities, requires the transaction to be made through a registered securities dealer. The investor must first open an account, and then make a monetary deposit equal to the value of securities to be purchased. In such transactions, security ownership is usually registered with the securities dealer in "street name" form of ownership. However, certificates of ownership of stock can be obtained by directing the securities dealer holding shares in street name in a brokerage account to request the transfer agent to issue a certificate in the owner's name. When such request is made, ownership is transferred from the name security dealer with the company issuing the stock, to the names of persons registered as owners of the security account. The advantages and disadvantages for the various share ownership forms are explained below.

Holding Stock Certificates

Stock certificates are issued by the company, or its agent, indicating the names of the owners, and the number and class, if any, of shares represented by the certificate. The main benefit for holding share certificates, beside personal satisfaction of possession, is that some companies have a "dividend reinvestment plan" (called DRIP). Periodic cash dividend payments will accumulate on the books until there is a sufficient amount to purchase additional shares from the company, which is performed without paying any commissions. Other companies have other advantages, such as Warren Buffett's Berkshire Hathaway Corp., where the registered stockholders can declare the charity of choice to which their share of the annual, corporate charity contribution is to be distributed.

The main disadvantages are not being to be able to sell covered Call stock options, and using the leverage of margin to purchase securities or sell securities short. In addition, the owner has the responsibility for the safekeeping of the stock certificate, making sure it will be in "good delivery" form (not defaced or mutilated) on sale. A sale of stock designated by a certificate requires bringing the certificate to a securities dealer; establishing an account, if one has not been established; signing a "stock power" form, which transfers shares represented by the certificate to the securities dealer; and finally, issuing a sell order with the dealer. All shares designated in the certificate must be deposited into the account; however, not all shares must be sold.

Street Name Ownership

Ownership form in *street name* is the term used for securities owned by clients of securities dealers who do not take possession of ownership certificates. Street name means that the companies issuing securities do not have a record of the names of the owners, only the name of the securities firm on The Street that holds the securities for clients. Since shares are purchased and held by the dealer, the issuer recognizes only the dealer as owner in street name.

Filling out a new account application form to open an account will establish book-entry ownership with a securities dealer. Securities are then purchased and sold, typically by telephone communication, with the broker filling out an order ticket using the assigned stock symbol. The client's securities are recorded in *book-entry* form with the securities dealer. The owner will receive periodic statements of account, annual reports, and proxy statements directly from the dealer, not the issuer of the stock. In addition, with this form of ownership, dividend payments are deposited directly into the client's account. The owner's name may be disclosed to the issuing organization, but only with the concurrence of the owner (typically by checking a box on the account application).

OPENING A SECURITIES ACCOUNT

Securities dealers are responsible for obtaining essential facts about investors upon opening securities accounts. Full-service dealers have a registered representative, who should have been selected by the client, assigned to each account. The broker is responsible for soliciting this information and recording such on the application form.

Most discount securities dealers, who do not assign a particular representative to client accounts, as well as online securities dealers both require clients to fill out an application and an investor qualification form. This latter form asks for additional financial information that is used to qualify acceptable clients and to eliminate "unqualified" individuals. The client typically must sign a statement that he or she acknowledges that the dealer provides neither advice on investments, taxes, legal issues, nor makes investment recommendations. However, despite these disclaimers, courts have still held discount dealers responsible for client losses in cases that have involved trading in "unsuitable" securities.

New Account Applications

Account applications are recorded on forms that are unique to each securities dealer, and are the basis for determining the suitability of investment purchases. Some of the financial information requested is extremely confidential, but it is necessary for the securities dealer to have on file. It allows branch managers of full-service dealers to supervise adequately the assigned broker. It also establishes the securities dealer liability should unsuitable activity have been allowed.

Accounts require the names of all the owners, their addresses, home and work phone numbers, age, marital status, occupation, employer, tax ID number, citizenship, banking and securities dealer references, and the registration status for the account (see "Securities Account Registration" discussed below). Retirement accounts must be in the name of an individual only, and beneficiaries are defined, which must comply with inheritance rules for the state of residence.

Business accounts can be opened for a corporation, partnership, or a non-incorporated association. Corporate accounts require a copy of the Articles of Incorporation which must show a resolution authorizing the trading of securities, the type of account allowed (cash or margin), and the names of persons authorized to make securities investment decisions. Partnership accounts require a copy of the Partnership Agreement that shows that investing in securities is permitted. Non-incorporated associations, such as investment clubs, are required to file a copy of the By Laws.

Accounts wherein individuals, or institutions, act on behalf of another are called "fiduciary" accounts. Copies of the trust defining the trustee, or the court order appointing a custodian or guardian as trustee for another, must be submitted with the account application. The types of securities investments allowed in fiduciary accounts are typically governed by state law. Some states require that such accounts hold only securities specified in the state's "legal list," which is a list of all securities approved by the state of residence for such accounts. However, the majority of states require fiduciaries to abide by the "prudent-man rule." This rule essentially requires that the securities held in such accounts must be reasonably prudent for income, and safety of principal purposes.

Financial information recorded on the application includes the individual's annual income, net worth, the total value of liquid assets owned, and banking references. Current securities dealer accounts as well as previous securities investment account histories, including the types of securities previously traded and the number of years trading such securities must all be disclosed.

The most important information required in the new account application includes the account investment objectives. This determines suitability (see the explanation below under "Investment Objectives") for all future securities investments. The client can also assign power of attorney, if another person has been so named, as well as the amount of authority so designated. Initial transaction must also be defined: the amount of a cash deposit and the type of transaction requested, if any; the deposit of a security certificate using a Stock Power form, and whether securities are to be sold; or, the transfer of securities from an existing account, and their disposition, if any. The securities representative who opens an account for a new client is required to sign the account application, indicating that the information recorded is correct. The branch manager, or a principal of the firm, must approve every account application.

Securities Account Registration

Securities account ownership may be registered in several different ways. The typical ownership form is a general securities account held by an individual or a couple. Another common form is the fiduciary account, an account wherein someone acts for the benefit for another as in a trust or custodial account. There are also a number of different forms of retirement accounts, such as an Individual Retirement Arrangement (IRA) or a Self-Employed Individual Retirement Plan (SEP IRA). The application forms for these different accounts may be different, but they all require disclosure of essential financial information.

Accounts for individuals may contain either "cash" or "margined" securities (see explanations for "Cash Securities Accounts" and "Margined Securities Accounts" given below). The individual owner of a securities account is registered as the sole owner. At death, the account passes to an heir designated by the deceased person's Last Will and Testament, or else under state law if no Will exists. "Put" and "Call" options can be traded in either cash or margin accounts, if the individual can meet financial and suitability requirements. Cash accounts require full payment for all securities purchased. Margin accounts allow securities to be both purchased on credit from securities dealer, as well as permitting "short sales" of borrowed securities (see "Margin Securities Accounts" below).

A joint account can be registered as either "tenants in common," or with "right of survivorship." All individuals listed in a joint account registered as "tenants in common" equally share the account assets. On the death of any individual listed as an owner, the deceased person's share becomes property of the heirs of that person's estate. The surviving individual in a joint account registered with "right of survivorship" assumes ownership of the entire amount. Married couples typically use this form allowing the surviving spouse to assume ownership without the need of a Will.

An IRA (see "Retirement Securities Accounts" below) can only be registered as a cash account, and securities cannot be margined. Call option contracts can be sold on stock held in the account, which is called "covered call writing." This allows the owner to receive a specific dollar payment (called the "premium") that is deposited in the account by selling the right to purchase fully owned stock at a specific price in the future. Therefore, covered call writing allows the owner of stock to lock-in a potential future sale at a specific price, if the holder of the Call option (to whom the stockowner has sold the right to buy the stock) elects to exercise the option. If not, the owner retains ownership of the stock, and the premium received remains part of the account's assets.

A custodial account for a minor can be established under the Uniform Transfer to Minors Act (UTMA). The account is registered in the custodian's name "for the benefit of" the name of the minor, but the tax identification number on the account is that of the minor. Current law allows any person to give any other person up to $10,000 per year without affecting the donor's exemption for estate tax liability upon death. Therefore, assets from wealthier individuals can be distributed to minors without income thereby avoiding paying annual income tax on investment income generated by the gift. (One should always seek qualified tax advice for such cases.) All such gifts must be irrevocable, and can be given by any individual to any minor, whether or not the donor is the custodian. The custodian has the fiduciary duty to comply with the requirements mandated for a fiduciary, and only a cash account and covered call writing is permitted. Custodians must appoint a successor custodian in their Will to avoid having a custodian for the account appointed by a probate court judge.

Power of Attorney

The account application also contains a section for establishing a "power of attorney": someone who is designated to act in place of the owner. The person so named can be any individual, even the broker of record on the account, and the authority allowed may be either "general" or "limited." General power of attorney permits the person to have full and complete authority, even to close the account and take receipt of the proceeds. Limited authority allows the power of attorney to trade securities in the account; however, withdrawing funds from the account is not permitted. The power of attorney has complete discretionary authority over what securities to buy or sell, and when. Therefore, this authority should be given only rarely, since most accounts with such authority eventually will incur problems, especially when the broker is given discretionary authority and the account loses value.

Investment Objectives

Every securities account application contains a section defining four investment objectives for the account. The four categories typically listed are "income," "safety of principal," "growth," and "speculation." The individual is requested to define the four objectives in preferential order, highest to least. Anyone considering investing in new issue equity securities, especially IPOs, should select "speculation" and "growth" as either first or second. "Income" and "safety of principal" should be three and four. In addition, the stated investment objective, which typically represents the individual's risk personality, must be consistent with the owner's financial status. Any account where safety of principal is rated higher than speculation is likely to be denied the opportunity for IPO purchases, especially for lower income and lower net worth clients.

The securities dealer assumes total liability for accepting an account with any inconsistency between objectives and financial status. The securities representative and dealer can be held liable for executing client orders that are inconsistent with stated objectives, as well as with the financial status.

Compliance rules require that should an investor change either investment objectives or financial status, the broker must be made aware of such, and record the change on an updated "new account application," which once again must be approved. Astute brokers will periodically review their client's investment objectives and financial status for changes.

CASH SECURITIES ACCOUNTS

Cash securities accounts contain fully paid securities held in street name, as well as cash monies. The client is usually required to sign a separate (from the new account application) "cash securities account agreement" which basically states that the client will make payment in full for all securities purchased, including transaction costs, within the allotted time period. If not, the dealer may dispose of the securities purchased for non-payment, even if at a loss. The client will then be responsible for such losses including transaction charges for both the purchase and sale. In turn, the dealer typically pledges to maintain all fully paid securities held in street name in a separate account, unencumbered from securities pledged as collateral in margin accounts. The last main provision is the acceptance of binding arbitration in case of any dispute between the dealer and client, thereby waiving all rights to seek remedy in court. The agreement is typically signed by the client, and approved by an executive of the firm.

Every product, with the exception of futures contracts and certain Put and Call options offered by the securities dealer, can be purchased and held in street name in a cash account. These consist of corporate stocks (including IPOs, which must always be paid in full), bonds, warrants, as well as U.S. Treasury and municipal government debt obligations. Also included are: both open-end and closed-end mutual funds; limited partnerships; real-estate investment trusts; and mortgaged-backed, pass-through certificates such as "Ginnie Maes." Purchasing Put and Call option contracts (depending upon investor suitability and financial status), as well as writing covered Call options, can be transacted in cash accounts.

Transaction Orders

Securities transaction orders that are ordered by the client are called "unsolicited" orders. A "solicited" order is an order that is recommended by the broker, and accepted by the client. Every order ticket must be marked as either *solicited* or *unsolicited,* and the order ticket is stored for a minimum of three years to maintain a record of the order in case of any future dispute. (It must be noted that in the now famous case charging Martha Stewart with lying to prosecutors investigating insider trading, the defense argument whereby an "understanding" existed between Martha and her broker was invalid. All such transaction "under investigators standings" must be reduced to writing, which in that case should have been a stop-loss order.) The different types of transaction orders for purchasing and selling securities for both the exchange and OTC markets were described previously in Chapter Five, "Securities Markets."

Settlement

All corporate issued securities require full payment for securities purchased, or the delivery of certificates for securities sold when not held in street name, within three business days after the trade date. However, both listed options and U.S. Treasury securities require next day settlement. Although buy orders are typically executed for existing clients without having sufficient cash in the account to pay for the trade, a new account client is unlikely to have an order processed without first making a cash deposit for purchase orders, or by delivering security certificates for sell orders.

Failure to comply with settlement requirements will cause the trade to be "busted," and the securities that the client ordered to be purchased will be sold. The broker of record (the assigned broker) is held ultimately responsible for any uncollected losses, including transaction charges that may be incurred. It will be deducted from the next paycheck. Therefore, both securities representatives and their branch managers are unlikely to effect transactions for new clients without adequate funds first being deposited in the account. (Note brokers are strictly prohibited from making personal loans to clients.)

MARGIN SECURITIES ACCOUNTS

A margin securities account allows investors to use leverage to buy various securities financed, in part, by the securities dealer and held in street name in the account. A margin account agreement (which is correctly called a "hypothecation agreement") must be signed by the client, and approved by an executive of the securities firm. Apart from the typical clauses that were stated previously for cash accounts, margin accounts have additional clauses. The client must further agree to adhere to the securities dealer margin requirements by maintaining a minimum equity position, as well as paying the stated interest rate charged as a defined percent above the current "broker call" interest rate (which can vary daily). Lastly, the client agrees to allow all margined securities to be pledged, by the securities dealer, to a commercial bank as collateral. The broker call rate is the charge imposed by a commercial bank for providing cash in the form of a secured loan, to the securities dealer for making credit available to clients.

IPOs must be initially purchased in a cash account. However, those that are listed to trade on the NYSE, AMEX, or the NASDAQ National Market typically can be transferred to a margin account at the end of the quiet period—typically 25-days after the effective date. All margin account securities are held separately from cash account securities. Therefore, an account holding margined securities—called a "long margin" account (described below)—allows these securities to be sold short by other margin account clients, in their short margin account (also described below). A "short sale" is the selling of borrowed securities by clients who then are obligated to purchase such shares in the future to replace the borrowed shares, which is called a "covering" transaction.

Margin accounts provide the speculative investor with leverage. Long margin accounts allow bullish investors to increase potential profits by buying, currently, up to two times the value of their cash deposit with great hopes that shares can be sold at a higher price in the future. Short margin accounts provide bearish investors the opportunity to sell borrowed securities at a high price, and later making a covering transaction at a lower price.

Initial Margin Deposit

Securities regulations require a minimum, initial deposit of $2,000 for all margin accounts before any trades can be made; however, individual securities dealers may, and usually do, have higher initial deposit requirements. The Federal Reserve Board (FRB or more commonly referred to as "the Fed"), requires immediate additional deposits to satisfy the "Regulation T" required margin rate (currently 50%) for every transaction made in the margin account.

Some day trading *emporiums* (day trading is described in Chapter Three, "Securities Dealers and Investors") require a $25,000 minimum initial deposit for margin accounts, but most *house rules* (securities dealers' rules) require at least double this amount for such activity. These high deposit levels are imposed because securities regulations require that no profit be taken without either paying for securities in full, or maintaining the required equity in a margin account.

Long Margin Account

Securities in a long margin account have been purchased using credit extended by the securities dealer. Interest charges accrue daily, but they are billed monthly. The rates typically are about 2% to 2½% higher than the broker call rates charged by commercial banks. (Broker call loan rates are reported daily in financial periodicals.) "Margin" refers to the percent ownership for owner at the market close for all securities held in the margin account. Therefore, a margin of 55% indicates that the client owns 55% of the value of all long securities (purchased securities) held in the account. The Federal Reserve Board dictates the *initial margin* requirement for each purchase transaction, with the current minimum requirement being 50%. The NYSE sets, for its members, a minimum margin maintenance rate of 25% for long margin accounts. However, member dealers can individually establish a higher minimum margin maintenance rate for client accounts.

The primary reason for using leverage by purchasing stock in a margin account, is when there is reason to believe that a particular stock, or the stock market or industrial sector in general, has the potential to significantly increase in price over a given period, This is called having a "bullish" sentiment. However, the percent appreciation anticipated must be much greater than the interest charged by the dealer on the amount of the purchase made on credit.

For example, assume that a particular stock is expected to increase by 30% over the next year, and the annualized charge on the amount borrowed for margin purchases is 10%. If the investor were correct, the margined purchase would generate a return 67% greater than the 30% return that would have been achieved if only half of the stock had been purchased in full. A $50,000 margin purchase would have increased by $15,000, which would be reduced by about $2,500 in margin interest paid during the year. The net gain of $12,500 would represent a 50% return on the initial deposit of $25,000, and would be greater by 67% than the $7,500 gain possible if only $25,000 worth of fully paid securities had been purchased.

However, the sword cuts both ways in such accounts. A declining market value will result in losing twice the amount that would have been lost by owning fully paid securities with the same initial dollar investment. In addition the monthly margin interest charge is assessed on the initial borrowed amount, and is typically added to the amount financed thereby compounding the loss.

Initial Margin Requirement

Most securities listed on the NYSE and AMEX, or on the NASDAQ National Market can be margined. However, initial public offerings and all new issue offering securities listed for trading on these markets cannot be margined and must be purchased and paid in full. They may be placed in a margin account after the *quiet period* following the offering (see Chapter Seven, "New Issue Offerings"). The initial margin requirement is set by the Federal Reserve Board for all equity securities held in margin accounts, including stocks, warrants, convertible securities, and mutual funds. The current requirement is set at 50% of the transaction amount at purchase, and is called the FRB's Regulation T, initial margin requirement.

If account funds are insufficient to cover the initial margin requirement of 50% at the time of the trade, a FRB *Reg. T call* is issued for the balance due, and must be met within five business days. Once issued, a Reg. T call must be met. It does not matter if subsequent price increases occur within this five day period, which would result in achieving a margin of 50%, or greater, in the account. Failure to meet the Reg. T call will immediately put *a freeze* on the account for 90 days. A frozen account where the initial margin deficiency is greater than $500 requires that sales not be permitted without first fully paying for the securities. In addition, other security purchases during the freeze period must be fully paid in advance prior to executing the trade.

The initial margin requirement is determined by the purchase price, while the "Reg. T retention margin" and "maintenance margin" requirements (both explained below) are determined by daily closing prices. The expression for determining the amount of long margin account equity is as show by Table 6-1, "Long Margin Equation."

Table 6-1
Long Margin Equation

Long Market Value less Debit Balance equals Account Equity

The "long market value" (LMV) is the total value determined by the current closing market prices for all securities purchased on margin. Therefore, the LMV will change daily (either increase or decrease) as the market prices of securities held in the margin account change. In addition, it will increase for additional margin purchases and decrease when margined securities are sold.

The "debit balance" (DB) is the amount borrowed from the dealer for the initial purchase of margined securities. It includes amounts borrowed for securities purchases, dealer commissions, and all subsequent interest charges. The DB does not change daily, as does the LMV, since it represents the dollar amount borrowed. It increases with additional margin purchases, as well as on the day of the month in which the dealer debits the account for the monthly interest charge. The DB will decrease when margined securities are sold without withdrawing any of the proceeds of the sale from the account.

One can determine the account's *equity position,* which is typically given as a percent of the LMV, by subtracting the DB from the LMV. Account equity will change daily as a function of changes in market prices for securities held in the account. This is called being "marked-to-the-market." Therefore, the equity position can be greater, or lower, than the 50% Reg. T retention requirement at the close of each trading day.

Reg. T Retention Requirement

The FRB also requires that the subsequent, daily percent equity for margin accounts be *retained* at 50% of the current long market value (and therefore called the Reg. T retention amount). If the margin falls below the Reg. T retention amount, as established by the daily closing prices of securities held in the account, the account will become *restricted.* Restricted accounts do not require additional monetary deposits unless the margin falls below the securities dealer's "maintenance margin" level. However, restricted accounts prohibit further purchases. In addition, up to 50% of the proceeds of any sales in restricted accounts can be withdrawn by the owner, as long as the account does not drop the margin below the dealer's maintenance margin level. The balance must be applied toward the Reg. T retention deficiency.

Margin Maintenance Requirements

The NASD and the NYSE set the minimum margin maintenance requirement for long margin accounts at 25% of the long market value (LMV), but many securities dealers set the minimum at 0%, or higher (called "house rules"). When the equity drops below the maintenance margin level, the securities dealer issues a *margin call.* This is a demand to deposit cash immediately to bring up the margin to the margin maintenance level. In a declining market, successive margin maintenance calls may be issued daily as the market prices continue to decline. Failure to act will result in the forced liquidation of securities in the account.

Securities dealers can have more restrictive margin maintenance requirements. For example, some securities dealers may increase the margin maintenance level in an account with only one stock position (either long or short) to 40%. House rules, typically, are never all presented to the client at the time of the transaction. Most brokers are not completely aware of them all. The client and broker will only realize that an obscure house rule exists when some transaction violates a house rule and requires immediate action from the client. Securities representatives learn from the actions of their clients, just as teachers learn from their students.

Margin Account Bookkeeping

Margin account bookkeeping is performed by the securities dealer and is seldom, if ever, presented to the client. However, when one decides to have a margin account, it is important to understand the basic elements of how margin is computed, as well as the risks for such accounts. This bookkeeping can be explained by using a tabular example to shown the relationship between the long margin equation, and both the Reg. T retention and margin maintenance requirement computations for a series of events within a hypothetical margin account. A hypothetical margin account example is illustrated below in Table 6-2, "Hypothetical Long Margin Example."

Table 6-2
Hypothetical Long Margin Example

Action, or Transaction	LMV	Debit Balance	Account Equity	Reg. T Retention	Excess Equity	SMA	30% Margin Maint'nce
Deposit $10 k	0	0	10 k	0	0	10 k	0
Buy $20 k	20 k	10 k	10 k	10 k	0	0	6 k
20% increase	24 k	10 k	14 k	12 k	2 k	2 k	7.2 k
20% decline	20 k	10 k	10 k	10 k	0	2 k	6 k
Buy $4 k	24 k	14 k	10 k	12 k	0	0	7.2 k
20% decline	20 k	14 k	8 k	10 k	0	0	6 k
Sell $10 k	10 k	4 k	6 k	5 k	1 k	1 k	3 k
Withdraw $1k	10 k	5 k	5 k	5 k	0	0	3 k

Note: All amounts in thousands of dollars.

In the hypothetical example of Table 6-2, an owner establishing a long margin account with a $10,000 cash deposit can purchase $20,000 worth of stock on margin, thereby complying with the initial margin requirement of 50% of the

LMV. The debit balance and initial account equity are $10,000 each. Assume that after a few weeks, the market price increases by 20% thereby resulting in a LMV of $24,000; however, the debit balance remains at $10,000. The owner's equity then increases to $14,000, which is $2000 more than the $12,000 Reg. T retention amount (50% of the LMV). The bookkeeping for these transactions is shown in the first three lines of the table.

Excess Equity and the Special Memorandum Account

When the equity position exceeds the Reg. T retention level of 50%, the excess amount is considered as a line of credit, and is called "excess equity." Excess equity is maintained in what is called a Special Memorandum Account (SMA). Either this amount can be used to finance additional margin purchases, or it can be withdrawn. The SMA amount may not always be equal to the excess equity (as explained below), but can always be withdrawn up to the extent of the amount of current excess equity. In a restricted account, the SMA amount cannot be applied to additional purchases. However, with the securities dealer's permission, it could be withdrawn to the extent that the margin maintenance level is maintained.

Excess equity, once it is generated, is protected from market declines. The SMA amount, therefore, can be greater than the current amount of excess equity, and probably would be in a declining market. In the example of Table 6-2, assume the market price subsequently declined back to the purchase price (line 4). The equity position would then decline to the $10,000 initial equity amount, thereby reducing the excess equity to zero. Nevertheless, the $2000 SMA generated by the previous price increase would remain intact.

The benefit of the SMA is that it can all be used for additional credit purchases even if the excess equity amount is zero. With the current 50% retention level, the purchasing power of a margin account is two times the SMA amount. As shown in the example of Table 6-2, an SMA amount of $2000 had been created with the price increase, as shown in line 3, after the initial purchase on line 2 (which was the same as the amount of excess equity at that point). However, with the subsequent price decline back to the purchase price, the excess equity declined to zero, but the SMA was maintained at $2000. Assuming that the owner then orders a purchase of an additional $4000 of stock, the debit balance will increase to $14,000, with the LMV increasing to $24,000 (as shown on line 5). The 50% Reg. T retention amount increases to $12,000, even though the equity position is maintained at $10,000. At this point, the account would then be restricted, and no further credit purchases would be permitted. A call for an additional cash deposit would not be issued since the equity position is still greater than the dealer's 30% margin maintenance level.

Continuing with the example cited in Table 6-2, assume that the market declined continued reducing the LMV to $20,000 (as shown on line 6). The owner then orders half of the LMV ($10,000) of stock to be sold (as shown on line 7). The $10,000 sale proceeds are applied toward the debit balance reducing it to $4000. The equity position would decrease to $6000, but with a Reg. T retention level requirement of $5000, an excess equity of $1000 is then created and the account restriction would be lifted.

If the client then withdraws the excess amount, as shown on line 8, the equity would then increase to the Reg. T retention level. The excess equity and the SMA would both drop to zero because of the withdrawal.

Proceeds of stock sales are typically applied to reduce debit balances, as was indicated in the above example. However, 50% of the proceeds of any margin account, stock sales can be withdrawn, regardless of the margin retention level, as long as the equity position does not drop below the dealer's maintenance level. In the above example, should the owner have requested a withdrawal of the proceeds of the sale shown on line 7, the most that could be withdrawn from the $10,000 sale is $3000, because the equity position would then be equal to the example's margin maintenance amount.

Answering Long Margin Maintenance Calls

A margin maintenance call is an immediate call to deposit cash into the account because the equity has fallen below the margin maintenance level. The client typically must meet this demand within 48 hours (unlike the 5-day, Reg. T initial margin call), and repeated margin calls for cash can be issued in a declining market. However, other actions, besides depositing cash, can be taken to satisfy the margin call.

The call is for cash, but it can be met by either depositing fully paid stock (transferred from a non-retirement cash account) into the margin account, or to sell some of the stock in the account (which is the action the securities dealer would take if neither cash, nor fully paid securities were deposited by the client).

To satisfy a call by adding fully paid securities, the value of the stock to be added must be at least 1.43 (10/7) times the amount of the cash demand with a 30% long margin maintenance level, or 1.33 (4/3) times the amount of the cash demand with a 25% maintenance level (the NYSE requirement). Selling margined stock to meet a call requires selling 3.33 (10/3) times the amount of the cash demand for a 30% long margin maintenance level, or 4.0 times the cash demand for a 25% maintenance level. The account owner, therefore, pays the severest penalty when selling stock to meet a maintenance margin call.

The question of whether a margin maintenance call should be answered by a cash deposit, adding fully paid stock, or by selling stock, is one that has been the subject of much discussion. Conventional wisdom advises answering a call with an order to sell out the position completely. This is likely to be correct for a low price stock (which may eventually decline to penny stock status). In this situation, it would be better to salvage whatever amount is possible by selling out the position completely, rather than by adding more cash that will probably go down the drain also. Answering a call by either adding cash or fully paid stock, however, may be the correct action for the longer term with a highly capitalized, high price stock that is unlikely to have any skeletons rattling around in the closet (as may be likely with low priced stocks). Unfortunately, no one rule can be stated that will cover all situations. Each will be different.

Debt Securities Margin Requirements

Margin requirements for debt obligations are different from margin for equities. Non-convertible corporate debt securities require an initial deposit of 20% of the purchase price, or 7% of face value, which ever is greater. Municipal bonds require 15% of the purchase price, but are also subject to the 7% of face value rule. Margins for U.S. Treasury securities range from 1% of face value for securities whose maturities are less than one year, to 6% for 20 years or more.

The maintenance margin requirement for a non-convertible debt obligation is identical to the initial margin requirement, and is "marked-to-the-market" daily. One could then expect frequent maintenance calls on a position holding $100,000 of 20-year T-bonds purchased with $6000. Convertible debt obligations are governed by the 50%, Reg. T initial and retention margin levels, as well as house margin maintenance.

Holding fully margined debt obligations in a margin account is not encouraged for the average individual investor. Interest charges on margined debt obligations will far exceed the nominal rate of return available for these securities. They are more suitable for accredited investors having deep pockets who will attempt to reap capital gains by anticipating short-term decreases in interest rates.

Short Selling Securities

Short selling marginable equity securities (securities listed on exchanges and on the NASDAQ NM) is also performed in a margin account. A short sale is the legal sale of securities borrowed from the securities dealer that is held in street name for clients holding long margined positions. Unlike buying on credit, short selling incurs no interest charge since no money is borrowed. The only requirements are that the account equity must be maintained at a specified minimum level, and that a covering purchase be made sometime in the future in order to replace the borrowed shares that were sold short. However, accounts with short positions in dividend paying stock are debited the amount of the dividend payment on the exdividend date. This allows the securities dealer to credit the dividend amount to the accounts of the holders of margined stock held in street name, from which the stock was borrowed and sold.

There are various reasons for short selling. The primary reason is for short-term speculation when there is reason to believe that a particular stock, or the stock market in general, has been overbought, and the current market price is likely to decline (called having a "bearish" sentiment). Another reason is for hedging a convertible issue to protect against a potential price decline. Short selling can also lock-in a capital gain on stock that is owned, which defers the tax liability into the next tax year, and is called selling short "against-the-box." The covering transaction can then be ordered in the new tax year by informing the broker to deliver the "long" stock.

A less common use for short selling is by performing arbitrage with marginable securities. It takes advantage of a difference in prices of a security traded in different marketplaces and hence buying long in one market at a lower price while selling the same stock short in another market at a higher price.

Short Margin Requirements

"Margin" as used in a short sales transaction means the amount of equity in a short margin account that is above the current, obligatory covering amount. The 50% FRB Reg. T initial margin requirement necessitates an initial cash deposit equivalent to one-half of the value of the short sale, prior to, or within five days of the sale. The Reg. T retention and dealer maintenance margins are determined by the subsequent daily closing prices, which is called being marked-to-the-market as previously stated. The expression for determining the amount of owner equity for short positions is show below by Table 6-3, "Short Margin Equation."

The *credit balance* (CB) of Table 6-3 includes both the cash margin deposit and the net proceeds (sales amount less transaction charges) of the short sale. The *short market value* (SMV) is the amount that the short seller is obligated to cover, and represents the current value of the stock sold short. The difference between the CB and the SMV is the amount of equity in the short margin account, which when expressed as a fraction of the SMV, represents the percent margin.

Table 6-3
Short Margin Equation

Credit Balance less Short Market Value equals Account Equity

Both the NASD and the NYSE set the maintenance margin requirement at 30% of the current market value of short stock. Securities dealers typically impose this on short margin accounts, as well as on long margin accounts (as noted previously) for accounting convenience. However, margin maintenance for a short sale of marginable stock that has declined to less than $5 per share is set at 100% with a minimum of $2.50 per share. For example, in 2003, shorting Lucent Technologies stock, when it was at $1 per share (declining from $80 in 1999), would have required a $2.50 per share margin deposit.

Excess Equity and the Special Memorandum Account

Excess equity, special memorandum accounts (SMA), and Reg. T amounts, as well as margin maintenance requirements are essentially similar to long margin accounts. Account equity increases with decreasing stock prices, and excess equity and SMA are created. Price increases will decrease equity, but SMA, if any, is protected from adverse market conditions (price increases) once generated. The SMA represents a line of credit; therefore, short sales can be transacted for up to two times the value of the SMA (called "shorting power") with the current, 50%, Reg. T initial margin requirement.

Adding cash to the account equally increases both the credit balance and equity by the same amount. Likewise, removing cash from the account (which would occur to credit dividends paid to the owners of short stock) will decrease equity by the amount withdrawn. In addition, every $2 decrease in stock price will increase the equity by the same $2 amount; however, because the Reg. T retention level decreases by only $ 1, the excess equity and SMA will increase only by $ 1.

Answering Short Margin Maintenance Calls

A short margin maintenance call is issued when the equity has fallen below the maintenance equity level. Requirements for answering a short margin maintenance call are the same as for a long margin call. The owner is typically required to meet this demand within 48 hours (unlike the 5-day allowance for a Reg. T initial short margin call), and repeated margin calls will be issued in a rising market. However, other options, besides depositing cash, can be taken to satisfy the short margin call.

While the demand is for cash, the call can be met by either of two other actions. The first is by depositing different, fully paid securities into the margin account. This will result in combining long and short positions with two different stocks. The second is by making a covering purchase of some of the stock shorted in the account, which the dealer would perform if neither cash nor fully paid securities were deposited.

Adding fully paid securities to the margin account can satisfy a margin call. This requires that the amount of stock to be added must be at least 1.43 (10/7) times the amount of the cash demand for a 30% combined account margin maintenance level (short margin maintenance minimums typically being 30%). A covering purchase of stock to meet a call requires buying 3.33 (10/3) times the amount of the cash demand for the 30% short margin maintenance account. The covering purchase is funded with the existing credit balance. Therefore, as in the long margin account, the account owner pays a severe penalty when "covering" to meet a short maintenance margin call.

Whether or not to answer a short margin call is also a question that has raised much discussion, and again, no one rule can be stated. Conventional wisdom advises against answering a call with cash, and may likely be correct for most short positions. A maintenance margin call for a short stock with deteriorating financial status of the company may be tempting to answer. However, should it be on a high-priced, large-cap stock, it might be better to salvage whatever amount is possible with a covering buy for the entire short position, rather then to add cash. Answering short margin calls on low price stock, which could eventually achieve penny stock status, may be justified either with a cash deposit, or by adding fully paid long securities to the margin account. However, margin requirements for stocks below $5 a share increase significantly, as noted previously, and are extremely risky because of the potential that a sudden spurt in prices will occur.

Plus Tick Rule for Exchange Stocks

Some short sellers, typically short selling syndicates, attempt to drive down the price of a marginable security by creating a disproportionate number of sell orders. It is hoped that this will subsequently induce panic selling by the current stockowners, thereby driving the price down and creating huge profits for the short sellers after making covering sales in the depressed market. To prevent this type of activity, exchanges apply a *plus tick rule* (a price greater than the last transaction) for all short sales. Therefore, it is unlikely that short selling syndicates can achieve much success in driving down prices of exchange stocks.

However, the OTC market, by virtue of the multiple market maker system, does not impose a plus tick rule for short sales. Therefore, selected NASDAQ stocks are frequent targets of short selling syndicates. These are typically low cap, low priced stocks with a small float (number of outstanding public shares), and typically having a low daily volume of shares traded (thinly traded).

Combined Margin Account

Margin accounts combine long and short positions with one general accounting equation. This equation is shown in Table 6-4, "Combined Margin Account Equation." It is a composite of the expressions stated in Table 6-1 and Table 6-3.

Table 6-4
Combined Margin Account Equation

LMV plus CB less DB less SMV equals Combined Equity

Long and short securities held in a combined margin account are market to the market daily, and establish the combined equity for the account. The Reg. T retention and maintenance margin requirements are compared with the combined equity amount. The account is restricted when the equity drops below the Reg. T retention amount, and a margin call is issued when the equity falls below the margin maintenance level of the house.

RETIREMENT SECURITIES ACCOUNTS

Small businesses and the self-employed have a number of retirement plans available. These plans include Keogh, SEP IRA, and SIMPLE retirement plans. The wage earners of large corporations are typically offered participation in a 401(k)-retirement plan. However, wage earners have a choice of the benefits of a traditional IRA, or a Roth IRA, whether or not they belong to an employer's retirement plan. The Keogh, SEP IRA, SIMPLE, 401(k), and IRA retirement plans are "defined contribution" plans with contributions limited by law. The benefit at retirement depends on how much was contributed over the years, and the degree of success of the investment vehicles used. These plans are available through most financial institutions, mutual funds, and securities dealers. (It should be noted that the Individual Retirement Annuity is also confusingly called an IRA. This is a "defined benefit" qualified plan issued by an insurance company in which defined retirement benefits are payable over the individual's life expectancy.)

Contributions to a traditional IRA can be made by every wage earner up to the maximum allowable annual limits. It may shelter annual income from taxes up to the extent of the contribution for those not covered by an employer's retirement plan. Wage earners that are so covered can still contribute the maximum amount allowed; however, the amount that can be deducted from income to reduce tax liability may be limited, depending on annual income. In this case, the contribution is called "non-deductible."

Contributions to a Roth IRA do not shelter annual income from tax. However, distributions in retirement are tax-free since they consist of a return of previously taxed capital contributions and accumulated, tax-free earnings and capital gains. It should be noted that the ability to contribute to a Roth IRA is limited by annual income. High-income wage earners are precluded from contributing to a Roth IRA.

Each of these IRA types can be funded by annual contributions, as well as by *rolling over* an existing retirement plan, such as a 401(k) pension plan. However, there are different consequences for each of these type rollovers. For some, the benefits of the Roth IRA have warranted the conversion of an existing traditional IRA into a Roth IRA despite the current tax liability incurred upon conversion.

Anyone who has, or is considering establishing a self-directed retirement account should be acquainted with all the rules for there type accounts. There are substantial penalties for violations, especially the rule governing *prohibitive transactions*. Any violation may result in the entire account being declared invalid, thereby incurring income tax and penalties on the total amount of the IRA account. All retirement plans are required to be cash accounts with no leveraged investments permitted (such as using margin or listed stock options). IPOs may be purchased in such accounts providing that the owner has stated speculative and growth as being the first two investment objectives. He or she must also have a history of purchasing IPOs, and has an appropriate financial status (high annual income as well as high net worth).

However, it should be understood that losses from speculative IPOs in retirement accounts are doubly treacherous. They invalidate the past annual contributions made to the account, and cannot be applied toward capital gains made (as in a self-directed, individual or joint securities account). Therefore, the average individual investor, regardless of his or her risk personality should avoid buying IPOs in these accounts.

Seven
New Issue Offerings

♦

The Business of Tendering Securities!

The types of securities that business organizations and government offer to provide capitalization were explained in Chapter Two, "Business Capitalization Securities," and the roles of securities dealers and investors, with regard to trading public securities, were discussed in Chapter Three, "Securities Dealers and Investors." This chapter explains how securities are offered to the public. It describes the roles of the different securities distributors; the types of distribution agreements; the offering procedure; the information presented in the prospectus; and the types of securities exempt from SEC registration.

The probable success of many new issue equity securities, especially initial public offerings can be detected not only from the required disclosure material presented in the prospectus, but also by the type of legal relationship between the issuer and the underwriters participating in the offering. In other words, the probability of success is greatest when the underwriters guarantee that the issuer will achieve the desired capitalization level with a "firm commitment" type underwriting agreement. Success is least probable success the underwriter only makes a "best effort commitment" to the issuer. If the underwriter will not risk guaranteeing the issuer the level of capitalization desired with a firm commitment, public investors should not feel compelled to subscribe to the issue, regardless of touts from sales representatives.

New issue offerings require purchase in full. Therefore, securities dealers typically require a cash deposit for the indicated offering price when the investor submits an indication of interest in the offering. However, investors in some best efforts offerings may have to wait for a better part of a year before the issue becomes public, whereas firm commitments typically go public in less than 30 days.

In recent years, Internet securities offerings have become exceedingly popular with uninformed, risk-taking individual investors. These offerings are typically listed on the OTC Bulletin Board, usually having limited information disclosure. They typically take advantage of small cap or other exempt security rules, and the only benefit is capitalization for the issuer and distribution fees generated for the online offering dealer. The investor receives illiquid securities.

There have been a number of attempts to "reform" securities regulations by individual lawmakers claiming that they are too archaic for these modern times with instant, high speed, electronic communications. Attempts to repeal securities laws, as well as online offerings, both revert to the *let-the-buyer-beware era,* instead of the current requirement, which is for *full and fair disclosure.*

SECURITIES DISTRIBUTORS

Investors are required to employ securities dealers to purchase and sell marketable securities. The securities dealers therefore engage in the retail securities business by effecting public securities transactions for their clients. However, many securities dealers also engage in the wholesale securities business when helping government and corporations acquire capitalization through the distribution of new issue securities.

The Investment Banker

An *investment banker* is a securities dealer that is in the business of raising capital for businesses and governments. Organizations engage an investment banker to advise them with respect to recommending the most appropriate form of security to offer, and to promote the distribution of these securities to the public. Investment bankers are also called "underwriters," which has become a generic term. However, it correctly refers to a particular type of underwriting commitment; that which the investment banker is contractually obligated to fully fund (underwrite) the issuer, while soliciting public interest for the purchase of the securities offered. As such, a firm commitment provides the greatest assurance of all possible underwriting commitments for the new issue investor (see "Underwriting Commitments" explained below).

However, for some offerings, the investment banker has no liability other than to make a reasonable effort to distribute the desired amount of shares to the public for the issuing company at the desired offering price. By acting as an agent, not as an underwriter, the only liability for the securities dealer is the loss of underwriting compensation for shares not sold to the public.

Underwriting Agreements

Securities laws require a written underwriting agreement, which defines the terms and conditions between the investment banker and the issuing organization. The agreement also defines the type of commitment that the underwriter makes to the issuer of the security. The type of commitment is a reflection of the underwriter's opinion of the offering, since it indicates the degree of risk that the underwriter is willing to take.

However, every firm commitment also contains a *market out* clause. This gives the underwriter the authority to cancel the new issue for any unforeseen event that would seriously affect the distribution. Underwriters can suffer a major financial loss by being forced to underwrite an offering that it subsequently discovers may have difficulty in distribution to the public: either because of circumstances developing within the issuing company, or because of a geopolitical event affecting the markets. New issue capitalization is typically the greatest in the later stages of a bull market, and is the least at the bottom of a bear market. New issue activity is an indication of the willingness of investors to invest in new issues, as well as a reflection of the current state of the economy.

Mergers and Acquisition Activities

Corporations seeking growth by acquiring other existing businesses also employ investment bankers. Absolute secrecy is required in the initial stage of such activity; else, the proposed acquisition would fail due to premature disclosure of such intentions. Most all investment bankers also engage in the business of making securities transactions for their own account, as well as for clients. Therefore, corporate finance activities are kept separate from the retail half by what is referred to as a *Chinese curtain*. However, this pseudo barrier does little to keep sensitive corporate finance activities from being disclosed to the freewheeling activities of the retail securities representatives looking for a score for their clients. In order to minimize loose talk around the water cooler, many firms physically separate these activities by establishing offices in different physical locations.

Underwriting Syndicates

Investment bankers engaged in new issue offerings often form an alliance with other investment bankers, thereby creating an *underwriting syndicate*. This occurs either when the investment banker feels that the offering is financially too large to handle by itself, or else as a goodwill gesture to other underwriters for having been included with other underwriting syndicates in the past. However, there is always, only one managing underwriter.

By law, new issue purchases are intended to be long term-investments. Therefore, all syndicate underwriters are obligated, by the *speedy profit clause* in every syndicate agreement, to prevent clients from flipping stock. "Flipping" is the term used for making a quick profit by selling after a modest price increase has been achieved in the marketplace. Securities dealers, whose clients engage in this practice, can be penalized by not receiving the underwriting concession for shares flipped within a certain period after the effective date, (typically 25 days). The threat that the managing underwriter can withhold the underwriting concession for selling securities dealers whose shares flip shares, results in this practice being greatly discouraged.

Underwriting Commitments

The various types of underwriting commitments can provide an indication of the underwriter's opinion of the new issue. The two basic commitment types are the "firm commitment" and the "best effort commitment," the latter of which has several variations.

Firm Commitment

A firm commitment guarantees that the issue will become public on a particular date, called the "effective date." Therefore, the issuer is assured of receiving the desired amount of capitalization being sought, less the underwriting concession, from the managing underwriter. The underwriters of a firm commitment, which is also referred to as a *bought deal*, assume full liability for any shares not publicly distributed on the effective date. The underwriting syndicate members act as principals, which is the classic definition of underwriting.

Two types of firm commitments define the liability arrangement between the underwriting syndicate members. In a Western Account, liability is limited to the allotted amount for each member. On the effective date, each underwriter "purchases" its share of securities from the managing underwriter, and is only responsible for distributing this amount to the public. The Eastern Account requires that all members be held responsible for all other members' unsold shares on a *pro-rata* basis. For example, should one member of a three member underwriting syndicate having equal liability in an Eastern Account not distribute its allotted amount, all three members would then share the liability for the amount unsold by the one member.

Another type of firm commitment is the "standby commitment." This is typically given by an underwriter to an existing public company that desires to raise additional capital by issuing additional shares to existing shareholders with a rights offering. In this type offering, the underwriter *stands by* to purchase, and then distribute to the public, all shares not purchased by shareholders holding expired rights.

Best Effort Commitments

A best effort commitment is essentially no commitment at all from the underwriters. They promise to make the best possible effort without any liability; therefore, they act strictly as selling agents. The concern for the issuer is the uncertainty that an adequate number of shares will be issued to provide a reasonable amount of capitalization. The concern for the investor is the uncertainty that the amount of shares sold will provide sufficient market liquidity. As a result, best effort commitments typically contain either of two clauses that can provide some degree of certainty to the offering.

The first is an *all-or-none* best effort commitment, which provides that the entire issue will be canceled at the end of the stated offering period if shares are not all sold. However, the disadvantage here is the long duration for the offering period, which is typically about three months compared to about 30 days for a firm commitment. In addition, the underwriter is usually authorized to extend the offering for an additional period, which could be up to six months. Both the issuer and investor may have to wait the better part of a year to determine whether the issue will ever become public. Meanwhile, investors' subscription deposits, for shares that may never be issued, are held in an escrow account.

The other type of best effort commitment is the "mini-max" commitment. Here, the underwriters make a best effort to sell the maximum number of shares offered, but the issuer will accept a lower, minimum amount. The offering will be canceled should the defined minimum number of shares not be sold by the end of the offering period, which also may be as long as three months with an additional six-month extension. Again, the disadvantage is the long period of uncertainty before the issue becomes public, or is finally canceled.

Best effort issues that are "turkeys," new issues with very little public interest, are especially difficult for both front line securities brokers, and their clients. Brokers are typically fed misinformation about the status of such offerings, so that it will be repeated to anxious clients who have subscribed to the offering and are waiting for it to go public. This provides only temporary satisfaction, and invariably results in client total dissatisfaction, even anger, after realizing that the information received is untrue. Many well-developed, long-term relationships between brokers and clients can become irreversibly destroyed in only a few months.

Underwriting Compensation

The cost of underwriting a new issue is built into the *public offering share price* (POP); therefore, the difference between the POP and the amount the issuer receives is called the "underwriting compensation." This includes the total amount taken by the managing underwriter, underwriters in the underwriting syndicate, selling group members, and participating securities dealers who are not members of the selling group.

Underwriting compensation is typically between 8% and 10% of the POP for firm commitments on new issue equity securities. However, firm commitments on risky, small capitalization IPOs can be as high as 25%. The underwriting compensation for a direct participation, limited partnership (DPP LP) that is a "managed offering," underwriters acting as principals, is limited to 10% of the POP. However, an unmanaged, best effort, DPP LP offering typically is, about 20%. (Limited partnership securities were discussed in Chapter Two, "Business Capitalization Securities.")

For a typical 10% underwriting compensation, the managing underwriter's fee is about 1% of the POP on all issues distributed. The remaining 9% is called the "underwriter's concession," or sometimes called the "takedown."

Selling Group Members

Selling group members, also called the *selling syndicate,* are securities dealers who sign a written agreement with the underwriters to help distribute new issue securities. These agreements are executed as a goodwill gesture to provide new issues to investors of other securities firms that are typically not underwriters. Selling group members act as agents for the underwriters and receive a "selling concession" as compensation on the amount sold. They have no liability for any commitment, nor do they have a quota for the quantity to be distributed. They operate on a best effort basis only. Typically, the "selling concession" is about 7.5% of the POP, for a 10% underwriting compensation amount, and is taken out of the underwriter's concession.

Non-Selling Group Members

On occasion, underwriters will allow some securities dealers to participate in a new issue distribution without the formality of signing the selling group agreement. This occurs typically as a personal favor to acquaintances in other securities firms that may ask to participate in an offering. The small quantity of shares offered to non-selling group members are typically taken from the underwriters' distribution quota. The typical compensation for non-selling group members is about 1.5% of the POP.

Internet "Underwriters"

Historically, all new issue offerings were once only available from established full service securities dealers performing as underwriters (the wholesale function), and assisted by underwriting syndicate members and/or authorized selling group members (as explained previously). However, many popular online securities dealers currently offer access to IPOs for frequent trader clients, as well as those with high-balance accounts ($100,000 or more). The capitalization dollar amount for IPOs currently available online is not significant when compared with the total of new issue offerings offered through traditional investment bankers.

It was inevitable that, given the Internet explosion, securities would readily become offered to the public directly through Internet "underwriters." These are known as Direct Public Offerings (DPOs). These firms do not underwrite offerings; they simply assist companies to raise capital by distributing self-underwritten new issues to the public for a fee. The focus is on micro-cap offerings, from $5 to $20 million. Such offerings are of little interest to the traditional, large, national underwriters, and would otherwise have been offered by smaller, regional investment-banking firms. Internet underwriters assist client companies with the registration process for a modest underwriting fee (typically about $100,000), and offer the new issue shares to online clients typically with a best effort "Dutch auction." Those wishing to purchase these Dutch auction IPOs then make a bid at a particular price, which should be within a specified price range. The higher the bid price, the more likely the bid will be accepted. The issuer will receive most all of the funds raised, with the distributing dealer receiving a fractional percent of the shares sold. This is typically less than the best efforts underwriting compensation charged by conventional underwriters.

The securities offered by such online dealers should be considered as the riskiest of these high-risk securities. There is no "due diligence" provided by these Internet underwriters, and the offerings are typically too small to be listed on an exchange or on the NASDAQ. Therefore, online subscribers find they own shares in companies that they cannot sell. Moreover, with a best effort type commitment, the subscribing shareholder and the company are both unsure whether the offered shares will be all sold, as well as what the actual offering price will be. Consequently, the company may not be capitalized as desired, and the investors who subscribe to the offering may find that they own an illiquid security.

THE OFFERING PROCESS

The type of stock being offered to the public should be understood by potential investors of new issue securities, as well as the type of underwriting commitment. Fortunately, most public offerings require full and fair disclosure. Adherence to specific rules and regulations is required by the offering process in order to be a *bona fide* distribution to the public. These rules and regulations apply during the period of the offering process, and for a limited period after the stock becomes public.

Types of Public Offerings

Most public offerings provide capitalization for the company. However, beneficial owners (officers, directors, and owners of more than 5% of outstanding common stock) can offer a new issue that only distributes existing, private, restrictive stock to the public for personal gain. These offerings can be made for IPOs, or for quantities of restrictive public stock held by insiders of public companies that would otherwise either exceed the limit for individual insiders to sell in the marketplace, or dramatically lower the share price if such quantities were exposed at one time in the marketplace. Therefore, it is important to understand the meanings of the terms used in the distribution of new issue offerings.

Primary Offering

A primary offering is the sale of new issue equity securities to the public from the business organization's authorized securities (as specified in the articles of incorporation). The offering may be the same or a different class of equity security from that previously issued. Net proceeds from a primary offering go directly to the company to be used as described in the prospectus. The term "primary offering" is often used interchangeably with the term "primary distribution"; however, the latter term is more correctly used for a new issue of debt obligations.

Initial Public Offering

An initial public offering (IPO) is the offering of common stock to the public for the first time. IPOs usually represent a primary offering of common stock that provides capitalization; however, they could also be a "secondary" or "split" offering, which are explained below.

Secondary Offering

On occasion, beneficial owners of either public or closely held companies desire to sell stock obtained from distributions other than a public offering, such as unregistered stock from either a private placement or stock allocated to individuals at incorporation. These shares may be offered to the public in a "secondary offering" when the amount of stock to be sold would represent too great a volume to be allowed under Rule 144 (as was explained in Chapter Four, "Securities Regulations"), or would otherwise be too great for the market to assimilate. All proceeds go to the individual beneficial owners of the stock. The company receives no capital from a secondary offering.

Split Offering

A split offering is a combination a primary and secondary offering. A portion of shares being offered represents non-issued, authorized stock for capitalization purposes, with the balance being restricted shares previously issued to insiders. The capital raised by this offering is split, on a pro-rata basis, between the company and the major stockholders tendering their shares.

Rights Offering

Public companies seeking additional capitalization sometimes offer non-issued, authorized stock by issuing rights to existing shareholders to buy additional stock. Existing shareholders therefore have the opportunity to maintain their percent ownership in the company (called "pre-emptive right"). Rights have value and a limited duration beyond which they will expire worthless. Some may be traded as a security in the same market on which the stock trades prior to expiration. Rights offerings to shareholders are never fully subscribed; therefore, an investment banker typically will distribute the unsubscribed amount as a primary offering to the public as either a firm or best effort commitment (explained previously under "Underwriting Commitments").

New Issue Offering Procedure

Preparations to bring the issue public then begin with the culmination of negotiations between the issuer and the managing underwriter, and the signing of an underwriting agreement. These negotiations determine what type of security to offer to the public, and what price range per share would generate the most interest, yet still meet the requirements of the issuer for capital to be raised. Most startup and emerging growth companies with current shaky finances and uncertain future income will only be able to offer common stock. No one would subscribe to an offering of dividend paying preferred stock, or interest paying debt obligations, without adequate assurance of future income from which dividends or interest payments can be made.

On occasion, the underwriter may suggest offering units consisting of common stock and warrants in various proportions. A warrant, as explained in Chapter Two, "Business Capitalization Securities," is a long term right to purchase additional authorized common stock at a specified price that is set higher than the offering price of the common stock. These offering units consist of stock bundled with warrants, and are of interest to the more speculative of the new issue enthusiasts because of the potential for leveraged returns from the warrants. The issuer can also expect additional capitalization in the future from the exercise of the warrants.

Other underwriting firms, as well as selling group members, are solicited to participate in the offering after the signing of the underwriting agreement.

S-1 Statement

The managing underwriter prepares an S-1 Statement seeking registration for the issue with the SEC. The S-1 Statement provides information disclosure of all material facts about the organization seeking capitalization; therefore providing full disclosure to the public. It includes the following information:

1. the name of the company

2. the names and biographies of the officers and directors

3. the amount of capital to be raised

4. the type of security, or securities, to be issued, the number of shares to be issued, and the indicated price or price range

5. disclosure of how the proceeds are to be used

6. audited financial statements for the past three years

7. the amount of stock held by insiders

8. the Articles of Incorporation

9. statements of pending legal action, and a legal opinion

10. the amount of the underwriting compensation

State registration documents (also called "blue sky" registration) are prepared and typically filed after filing the S-1 statement with the SEC, if the security has not been listed for trading on either the NYSE, AMEX, or on the NASDAQ National Market. The different types of blue-sky registrations were stated in Chapter Four, "Securities Regulations."

The Preliminary Prospectus: "Red Herring"

A preliminary prospectus is distributed to all underwriters and selling group members after filing the registration statement with the SEC. These are used to solicit indications-of-interest (IOIs) from investors who have adequate financial resources and have listed speculation as either the first or second investment objective. The document is typically referred to as a *red herring* because a portion of the cover page consisting of mandatory disclaimers is printed in "red."

New issues can only be sold by prospectus; therefore, all *material facts*—a legal term referring to important information about the business organization—must be disclosed in the prospectus so that public investors can decide the merits of the issue for themselves. The preliminary prospectus contains all of the information contained in the S-1 filing statement as well as some additional information.

The prospectus identifies the managing underwriter and underwriting syndicate members, but not the selling group members, on the first page. The share price will be stated on the summary page, and will be indicated by price range on firm commitments. The effective date does not appear because of the many factors that can delay or cancel the offering. The actual effective date for firm commitments depends on the amount of IOIs received and on market conditions in the days just before the "cooling off" period (discussed below).

A *green-shoe* clause is typically included in the preliminary prospectus for firm commitments. This clause indicates the underwriter's right to purchase an additional amount of securities (typically up to 15%) from the issuer after the effective date to allow underwriters to cover over-allotments. The "red herring" notice will appear across the top, or side, of the cover page in bold red lettering. This notice will state that:

1. the information presented is subject to change or completion

2. a registration statement has been filed with the SEC

3. the security described is not to be sold, nor offers to buy will be accepted, until the effective date

4. the preliminary prospectus does not constitute an offer to sell, nor a solicitation to buy shares described

5. sales of securities are not to be sold in any state without registration in the state

Another bold disclaimer statement is also required on all prospectuses, stating that, "The securities offered have neither been approved nor disapproved by the SEC, the SEC has not verified the accuracy of information presented, and any representation to the contrary is a criminal offense."

SEC Review: The "Cooling-Off" Period

After filing the registration statement with the SEC, a minimum period of 20 days is required for the SEC's review; although, underwriters typically extend this to 30 days for firm commitments. This period is called the "cooling-off period. The SEC review only confirms that all the information required to make an informed decision about the offering is included. It does not verify the correctness of the offering documents, but relies for such on the independent auditor's report.

The issuer and underwriters expect and hope not to receive any communication from the SEC during the cooling-off period. This would indicate that the offering, and its prospectus, are not deficient. An SEC response will be either a *deficiency letter* or a *stop order*. A deficiency letter will indicate specific amendments that must be included in the prospectus. A stop order is issued when there is an obvious omission of material facts.

Securities representatives for the underwriting syndicate members, as well as selling group members, solicit indications-of-interest (IOIs) during the cooling-off period. IOI solicitations are limited to existing individual clients for which the new issue would be a suitable investment. Indications-of-interest determine the amount of public interest in the offering, and establishes the final share price of firm commitments. IOIs may also indicate that the issue should be modified or canceled for a lack of interest.

All public offerings of securities are sold by prospectus only. Therefore, sales representatives cannot provide other information, such as research reports, nor can they puff-up or speculate on share price appreciation. They may discuss only the information stated in the prospectus with their clients, *when* asked.

Securities dealers' management personnel, typically those with vice-president status, will also solicit indications-of-interest from institutional investors with whom they have had a personal or business relationship. These are the main targets of every new issue offering, since institutions subscribe to large quantities of stock being offered. However, institutional investors can also be detrimental to the offering after the effective date. They typically have a *short investment fuse* with IPOs, and will unload their entire position should the price either decrease in the marketplace after the effective date, or not increase as much as they would have expected.

Blue-Sky Registration

If the issue is to be listed for trading on the NASDAQ Small Cap after it goes public on the effective date, blue-sky registration is required in every state that a new issue is to be offered,. During the cooling-off period, the underwriter prepares and submits registration documents for each of the states. However, "blue sky" registration is not required for issues that are to be listed for trading on the NYSE and AMEX exchanges, as well as on the NASDAQ National Market (see Chapter Five, "Securities Markets").

In addition, issues that are to be listed on one of the regional exchanges do not have to be registered in the states covered by the exchange. However, registration is required for every other state in which it will be offered that is not covered by the regional exchange on which it is to be listed.

Due Diligence

"Due diligence" is a term that refers to the requirement for the underwriter to provide a fair, and legitimate, new issue public offering. This is typically performed in two stages. The first stage is a series of informal, open meetings between the issuer and public investors. The second, more important stage is the formal, closed meeting between the managing underwriter, underwriting syndicate members, and the issuer before the issue becomes effective.

The underwriters arrange for informal meetings that are typically held throughout the cooling-off period in the branch offices of the underwriters in various locations throughout the distribution area. Select public and institutional investors, as well as securities sales representatives, are invited to question executives of the issuer who attend these meetings. However, neither the issuer's representatives nor the underwriter's representatives are allowed to tout or hype the issue. They are only available to clarify matters that may be unclear or in question in the red herring. However, the major benefit is the opportunity to get to know executives of the company in which they are being asked to indicate an interest in financing.

A formal due diligence meeting is held at the end of the cooling-off period. It includes the managing underwriter, underwriting syndicate members, and the issuer's officers, attorneys, and accountants. All aspects of the offering are reviewed. This includes the validity of all information in the registration statement, the purposes for the capital being raised, actual and potential legal issues, and the indications of interest.

The final offering price is negotiated between the underwriter and issuer. The final offer price will be at the top of, or higher than, the price range given in the red herring when IOIs exceed the number of shares being offered (called a "hot" issue). Likewise, the final offer price will be at the lower end of the stated price range if IOIs appear not to be able to support full subscription to the offering (thus called a "turkey"). An issue may be canceled if there is too little interest, or if market conditions develop which may be detrimental to a successful offering.

Hot Issues

Hot issues are also called "blowout" issues. They are determined when IOIs indicate that there is public interest for more shares than the quantity being offered, including the green-shoe clause allocation. Hot issue share prices can be expected to skyrocket after the effective date because of the insufficient quantity of shares available for all who have indicated an interest in purchasing the issue. Moreover, the final share price will be set at the high of the indicated price range, or even higher.

Securities laws demand a *bona fide* (genuine) offering to the public. Therefore, underwriters, selling group members, non-selling members as well as their employees, brokers and family members are all precluded from buying shares as a new issue offering (although they can purchase shares in the marketplace once trading commences). To do otherwise would be to practice "free-riding," an illegal act of withholding new issue shares from the public.

Turkeys

Turkeys, which are also called "sticky issues," are offerings that are expected not to do well in the marketplace after the effective date. They are indicated by a lack of interest with poor results from brokers soliciting indications-of-interest during the cooling off period. When this occurs, the managing underwriter may then notify both the syndicate members and selling group members that they, their employees, brokers, and family members are allowed to subscribe to the offering. Clearly, there would not be a problem with illegally withholding shares when the public has shown little interest. The theory here is that securities dealers and brokers that have an added interest in the offering, besides sharing in the underwriting concession, will work harder to convince the public of the merits of the offering.

Turkeys will be priced at the low of the indicated price range. They are also likely to be bundled with warrants and offered as units to generate interest. The managing underwriter may offer to stabilize the issue in the marketplace as an additional incentive for investors to subscribe to the offering (see "Price Stabilization" defined below). Should none of these incentives appear to generate much public interest, the underwriter is likely to cancel the offering, or may renegotiate the underwriting agreement with the issuer into a best effort type of agreement to proceed with the offering.

Effective Date

Solicited shares are distributed to investors on the *effective date*. This date, which is established by the underwriters with concurrence by the issuer, is stated in the final prospectus (as described below), and typically is not available until that time. Securities representatives of both the underwriters and selling members contact clients that have previously indicated an IOI, and ask them for firm orders. At least this occurs in theory. In practice, select clients that have previously given IOIs will find their account debited cash by the amount of the offering price and shares deposited in street name on the effective date.

During the cooling-off period, soliciting brokers typically record IOIs on the securities dealers' standardized buy-ticket form by the marking "IOI" written across the top. They are collected, and held by the underwriters and selling group members until the effective date. On this date, the management of each distributing securities dealer allocates the number of shares allowed for each client submitting an IOI. Underwriters attempt to allow as many public investors as possible to participate by allocating a reduced number of shares of popular issues to as many interested clients as possible.

Unfortunately, a great many individual investors seeking hot issues may find that they have been shutout completely. This situation is difficult for the securities account representative for he or she has the job of pacifying a disappointed client (typically a futile attempt). On the other hand, clients submitting IOIs on sticky issues will get their order filled in full. Therefore, any client who has previously given an IOI, but later relents, should immediately contact the securities representative to pull the IOI, because the effective date can never be certain.

Final Prospectus

A final prospectus is officially called the "statutory prospectus," but is typically referred to only as the "prospectus." It is issued to each investor with the statement confirming the purchase at the offering price. At this point, the preliminary prospectus no longer has relevance. The final prospectus is devoid of the Red Herring Notice, and the final price and effective date will be stated. All underwriters will be listed, including those becoming underwriting syndicate members since the printing of the preliminary prospectus.

Public Trading of IPOs

On the effective date, investors that have subscribed to the offering will have had their accounts debited cash and credited with the new issue shares. Shares also start public trading in the stock market under the stock symbol as stated in the prospectus.

Prices for shares of hot issues typically skyrocket in the marketplace on the effective date, and for some days thereafter. The limited supply of shares available for public trading on the effective date will result in the hot issue opening at a much higher price than the offering price. This phenomenon occurs as investors that have either been shutout of the offering or given a reduced allocation, along with others who become intrigued by the explosive market prices, attempt to purchase shares in the marketplace. However, the only shares available for fully subscribed offerings are those obtained by the underwriters from the issuer under the green-shoe clause, and from some subscribers desiring to make a quick profit by flipping shares.

Flipping shares during the quiet period (defined below) is legal, but is considered as an egregious activity that is discouraged. The concept behind underwriting is for securities distributors to seek long-term investors for issuers. Therefore, the managing underwriter typically threatens to withhold the sales concession for dealers whose clients flip shares during the quiet period. Securities representatives then "jawbone" clients that try to place sell orders of IPO shares in order to preserve their selling commissions.

On the other hand, market prices for sticky issues will languish and may decline to levels at which speculative investors may take *a flyer* and purchase shares in the marketplace. These shares become available from nervous investors who purchased shares at the offering price and are now looking to minimize their losses. The eventual success of a sticky issue depends primarily on the strength of the underwriter, who may provide price stabilization (defined below) during the quiet period, with a sales force that is should be sufficient to find additional interested investors thereafter.

Quiet Period

The "quiet period" is a specified period after the effective date in which a hold is placed on any advertising for the new issue. The one exception is a public announcement of the new issue with a "tombstone ad" (as explained below). Throughout this period, securities dealers and brokers are precluded from soliciting, touting, making predictions, or issuing research reports on the new issue security. In addition, all purchases made in the marketplace during the quiet period must also be by prospectus only. This covers sales made to clients of underwriters that represent distribution of shares obtained from exercising the green-shoe clause allotment option of the underwriting agreement (this is described below in "The Prospectus").

The extent of the quiet period depends on the type of new issue security offered, and the marketplace on which it listed. Quiet periods are defined as shown in Table 7-1, "Quiet Period Duration."

Table 7-1 Quiet Period Duration		
Market	**Type Issue**	**Duration**
Exchanges, or NASDAQ	All Issues	25 Days
Non-NASDAQ:	IPOs	90 Days
Non-NASDAQ	Primary or Secondary Distributions	40 Days
All Markets	Blank Check Company (1)	90 Days

Note: (1), Companies that cannot, or do not, describe in the prospectus the exact use of the proceeds of the offering.

Unbundling of Units

As stated previously, public offerings consisting of stock and warrants are initially offered as units. These securities start trading as units on the effective date, and all during the quiet period. At the end of the quiet period, the units will become unbundled (separated), and thereafter will trade as separate securities in the same stock market.

Tombstone Ads

Underwriters, selling dealers and their sales representatives cannot solicit trading in new issues during the quiet period. However, a public announcement of the new issue is permitted after the effective date to inform the public of the new issue. The announcement is not a solicitation, but it is intended to generate additional public interest that will result in requests for a prospectus by the public. This announcement is called a "tombstone ad."

The tombstone ad includes only the following information:

1. the name of the issuing organization

2. the type or types of security being offered

3. the total dollar amount, or the number of shares or units, being offered

4. the price per share, or per unit

5.   the name of the managing underwriter and the underwriting syndicate members

Tombstone ads are displayed in most financial periodicals and magazines. An example of a tombstone ad for a new issue is shown in Figure 7-1, "Tombstone Ad Example."

Figure 7-1
Tombstone Ad Example

This announcement is neither an offer to sell, nor a solicitation of an offer to buy, any of these securities. The offer is made only by the Prospectus.

New Issue   **March 24, 1994**

1,500,000 Shares

Common Stock

Price $5 Per Share

Copies of the Prospectus may be obtained in any State from the undersigned if it may legally offer these Securities in compliance with the securities laws of such State.

Baraban Securities
incorporated

Associated Investors Corporation   **Dunhill Equities, Inc.**
                Tamaron Investments, Inc.
Barclay Investments, Inc.   **First Colonial Securities Group, Inc.**
Frederick & Company, Inc.   **Lew Lieberbaum & Co., Inc.**
            Société Financière du Seujet SA

The Figure 7-1 example shows that 1.5 million shares of a new issue of common stock in *Hi-Shear Technology Corp.* were offered on March 24, 1994 (the effective date) at $5 per share. The name of the managing underwriter, Bara-ban Securities Inc.—formerly a regional, West Coast, securities underwriter—is shown predominantly in large bold print. The names of the underwriting syndicate members are listed below the managing underwriter's name in smaller print.

Price Stabilization

The managing underwriter may state in the prospectus that it will act to support the stock price during the quiet period. This may occur for an offering whose success in distribution may initially be doubtful, but not necessarily a turkey. The underwriter, acting as a market maker, will set a bid price at the offering price in order to keep the market price from falling below the offering prices. This is called price stabilization. In effect, the managing underwriter is prepared to buy the stock back from nervous subscribers at the POP to stabilize the price in the marketplace. However, the duration of price stabilization activity is at the discretion of the underwriter. There is no legal requirement for the underwriter to perform such an activity, and when so performed, it will have been mentioned in the prospectus. Price stabilizing in this situation is allowed as an exception to what otherwise would be price manipulation in the securities markets.

Distribution of Corporate Debt Obligations

Corporate debt obligations are registered with the SEC, and with the individual states in which offered. The distribution process is the same as described above for equity issues, with the requirement being for sale by prospectus only, and for full and fair disclosure and distribution. However, new issue debt obligations are not a focus of this work since they are typically of interest to investors seeking income, not explosive growth. Therefore those interested in debt obligations for income purposes should seek advice from a registered general securities sales representative, or a registered investment advisor.

THE PROSPECTUS

New issue securities are offered as investments to the public through a *prospectus,* which contains all material information that an investor will need in order to decide whether to invest in the new issue, or not. By law, it is the only source of information that can be conveyed to potential investors during the *cooling-off period* (20 days or more prior to becoming public), and during the *quiet period* (25 days, or more, after going public). Therefore, conscientious securities representatives will offer a copy of the preliminary prospectus as a potentially suitable investment to select clients during the cooling-off period.

Any other type of promotional activity puts the securities representative, and the employing securities dealer, in legal jeopardy. Information disclosed to the client that is considered non-public information, even if just a rumor, will put the client in jeopardy of a criminal act simply by acting on this information. Therefore, a decision to submit an indication of interest to a new issue offering must only be made after the prospectus is thoroughly read and evaluated.

Sections of a Typical Prospectus

The prospectus is a lackluster document, unlike an annual financial report that has a colorful, eye-catching appearance. However, it contains all the information that an astute investor would require to form an opinion about the offering. Each section conveys information that is germane to understanding the merits of the offering; however, one initially needs to read only two sections to be able to determine an interest in the offering (see "Reading the Prospectus" presented in Chapter Nine, "Guidelines for New Issues").

Front Cover

The front cover contains far too much information for it to have an eye-catching appeal. The name of the issuing company, or organization, is prominently displayed and is followed by the number of shares or units (stock bundled with warrants) being offered, or by the dollar amount for a fixed-income security offering. A description of the securities being offered is then given; and, equity offerings will also state the stock symbol and securities market on which they will trade after the effective date. The managing underwriter is identified as well as all of the underwriting syndicate members. On firm commitments, the *green-shoe* clause discloses the underwriters' right to purchase a specific amount of additional securities from the issuer for their own account after the effective date as an over allotment award. (This clause is exercised for new issue offerings that increase in price in the marketplace after the effective date.)

Offerings of common stock shares (or units) will disclose the expected price range on the preliminary prospectus for firm commitments. The final public offering price (established at the due diligence meeting), underwriting compensation, and the proceeds to the issuer are stated on the statutory (final) prospectus, but is left as a blank number on the preliminary prospectus. A best effort commitment will state the public offering price, and the amount of the "underwriting," sales agent's compensation on the preliminary prospectus as well.

Required disclaimers are typically listed last. These are statements to the effect that:

1. the securities described have not been approved, nor disapproved by the SEC

2. the SEC has not verified the accuracy of the information contained in the prospectus

3. anyone making a representation to the contrary about either of the above two is committing a criminal offense

The cover page of the preliminary prospectus also contains a "red herring" notice, so called because of its required, bold, red lettering. It is usually found across the top of the front cover, or along the vertical outside edge. The notice informs the reader that:

1. the information contained is subject to change or completion

2. a registration statement has been filed with the SEC

3. the securities described are not to be sold, nor offers to buy accepted, until the effective date

4. the preliminary prospectus does not constitute an offer to sell, nor a solicitation to buy the securities described

5. the securities are not to be sold in any state without registration in that state

The inside of the front cover is the only section in which the issuer has the opportunity to present a visually appealing display consisting of illustrations of products and services that may be offered by the company.

Prospectus Summary

The first page is typically a summary of the offering. It presents a description of the company or organization, a restatement of the security being offered to the public, and *pro-forma* financial statements. This statement presents a hypothetical summary of the Balance Sheet (see Chapter Eight, "Business Life Cycles, Financial Statements and Analyses") should the offering be fully subscribed.

Use of Proceeds Declaration

A required statement disclosing the use of the proceeds of the offering is presented in the prospectus. Primary offerings will define the purposes that the capitalization received is to be used. For example:

1. paying down existing debt

2. purchase of capital equipment

3. reserve allocations for contingency purposes for potential abatement of factors posing a potential risk

4. all other business related items, such as research and development, requiring capital that are beyond the current income capacity of the organization

Secondary offerings disclose the dollar amounts to be paid to each holder of private stock being offered to the public. Split offerings will specify the amounts to be used by the organization for business purposes, as well as amounts to be received by private shareholders.

Statement of Risk Factors

This section describes all factors, in detail, that may pose a risk in the future. This includes business risks, as well as potential legal risks, which may affect the financial position of the company.

Capital Securities Disclosure

A listing of all capital securities is required—common and preferred stock, warrants, and debt obligations, as applicable—presented as if the amount for a full subscription offering would be received.

Summary of Selected Financial Data

This section presents summaries of past Balance Sheets and Income Statements (see Chapter Eight for explanations of financial statements). These are given here in summary form for information disclosure purposes, and are not as detailed as is shown later in the section on "Financial Statements," which discloses the current financial condition in greater detail.

Management's Discussion and Analysis

This section requires management to discuss and analyze the organization's financial condition and business operations. It is not intended here for management to engage in puffery, as they typically do in an annual report, but to provide an explanation for every item that could affect the financial condition; both positive and negative impacts.

Under the Sarbanes-Oxley Act of 2002 (see Chapter Four, "Securities Industry Regulations"), this section must include any off-balance sheet arrangements and unconsolidated entity connections that could have a material effect (legalese for significant) on current or future finances. It must describe the nature and purpose of such arrangements, and the potential risk and impact to shareholders. These should have previously been disclosed under the full disclosure doctrine; however, they are now specifically to be addressed in this section by law.

Business Description

This section provides an overview discussion of all the industries (if more than one) in which the issuer is doing business, and a disclosure of all products or services provided. The business strategies of the organization are explained and a review of the competition is presented as well.

Management Disclosure

The management of the organization issuing securities is revealed in this section. This includes identifying the directors, officers, and key employees by name along with brief biographies for each.

Recent Major Transactions

Spending within the past year on significant, major expenditures is considered material to an offering. Therefore, all major transactions for acquisition of plant and equipment are described and explained. This also includes disclosure of business mergers and acquisitions.

Dilution

New issue offerings of securities for companies, in which public shares are outstanding, can dilute the book value per share. This is especially true for secondary and split offerings, or offerings of convertible securities. The amount per share of the POP that is above the *pro-forma* book value is specified as the dilution.

Principal Shareholders

This section lists the identities of all current principal shareholders—shareholders holding more than 5% of equity—and the percent amount of ownership for each.

Underwriting Agreement

This section summarizes and describes the agreement between the underwriter and the issuer of securities. It will indicate how much risk is involved for the underwriters. A firm commitment means that the underwriters have contracted to purchase the entire issue from the company, distribute all shares to the public, or else purchase them for their own account. A best effort commitment is no commitment at all. Here the distributing securities dealers are pledging to make the best effort possible to distribute all shares. However, they are under no obligation other than to make a reasonable effort. (See explanations given previously for the different types of underwriting commitments.)

Financial Statements

Detailed financial statements, as they would appear in an annual report, are presented here. Startup stage businesses can only show a *pro-forma* Balance Sheet since they typically will have no income yet. Development stage and later business life cycle stage organizations should present current financial statements (Balance Sheet, Income Statement, and reconciliation statements are explained in Chapter Eight, "Business Life Cycles, Financial Statements and Analyses"), as well as a *pro-forma* balance sheet assuming a full subscription offering. Items that need further explanation are identified with numerical footnote markers, and will be discussed in the section under "Notes to the Financial Statements" (as explained below).

Auditor's Report

This section is also called "Auditor's Opinion," or "Report of Independent Auditors." It provides an independent, certified opinion of the financial condition of the company (required in every annual report). Typically, one of the most important statements in an annual report, this report should consist of only two paragraphs. The first explains the scope of the audit. The second paragraph typically states the opinion, and should contain both phrases, "*presents fairly the financial position*" and "*in conformity with generally accepted accounting practices.*" These indicate that the company's financial statements meet accepted accounting standards: an "unqualified opinion."

The words *"subject to"* or *"except that"* used somewhere in the middle of the opinion paragraph, will indicate that there may be a problem. These indicate that the auditor is giving a "qualified opinion," which is an alert about a problem area that probably can be corrected by appropriate action. When so stated, an explanation is usually provided in a third paragraph. In the qualified opinion, the auditor presents the facts and lets the readers draw their own conclusion.

However, a "disclaimer of opinion" is issued when insufficient documentation is available to verify the financial statements. Consequently, the opinion paragraph will make a statement that *"We do not express an opinion on the financial statements presented."*

Lastly, an "adverse opinion" will occur when the financial documentation is sufficient to form an opinion, but the auditor does not agree with the accounting methods used. In this case, the opinion paragraph would contain a statement that the financial statements *"Do not present fairly the financial condition of the company."* In the adverse opinion and disclaimer of opinion, the auditor essentially announces that there could well be a serious problem.

Notes to Financial Statements

This section is an important part of any financial report. The first part is typically a summary of the accounting policies, such as:

1. inventory pricing methods (FIFO versus LIFO)

1. the methods used for fixed capital property and depreciation and amortization

2. how deferred income tax payments and investment tax credits are treated

3. how earnings per share are computed, as well as disclosing what differences result when losses from discontinued operations are removed

The Notes also disclose information about items in the financial statements that require clarification. Unfavorable financial events cannot be omitted, but they typically are buried in the notes for obfuscation purposes. They also provide, for informational purposes, disclosure on the types, classes, and amounts of all capital stock issued and outstanding, as well as listing the maturity dates and face value amounts for all long-term debt.

Inside Back Cover

The inside of the back cover typically presents demographic information on the locations of business operations, and branch offices. Graphical illustrations are also typically given here showing aerial views of plant and facilities.

Back Cover

The back cover contains a table of contents, and page location for each section of the prospectus. It also will contain a last warning that any representation or information other than that disclosed in the prospectus is unauthorized and unlawful. Lastly, it will provide information on the availability of the prospectus (the sole information source during the cooling off and quiet periods).

EXEMPT OFFERINGS

Most equity and corporate debt obligation securities are considered as non-exempt securities; they are registered with the SEC before being offered to the public. However, all government and certain corporate securities are exempt from SEC registration, and may be offered not only to accredited investors (defined below), but in many instances, they are also offered to the public.

Even though some securities may be exempt from SEC registration, no security is exempt from the anti-fraud requirements of securities laws. Therefore, exempt securities are briefly discussed below to understand more fully the distribution requirements of exempt securities for investors that may be interested.

Private Placements

A *private placement,* also called both a "Reg. D" offering or a "letter security," is the distribution of securities (common or preferred stock, bonds, limited partnerships, and ADRs) only to "accredited investors" (SEC Rule 501). These offerings are exempt from SEC registration; therefore, they are neither to be offered to the public, nor traded in a public marketplace once issued. They are illiquid securities that must be considered as a long-term investment with only the possibility of someday becoming a tradable public security through the registration process. Even though there is no public market for private placements, some may be found offered by market makers in the OTC Bulletin Board, or the NQB's Pink Sheets (see Chapter Five, "Securities Markets").

Offerings for more than $5 million over a 12-month period must be registered as a public offering with both the SEC and with the individual states in which offered. However, because most private placements are for capitalization amounts less than $5 million, a regional, or online, investment banker having a best effort commitment with the issuer will typically distribute these securities.

In this age of the Internet, scores of online investment bankers offer their services to organizations seeking capitalization with a private placement offering. These type firms advertise their services to assist in acquiring capitalization for business organizations with a *direct public offering* (DPO). The term "direct," means that securities purchases are made directly with the issuer. The underwriter acts as an agent only. The term "public offering" is misleading in that the shares are to be distributed to only accredited investors, and are not registered with the SEC for sale to the public.

Securities that are not registered with the SEC and sold by the issuer as a private placement must be accompanied by a "letter of intent" (also called an "investment letter"). This letter is signed by the purchaser establishing that the securities are intended as an investment and not for resale. Therefore, the term *letter security* is often used for private placements. Private placements must comply with all the anti-fraud regulations established by law, in spite of the fact that they are not registered with the SEC. They are sold by an "offering circular" for offerings of more than $500,000, and the disclosure of information contained is typically limited. There are no disclosure requirements for private placements of $500,000 or less. It is up to the institution or accredited investor to determine whether the financial information contained in the offering circular is complete.

Securities sales representatives offering private placements must solicit only from known, accredited investors. The very successful technique of "cold calling" (making telephone solicitations to phone numbers obtained directly from a phone directory) is strictly prohibited. However, anyone who has ever subscribed to one or more financial periodicals, or has ever had an account with a financial services organization, has probably been contacted by a cold call sales rep soliciting private placements from a purchased list of names. This effective sales technique would appear to be illegal, but is allowed by SEC Rule 506, which waives the *accredited investor purchase only* rule for non-accredited investors, if they are represented by a professional Investment Advisor, or if they have sufficient financial sophistication and status and sign an investor qualification form. Another waiver is granted by SEC Rule 504, which applies to offerings that are less than $1 million.

Accredited Investors Beware!

The class of investors called "accredited investors" consists of financial institutions, certain organizations, and high net worth individuals. Financial institutions include banks, insurance companies, venture capitalists, pension funds, investment pools managed by a professional investment manager, and securities dealers buying for their own account. Organizations include both private businesses and non-profit organizations with assets over $5 million. Lastly, accredited investors include private individuals having a net worth of over $1 million, with an annual income of at least $200,000 per year ($300,000 per year if married with joint income) and with every expectation that this income level will continue in the future.

Accredited investors are generally not protected by current securities laws, which are mainly designed to provide the public with full and fair disclosure. The rationale is that they should have the financial expertise to provide a reasonable assessment of the offering, and if not, they have the resources to hire someone that does. Therefore, accredited individual investors are prime targets for securities sales reps distributing high-risk, illiquid securities.

Venture Capitalists

Venture capitalists are private accredited investors, or firms, that provide capital for startup and development organizations. They typically seek a "liquidity event" within 3 to 5 years for the unregistered shares. Their goal is a capital gain in the range of from 300% to 500% on their investment. The liquidity event typically consists of a public offering in which private investor shares will either become registered, or will be offered to the public, as well as also offering additional authorized stock with a split offering. Therefore, private investors have to be convinced of the integrity and capability of management to be able to expand the business within this period in order to meet these criteria. This can only be accomplished by having one-on-one meetings, something that public investors are not likely to get a chance to perform.

Small Capitalization Public Offering

Small capitalization offerings are also called "Reg. A" offerings. A small capitalization, public offering is defined as any offering with a capitalization of less than $5 million to be distributed in any 12-month period. These are exempt from SEC and state registration and from the requirement of *for sale by prospectus only.*

However, an Offering Circular, which is a simplified disclosure document, is to be filed with the SEC at least 10 days before the initial offering date for all such offerings over $100,000. It must be delivered to subscribers of the offering at least 48 hours before the confirmation is mailed. All other distribution rules discussed for non-exempt public offerings are to be observed, with only a tombstone ad being allowed during the quiet period.

However, small cap offerings less than $10 million can register with the SEC using Form SB-1. Small businesses offering securities with a maximum of $1 million in capitalization can register the securities in most states with a Small Corporate Offering Registration (SCOR) by filing Form U-7. The benefit of registration of these small cap offerings is that they can be listed on the Pacific Stock Exchange and traded on its SCOR Marketplace.

Intrastate Offerings

An intrastate offering, also defined as a "SEC Rule 147" offering, is a public offering made to only residents of a state, for securities issued by an organization doing business only in the state. Rule 147 offerings are exempt from SEC registration, but must be registered with the state in which it is offered, unless it also falls into the Small Cap public offering category. The stock certificates must carry a disclosure legend defining that the security must not be resold within nine months of the issue date, and then only to residents of the state of registration. It is the duty of the transfer agent to prevent illegal transactions.

Exempt Debt Obligations

New issue debt obligations exempt from SEC registration include U.S. Treasury bills, notes, and bonds; U.S. government agency obligations; and municipal debt obligations. U.S. government obligations are distributed both weekly and monthly by auction to major bond securities dealers. (Corporate debt obligations are non-exempt, and are subject to all distribution requirements for public securities offerings.)

Underwriters are selected by either a competitive or a negotiated bid with the issuer distributing municipal debt obligations. However, as stated previously, new issue debt obligations (either corporate, U.S. government or municipal governments) are not a focus of this work since they are typically of interest to investors seeking only income, not explosive growth. Again, those interested in debt obligations for income purposes should seek advice from a Registered General Securities Representative or a Registered Investment Advisor.

Eight
Business Life Cycles, Financial Statements and Analyses

✦

Assessing Securities' Values!

All business organizations require additional capital in each phase of their business life cycle. They first require capital in the startup phase, they require capital in the development phase, they require capital in the rapid expansion phase, they require capital in the mature growth stage, and they require capital to provide growth through acquisitions in the stability and decline phase. A variety of public securities is offered to investors throughout the life cycle. The type security offered is appropriate to both the life cycle stage, and the type of business organization (as discussed in Chapter Two, "Business Capitalization Securities"). The investment risk for these securities generally decreases with each successive life cycle stage.

Although the type of security offered to the public can reflect the current life cycle stage of the business corporation, it should not be, by itself, the sole determination of investment risk. The life cycle stage risk is secondary to the financial condition of a business organization. Therefore, understanding the financial condition is required before making any investment in a new issue.

The more traditional method for financially evaluating a business is called "Fundamental Analysis." This method is performed by first reducing financial data to form financial parameters, such as specific "ratios." The financial condition is assessed by making comparisons with the financial parameters reported for past reporting periods, as well as with financial parameters reported for different organizations within the same industry sector.

For many investors, having a clue about the financial condition of an organization may first appear to be beyond their comprehension. However, the financial condition can easily be assessed by applying a few, simple word statements. For example, everyone with reasonable deductive reasoning can understand the simple statement "net worth equals assets less liabilities." Assets greater than liabilities is good! However, the question then becomes, What is the quality of the assets carried on the books? This and other questions can be answered using the data provided. Financial data for all public businesses are disclosed to the public by law. The only difficult task is becoming acquainted with, and understanding the terms used in these statements.

Another method for evaluation is called "intrinsic value" analysis. Benjamin Graham, who is considered as the founder of fundamental analysis, initially espoused this method in the 1930s. Value analysis has been successfully championed by Graham's protégé, Warren Buffett, who is commonly referred to as the *Sage of Omaha,* and has arguably been the world's most successful investor over the last 40 years of the 20th Century. Although the short-term trading public largely ignores intrinsic value analysis, it can be a valuable tool for the long-term investor. The method can determine a theoretical dollar value for a security, which can then be compared with the current offer price. However, determining the intrinsic value requires historical financial data; annual earnings, depreciation, and capital expenditures. In addition, one must assume a probable growth rate in future earnings. The method can indicate a theoretical price valuation range although this may require a great leap of faith for nonbelievers.

Historical financial data of business organizations is required for each evaluation method, regardless of which method is used. These data are commonly found in annual financial reports that are required for every public business organization. Therefore, the IPO investor should understand how to read these reports and what information can be a precursor of a potential problem.

THE BUSINESS LIFE CYCLE

The type of security offered by corporations to raise capital depends upon the stage of the business life cycle in which the corporation is operating. Corporate life expectancy is mostly dependent on management expertise. For example, a company who started manufacturing leather buggy whips in 1900 would have eventually gone out of business as buggies gave way to autos, unless management recognized the industry's potential decline in time to take steps to diversify into other business areas. Even though if it may sometimes be difficult to determine exactly what stage a particular company may be in, most all corporations encompass five stages within their life cycle. These stages are identified as startup; development; rapid expansion; mature growth; and lastly, stability and decline. Each of these is discussed below.

Startup Stage

A "startup" stage company essentially consists of a business concept. It should be considered as being in a Stage Zero life cycle type business by default (since Stage One through Stage Four have been given classical definitions which are explained below). Startups are typically organized as privately held companies with the initial incorporators providing facilities, equipment, expertise, and limited seed capital. Throughout this stage, the emphasis is on verifying the product or service, and making initial sales to a limited number of customers. As soon as the business demonstrates that it can be a viable business organization with potential future, then outside capitalization is sought to get the company through the next three to seven years.

Startup companies typically do not offer shares to the public with a public offering. These business concept organizations would have extreme difficulty obtaining capitalization from either a public offering or a financial institution. It would be unlikely that anyone would invest only in a business idea, and most banks would require tangible assets for securing borrowed funds. Therefore, capitalization for startup companies is usually sought from private sources, with private placements with venture capitalists.

However, there are exceptions when public offerings are used for a startup company. One exception is a startup company that is spun off from well-known, financially sound company who retains a majority ownership in the startup company. Another is a company being started by a well-known, successful individual that has had a previous history of startup successes. These exceptions to start-up public offerings are made mainly on the strength of the name recognition of the sponsoring individual or organization.

Capitalization from Venture Capitalists

Venture capitalists are individuals, or organizations, that provide capitalization for new business ventures lacking the collateral typically demanded by established financial lending institutions. Venture capitalists look to the believability of management to assess the potential success rather than the type of business or the uniqueness of the product. A great business idea would be worthless without individuals that can make the business grow.

However, they often insist on majority ownership just to insure that, if necessary, they can control events to protect their considerable monetary investment. The high risk involved requires venture capitalists to make a minimum of 30% per year on their investment. They also require that within five years, an IPO would be completed so that their ownership shares would become liquid by being registered, and gain from 300% to 500% on their investment. The venture capitalist could then take profits by disposing of some, or all, of their ownership interest, either with a split offering or by selling shares in the marketplace.

Capitalization from Private Placements

When venture capitalists are not used for capitalization, the company may offer a small cap, private placement offering of less than $5 million (see Chapter Seven, "New Issue Offerings" for a discussion on the various type securities offerings). For this type securities issue, the company typically will employ an investment banker acting as an agent to distribute these non-public shares to accredited investors for a sales fee. Stock distributions are also available for intrastate offerings, as well as small cap offerings through online underwriters. Management does not surrender majority ownership with private placements, as is the case with venture capitalists, and those subscribing to the offering have no leverage to force a future liquidity event (public offering) should management later decide that it would not be in their best interest to do so.

Private placements represent an illiquid security. In addition, investors participating in private placements purchase shares with limited disclosure and without due diligence from the securities distributor, which would otherwise be required with a public offering (as described in Chapter Seven, "New Issue Offerings"). Without required audited financial reporting, private placements present the greatest potential for fraud from an unscrupulous management.

Development Stage

Development stage companies are classically referred to as Stage 1 companies in the business life cycle, are startup companies that have gone through the "knothole": they have achieved sufficient sales to demonstrate that the business enterprise has a product or service that can be expanded upon. Sales typically have been increasing consistently over the past several years. Earnings have started to materialize, which have been retained for business expansion, and have increased with each reporting period. Another term used for development stage companies is "emerging growth."

Stage 1 companies typically have a capitalization structure that is all equity with no long-term debt, and whose capit lization is less than $100 million. The additional capitalization required for exp nsion is typically obtained from a public offering of common stock; usually t' e IPO will provide a capital structure amount up to $500 million. Companies that seek less than $100 million with an offering will typically use a regional securities underwriter. The national firms are more interested in managing larger offerings that have a national appeal and can utilize the strength of all their branch offices to distribute the issue.

However, the proceeds from public offerings for Stage 1 companies may not all be used for business expansion. A portion may instead go to initial major stockholders distributing previously unregistered shares. Proceeds from primary offerings flow directly to the company for business expansion, while proceeds from secondary offering flow only to inside stockholders. Split offering proceeds are split between the company and the major stockholders. Therefore, the type of offering indicates where the capital raised by the offering will be used (offering types were explained in Chapter Seven, "New Issue Offerings").

Development stage companies do not have sufficient historical operational data on which to provide a meaningful financial evaluation. In these instances, the investor must use his or her judgment based on the *story*. The term "story" is nebulous. It cannot be defined. It is simply something about an offering that makes the investor feel excited about owning a piece of the business.

Shares of a primary public offering should be the same class of shares as that held by insiders. A different class would indicate a difference either in future dividend distributions or in voting rights. The quantity of public shares offered should also be a significant amount of the total outstanding shares (shares held by both insiders and the public). The shares may have insufficient liquidity in the marketplace if the amount of shares publicly offered represents less than 40% of the outstanding supply or ½ million shares. A lack of trading volume may cause some of OTC market makers to abandon the issue and may not even meet the required minimum of two to allow continued trading in the OTC markets. Therefore, the company may become "closely-held" by default, and public investors may find no market on which to sell their stock when they so chose.

In a secondary offering, all proceeds go directly to insiders distributing privately held shares personally owned to the public as an IPO, or a new issue. The company receives none of the capital raised by the offering. The majority owners, including initial incorporators and venture capitalists, are simply offering shares to the public to take profits. Public shares of secondary offerings consist of the same class stock as those held by insiders being offered to the public. The same rule-of-thumb amount of the float—40% of the total outstanding supply or ½ million shares as a minimum—applies to secondary offerings as well as to primary offerings, for the same reasons. A firm underwriting commitment would be required for offerings with marginal floating supply amounts.

A split offering is a combination primary and secondary offering. A portion, representing new stock issued from the authorized supply, is offered to the public along with an amount offered by inside majority owners. Shares offered to the public are typically the same class as those held by insiders. Again, the rule-of-thumb distribution amount of the outstanding supply also applies to split offerings, as well as having an underwriter's firm commitment.

Primary, secondary, and split offering shares offered to the public, as well as shares owned by insiders, will be registered with the SEC as "issued and outstanding" public stock. Insiders can therefore take profits by selling their stock in the marketplace, although they are subject to selling restrictions for control persons (as discussed in Chapter Four, "Securities Regulations")

Rapid Expansion Stage

A traditional rapid expansion company, also called a Stage 2 company, is characterized by exponential sales growth reflecting explosive earnings that have been retained for business expansion over the past three to five years. Rapid expansion occurs when the company has captured a market niche with few, if any, competitors. Stage 2 companies are typically "small cap" companies whose capital structure is less than $500 million (sometimes called "micro-cap" companies).

The market price for shares of rapid expansion companies is typically bid up to two or more times the average earnings rate. For example, a company with a 40% annual earnings increase over the past few years is likely to have share prices bid up to about 80 times current annual earnings (or higher). Whereas, prices of large cap stocks making up major market indices traditionally run between 10 and 20 times the current earnings per share. Stage 2 companies will frequently pay a stock dividend—otherwise called a stock split—because of the rapid increase in market prices. Stock dividends keep the nominal trading unit of 100 shares (a round lot) at an affordable level for the average individual investor.

However, expansion is typically so great that the retained earnings are not sufficient to provide for the anticipated level of capitalization needed for continued expansion. Therefore, new issue securities are usually offered to provide the amount of capital needed, typically through a national underwriting securities dealer making a firm commitment. The size of such offerings will be sufficiently large enough to interest a national underwriting firm, and national distribution is assured. The securities offered may either be a new issue of the same class common stock with a "rights offering" and a standby commitment from the underwriter; a new issue of a different class common stock with restricted voting or dividend rights; or convertible preferred stock or debentures.

A manic market should not be mistaken for a rapid expansion phase of the business life cycle. Most of the new technology and Internet companies collectively appeared to achieve rapid expansion in the absence of earnings over the last three years of the 20t^h Century. Here the emphasis was on accelerating sales, or in many cases, the anticipation of increased sales. Earnings, or more aptly the lack of earnings, were ignored. The new information age of instant electronic communications allowed investors to be confronted with manic touting of such investment vehicles on the Internet.

A phenomenon of such a magnitude had not been seen for 80 years, and the realistic consequences were largely ignored. Many of the traditionally conservative financial news analysts found flimsy reasons on which to justify this "new paradigm." Any reasonable person should have understood that this manic market could not be maintained. But, most reasonable investors could not help from jumping onto this bandwagon, especially in the latter phase when stock prices increased exponentially. The pre September 11, 2001 justification was that there could be no threat to the manic market as long as there was no threat to the global economy. Inflation was nil, and an event precipitating an economic collapse brought on by political upheaval in some other developed, or developing, country was inconceivable. None-the-less, the final blowout in March of 2000 occurred despite the lack of such news, and the end of this manic phase was not fully realized for nearly a year thereafter. By then, most dot-com securities investments had been wiped out.

Mature Growth Stage

Mature growth companies, which are also called Stage 3 companies, emerge from the rapid expansion stage. The company size increases, but the annual percent growth in sales and earnings both slow to a sustainable level from the Stage 2 pace. In this stage, earnings start to exceed the amount that is needed for business expansion, including amounts spent on research and development. Therefore, cash dividend distributions begin to be paid to the common stockholders. Stock splits become less frequent as stock price appreciation slows to an even slower rate than earnings, and the once lofty price-earnings ratios are gradually reduced to levels comparable with other companies having an equivalent growth rate. Typically, this occurs when the capitalization market value reaches the level of "mid cap" companies, between $2 billion and $8 billion. It may also occur with the "large cap" category where capitalization exceeds $8 billion in market value.

The large cap companies may engage in stock buyback programs to avoid corporate raiders from attempting a takeover to gain access to the excess cash in retained earnings. Buying back stock also increases public interest in the stock by the improving per share financial parameters on the remaining outstanding stock, thereby giving a specious indication of growth.

However, not every company reaches a healthy mature growth stage. Many of these are companies that are "closely held" corporations with a limited number of public shareholders. There is no genuine oversight of management with outside directors because management owns the majority of the outstanding stock. Although the business may have prospered within a narrow niche market, such management can easily reach their level of incompetence that precludes meaningful further expansion to mature growth status. Managements with inbred boards of directors usually do little to fund research and development for continued growth over the years, and most of the earnings typically are distributed to shareholders, the majority of which are insiders.

When the managements of these "sick" companies finally realize that additional growth is necessary for continued survival, their only recourse is to attempt to purchase growth by acquiring an existing business. The funds for such acquisition are typically obtained by issuing a different class common stock with limited voting rights (in order to prevent expanding the voting class stockholders) through a regional underwriter. The problem with these type offerings is that management usually does not have the competence to incorporate the acquisition successfully. In addition, market support by the regional underwriter for the new stock after issue may not be sufficient to maintain public interest after the new issue becomes public.

The challenge for managements of mature growth stage companies shifts from increasing market share by improving product lines or services (as had occurred in stages 1 and 2), to providing expansion by acquiring or developing other products or services, which is called business diversification. A classic example of such a company is Philip Morris. Once a king in the now endangered tobacco industry, it is now a globally diversified company where revenues from tobacco are a fraction of its annual earnings.

Cash rich companies may negotiate a buyout deal for majority control with either a cash offer or a combination of cash and authorized stock. Large cap acquisitions usually require obtaining the capital required through either a long-term debt or a preferred stock or a new issue offering. These are typically offered through national underwriting firms providing rigorous due diligence activities to assure that their firm commitment agreement has minimal risk.

Fixed-Income Security Offerings

Mature growth stage corporations will most likely attempt to secure capital required for business acquisition with a long-term debenture offering. These debt obligations provide capitalization without sharing voting rights. In addition to long-term debt securities, another fixed income security that is typically offered is preferred stock or a different class of preferred stock if other preferred stock issues are outstanding.

Convertible debentures or convertible preferred stock issues are usually not offered by large cap corporations. The name recognition of the company and investment quality rating should be able to support public interest in offering a fixed-income security offering competitive current yield from either interest or dividend payments. However, small-cap and even mid-cap, mature growth companies may find it advantageous to offer convertibles.

During the hostile takeover mania of the 1980s, Large-cap companies sought growth by acquisitions typically funded with "junk bonds." However, the junk bond securities fraud scandals that were publicly revealed later in that decade required intervention by the federal government. Both the savings and loan and the insurance industries—heavy investors in junk securities—needed rescue. Several major securities underwriters were cited for lack of due diligence. The principal junk bond underwriter was forced into bankruptcy. High yield debt obligations are still offered for capitalization when it is necessary to attract public interest, but the junk bond industry as it existed in the 1980s is no longer.

Equity Security Offerings

Mature growth stage corporations also may offer a new issue of same class common stock with a *rights offering,* followed up by a *standby offering* to the public to distribute residual shares not purchased by current owners. Occasionally, a different class common stock will be issued that will be backed by the operations of the new acquisition. Market price and dividend payments, if any, for the new class stock will be based on the business operation of the new acquisition. An example is General Motors' Class H common stock that was issued on the acquisition of the Hughes Aircraft Company.

Stability and Decline Stage

Eventually, business organizations find that annual sales have leveled off, or may have even declined. Earnings are still being generated, but are also in decline as profit margins become squeezed. Costs increase as competition forces price cuts. The lack of growth results in the stock competing as an investment vehicle. Share prices become a function of the cash dividends paid, which is typically the major portion of earnings. They are negatively impacted by either sentiment that dividends may be cut, or from increases in financial market interest rates. This *stability and decline stage* is also known as Stage 4, a precursor to the eventual demise of the organization.

Many of these Stage 4 businesses may never even reach a mid-cap size corporation, largely as the result of inept management. To have done do so would be an indication that management had successfully achieved growth, and should be able to continue to do so (unless taken over by hostile corporate raider intent on stripping it of all its assets). Stage 4 company management may try to buy growth with an acquisition (as described above), or may seek a merger with another corporation with the assistance of a securities underwriter.

Organizations that have achieved large-cap size by successfully growing into a diversified company may find that one of the business segments has started into decline. To avoid difficulties for the entire corporation, it will often spin off the declining business segment as a separate company, or seek another corporation to acquire it. This situation occurred with many defense contractors in the early 1990s upon the end of the Cold War. There are different terms for companies attempting to stave off Stage 4 status, but the term most often used is "restructuring." Restructuring implies that management (old or new) is attempting to reverse a declining situation with a "turnaround" strategy (another term used for restructuring). However, in the words of Warren Buffett, one of the world's richest men and considered by many the 20th Century's greatest investor, *"Turn-arounds seldom turn."*

FINANCIAL STATEMENTS

Organizations issuing public securities are required to provide audited financial statements both in the new issue, offering prospectus, and for each fiscal year thereafter. These statements define the financial condition on the date of the reporting, as well as the degree of success for business activities over the period since the last annual report. The three types of financial statements reported by those operating a business are:

1.   the Balance Sheet

2.   the Income Statement

3.   the Reconciliation Statements

Each statement gives different insights into the financial condition of the business organization.

The potential success of a new issue for an ongoing business should be able to be detected. An evaluation using current financial data and security market price to establish various parameters can indicate the financial health as well as value beside whatever else excites the investor about the offering (called its *story*). Two methods of evaluation can be used: analysis of the financial "fundamentals," which focuses on all of the data presented in the financial statements; and, "intrinsic" or "fair" value analysis, which attempts to put a current dollar value on the securities being issued. These evaluation methods are explained below, following the discussion of the individual financial statements. Both methods are more apt t be used to evaluate existing public company securities because of the availability of historical financial data.

However, many companies issuing new offering securities do not have sufficient historical operational data on which to provide a meaningful, if any, financial evaluation. In these instances, the investor must use his or her best judgment on the merits of the offering based on both the "story" for the company and the previous success of the management, both of which are presented in the prospectus. (As stated previously, the "story" is whatever it is that excites the reader about the organization's business prospects.)

The Balance Sheet

The Balance Sheet is a statement of the financial condition of the organization on a given date. It is the predominate statement indicating the financial health of an organization. It presents the organization's assets and liabilities, and the difference between these being the net worth, which is otherwise called "shareholder equity." Assets represent anything of value that is owned by the organization. Liabilities represent the value of all debt owed by the organization. Therefore, the Balance Sheet formula for any type organization is represented by Table 8-1, "Balance Sheet Formula" as shown below:

Table 8-1
Balance Sheet Formula

Assets = Liabilities + Net Worth

Assets

Assets can be either cash, or items of value that are owned by, or are to be paid to, the company. They are designated into two categories, either "current assets" or "fixed assets." Current assets typically consist of:

1. cash on hand or deposited in a financial institution

2. marketable securities that can be converted immediately into cash, such as stocks or bonds traded in a securities market

3. accounts receivable, which is the total of all unpaid receipts due by other business organizations that have purchased goods or services on an open credit policy

4. inventory, which consists of both the cost of finished goods on hand and ready for delivery, and the value of goods that are in the process of being manufactured, which is called "works-in-progress" (WIP)

Fixed assets, which are also called "slow assets," are all assets that cannot be readily sold or turned into cash. They are designated into two categories, "tangible fixed assets" and "intangible" fixed assets.

Tangible fixed assets consists of land, buildings, machinery and equipment, vehicles, furniture, fixtures, overdue accounts receivable (being on the books for more than a year), and illiquid or non-negotiable securities (such as private placement shares or non-tradable limited partnership interests). This later category has been used by some "creative corporate accountants" to hide some balance sheet debt to improve fictitiously the equity-to-debt ratio. This is described below under "Off-Balance Sheet Transactions."

Intangible assets represent money spent on items that are not "perceptible" or "touchable." They exist but cannot be seen, however an accounting of such must be made as an item on the Balance Sheet to keep the books balanced. Typical intangible assets consist of "goodwill"; money spent for acquisition of franchise, mineral, or patent rights; and, money spent for leasehold improvements (upgrading rented quarters). Goodwill represents the amount spent acquiring other businesses that was in excess of the acquired businesses' tangible net worth. Intangible assets represent money spent non-productively. It must be included to keep the books balanced; but for transparency, it must be subtracted from the book value of Net Worth to result in a "Tangible Net Worth."

Liabilities

Liabilities are either cash, or items of value that are obligations of the organization. They are designated into two categories, either "current liabilities" or "long-term liabilities."

Current liabilities represent debt that must be paid within one year. This includes:

1. principal amounts for loans or debt obligations that mature and must be paid within the year

2. interest payments for the year to be paid on loans and debt obligations

3. accounts payable for merchandise, services, or material acquired on open credit

4. corporate dividends declared but not as yet paid

5. reserve amounts for taxes to be paid and employee withholdings for income, Social Security and Medicare taxes

Long-term liabilities represent obligations that are payable on a date more than one year. For example, the principal balances on mortgages, loans, and long-term debt obligations.

Net Worth

Net worth is the difference between assets and liabilities It represents the amount of ownership equity in the business organization. Net worth for corporate Balance Sheets represents "shareholder equity." Separate line entries under shareholder equity include the "par value" of the issued and outstanding common and preferred stock; the amount of the "paid-in-surplus," also called "paid-in-capital"; which is also called "earned surplus." Retained earnings represent the accumulated annual net earnings not used for the business, or distributed to shareholders as cash dividends.

The par value for stock (as stated in Chapter Two, "Business Capitalization Securities") is an assigned value for each class share. It has little meaning for common stock because it is intentionally assigned a low value for purposes of state of incorporation tax. The difference between the offering price and par value is defined as the "paid-in-surplus." For example, assume that a hypothetical offering of five million shares of common stock is offered at $10 per share, and has an assigned par value of $1 per share. Assume the underwriter's concession is 10%. As a result, the *pro-forma* financial statement would show $5 million shareholder equity and $40 million paid-in-surplus. $5 million of the offering proceeds would have been paid to securities dealers as underwriting compensation.

However, the market price of common stock after distribution is established in the marketplace on which it trades. The term "market cap" is a value that is determined from multiplying the number of outstanding common shares by the current market price.

Unlike common stock, the par value of preferred stock does have meaningful value. It represents the amount of capital raised by the company, on which a specific annual dividend amount is promised. The market price after issue is set in the marketplace as a function of the parity between the nominal dividend yield and current cost for long-term money for equivalent quality securities. This is called its "investment value." The market price for a convertible issue is established by either its investment value, or on the common stock price when the conversion price is lower than the current common stock market price.

Corporate Balance Sheet Example

The Balance Sheet is typically presented in tabular form with a column for asset items on the left side, and liability and net worth items listed in the right column. The upper part shows current assets and liabilities, and the lower part shows "slow" assets, long-term debt and net worth. An example of a corporate Balance Sheet is shown below in Table 8-2, "Typical Corporate Balance Sheet."

Table 8-2
Typical Corporate Balance Sheet

Assets	Liabilities
Current Assets: Cash Marketable Securities Accounts Receivable Inventories	**Current Liabilities:** Loans Less Than 1 Year Interest on Loans & Debt Obligations Accounts Payable Dividends Declared Reserves for Tax & Withholdings
Fixed (Tangible) Assets: Real Property Physical Plant & Equipment Non-Negotiable Long-Term Securities	**Long-Term Debt:** Mortgages, Notes & Debt Obligations Due In More Than 1 Year
Intangible Assets: Goodwill Intellectual Property (Patents & Copyrights) Mineral, Oil, & Franchise Rights	**Net Worth** **(Shareholder Equity)** Par Value of Common & Preferred Stock Paid In Surplus, (Paid-in-capital) Retained Earnings (Earned Surplus)

As was stated previously, net worth for the corporate balance sheet is also called shareholder equity. It includes the initial proceeds of common and preferred stock offerings as well as retained earnings. Net worth for the sole proprietor's balance sheet would consist only of retained earnings (no stock is issued).

Note that the Balance Sheet, as stated above, is presented in two columns representing the Balance Sheet Formula shown by Table 8-1. The left column lists all assets, while the right column lists all liabilities plus shareholder equity. The dashed horizontal line represents the separation of items in the upper portion (current assets and current liabilities) from items in the lower portion (fixed assets, and long-term liabilities plus net worth). The dollar difference between these two "current" columns represents an important financial parameter called "working capital," which is explained below in "Reconciliation of Working Capital," and in "Balance Sheet Parameters" under section, "Fundamental Analysis."

Off-Balance Sheet Transactions

As mentioned previously in Chapter Four, "Securities Industry Regulations, "a too common accounting abuse that became public knowledge only after post-mortems of several well known, failed corporations was the hiding corporate debt using off-balance sheet transactions. The technique used was to create a wholly owned private organization, such as a limited partnership, to which significant amount of company debt would be allocated. The organization would not be financially incorporated (called an unconsolidated entity) into the corporate financial statements; therefore, the debt would then disappear from the liability side of the corporate balance sheet. These "off-balance sheet transactions" are complex; however, the following hypothetical example can illustrate how this worked.

Assume that corporation "Z" has assets of $500 million, including $300 million of intangible assets, and $400 million in liabilities including long-term debt. The net worth would then be $100 million as shareholder equity. Assume "Z" then transfers all the intangible assets and $250 million of the long-term debt to a wholly owned unconsolidated limited partnership. The LP balance sheet would consist of the $300 million in intangible assets, $250 million in long-term debt, and $50 million are placed under the partnership's Net Worth column as the value of partnership units issued to "Z" as the sole owner. Tangible fixed assets of "Z's" balance sheet would increase from $200 million to $250 million, while intangible assets shrink to zero and liabilities are reduced to $150 million. $250 million of debt is eliminated and $300 million intangible (worthless) assets disappear by not consolidating the financial statements of both "Z" and the partnership (wholly owned by "Z"). This off-balance sheet transaction vastly improves the balance sheet of "Z." Although this may have been considered legal by some, it was clearly intended to mislead. Under Sarbanes-Oxley, these trans-actions must now be clearly presented in the financial statements (transparency).

The Income Statement

The Income Statement is also called the Profit & Loss Statement. It is an accounting of business operations over a given period. Its purpose is to give an accounting between total revenues and expenses for a given period to determine the before tax earnings. Net earnings (profits) after taxes for the period are determined by subtracting an amount set-aside in reserve for taxes.

Items making up an Income Statement are shown below in Table 8-3, "Typical Income Statement." This statement is also valid for most all types of business operations, corporate and non-corporate organizations, offering either goods or services.

Table 8-3
Typical Income Statement

	Total Operating Revenues (Sales)
Less	Allowances (Discounts)
Equals	**Net Operating Revenues**
Less	Cost Of Goods Sold/Services Provided (1)
Equals	**Gross Operating Earnings (or Loss)**
Less	Non-Direct Expenses
Plus	Investment Income or Other Income
Equals	**Before Tax Earnings (or Loss)**
Less	Income Tax On Before Tax Earnings
Equals	**Net Earnings (or Loss)**

(1), See Table 8-4 below.

The "Non-Direct Expenses" entry consists of expenses that are not directly chargeable as costs for producing a product, or providing a service. These include: depreciation and amortization; salaries of non-direct employees (management and service departments); sales commissions; advertising; utility and product delivery costs; insurance; interest payments; legal and accounting fees; and bad debts written off as being non-collectible.

The "Cost of Goods Sold/Services Provided," in Table 8-3, is further defined below in Table 8-4, "Cost of Goods Sold/Services Provided Formula."

Table 8-4
Cost of Goods Sold/Services Provided Formula

Inventory Cost at Beginning of Period (if any)

Plus	Direct Labor Expense & Raw Materials Purchased
Less	Inventory Cost At End Of Period (if any)
Equals	**Cost of Goods Sold/Services Provided**

Table 8-4 represents the difference between inventories at the start and end of the accounting period plus the *works-in-progress*, (WIP). WIP includes direct labor expended plus costs of all material purchased during the period for products in the process of being manufactured. Inventory costs consists of *finished goods* ready for shipment, are carried either as the sum of the cost of materials plus direct labor charges or at the present market value (market price for goods manufactured), whichever is less.

A market value that is less than the cost of finished goods would indicate a problem. Competition may have forced prices down below costs, and not discounting the goods would result in bloated inventories of unsold goods. Corporate management tends to have difficulty with formally recognizing obsolete inventory. They often will carry such on the books at cost, because to recognize obsolete inventory by reducing it to market value would negatively affect both the Balance Sheet and the Income Statement.

In addition, an incompetent manufacturing department may not be declaring ruined WIP as scrap, and instead carrying it on the books as illegitimate WIP. This perpetuates a fraud on management as well as on investors. This will eventually become evident when the scrap value becomes so enormous that it will be discovered. However, it could take many years before this does occur. An astute reader of financial reports should be able to detect this type of problem.

Businesses providing services carry no product inventory. Therefore, the cost of services provided consists of the direct labor charges required to provide specific services plus all material purchases necessary to provide these services.

Reconciliation Statements

No financial statement would be complete without a statement on reconciliation of both net worth and working capital from one reporting period, typically the fiscal yearend, to another. These statements are discussed below.

Reconciliation of Net Worth

The Reconciliation of Net Worth is also called the "Statement of Change in Stockholder Equity." This reconciliation statement is required annually and gives insight into the reasons for any changes in net worth that may appear to be inconsistent with net earnings. It is of benefit more to the professional analyst than to the individual stockholder. None-the-less, it does indicate how dividend distributions, extraordinary receipts, and extraordinary charges affect prior yearend retained earnings as well as current period net earnings. For example, receipt of a judgment for monetary damages favorable to the company would be listed as an extraordinary receipt when received. On the other hand, if the judgment were against the company, an extraordinary charge would be shown when paid.

The typical formula shown below in Table 8-5, "Reconciliation of Net Worth," is used for defining line items affecting changes in net worth.

Table 8-5
Reconciliation of Net Worth

Net Worth at Beginning of Period

Plus	Current Period Net Earnings
Plus	Extraordinary Receipts in Current Period
Less	Dividends Paid (or Proprietor's Draw) in Current Period
Less	Extraordinary Charges in Current Period
Equals	**Net Worth at End of Period**

Also, amounts spent on stock buyback programs and held as Treasury Stock are also listed as extraordinary charges, but since it is still issued (although no longer outstanding), its value at issue is still carried under shareholder equity. However, a new issue of equity securities would be shown as an increase to the amount shown for common and preferred stock par value and paid-in-surplus at yearend, and will be accompanied by the amount received listed as an extraordinary receipt.

Reconciliation of Working Capital

The difference between total current assets and total current liabilities in the Balance Sheet (items above the dashed horizontal line in Table 8-2) is called "working capital." A positive value indicates that current assets exceed current liabilities; therefore, current bills can be paid. A negative value indicates that there are insufficient assets available to pay short-term bills.

The working capital of a well-managed business will be slightly positive, but not excessively so, for that would indicate inefficient use of capital. However, the managements of some organizations, as a matter of business strategy, keep consistently high levels of working capital. Therefore, the differences in the degree of excess of working capital between different companies are not that important, but significant changes in any given year require explanation.

The Reconciliation of Working Capital statement, also called Statement of Changes in Financial Position, shows the different sources of income that are from sources other than from normal business operations, as well as different expenditures, both of whom may have significantly affected the working capital. The changes are reconciled as shown below in Table 8-6, "Reconciliation of Working Capital."

Table 8-6
Reconciliation of Working Capital
(Statement of Changes in Financial Position)

	Current Period Net Earnings
Plus	Extraordinary Receipts In Current Period
Plus	Proceeds From Sales Of Assets In Current Period
Less	Dividends Paid (or Proprietor's Draw) in Current Period
Less	Extraordinary Charges in Current Period
Less	Purchases Of New Assets
Less	Pay Down On Long-Term Debt
Equals	**Change in Working Capital**

FUNDAMENTAL ANALYSIS

The traditional financial evaluation for business organizations is typically called "fundamental analysis." It is so named, because it evaluates the financial "fundamentals" of the organization as determined from items listed in the various financial statements that have been described previously. However, it also considers historical trends in earnings, sales, and inventories, as well as investor sentiment of valuation as determined by stock price ratios. Fundamental analysis is performed by analyzing different categories of financial parameters of a business organization. Fundamental analysis should be understood by every investor who is considering investing in any type of corporate security being offered.

Balance Sheet Parameters

The state of a business organization's financial condition can be evaluated in part with particular financial parameters using information obtained from the Balance Sheet. These parameters are explained below.

Working Capital

Working capital was defined previously as the difference between current assets and current liabilities. It is an indication of the ability of the company to pay current (short-term) debt. Current assets that are less than current liabilities suggest that some fixed assets may have to be liquidated. Management typically tries to minimize the amount of working capital by either putting excess cash into business expansion, or by distributing it to shareholders as dividends.

A review of the working capital reconciliation, as was shown previously in Table 8-6, can indicate whether the changes in working capital represent valid management business activities, or whether it may be an omen of bad times ahead. Comparing the changes in working capital for the current reporting period, to those reported for past reporting periods (typically from 3 to 10 years) is important. It gives an indication of the trend in working capital over the long-term, which may indicate continued financial success if positive, or may be an precursor of financial problems should the trend be negative.

Positive changes from consistent earnings increases are usually welcome news. However a significant increase from selling fixed assets or business segments should be carefully studied as it may indicate that the dismemberment of the organization is in progress, a typical strategy used by those that have acquired companies with hostile takeovers.

Negative changes due to either an operating loss or paying dividends that are in excess of earnings may indicate possible financial trouble in the future. However, some negative changes can be beneficial to the company's shareholders in the long-term. The beneficial negative changes could be due to: spending on fixed assets for business expansion; buying securities to gain a stake in another company; purchasing company stock in the marketplace for Treasury Stock; or accelerating long-term debt reduction.

Hazards of Excess Working Capital

A management that allows excess cash to accumulate will eventually attract the attention of a corporate raider. Corporate raiders are individuals, companies, or investment groups that look for cash rich companies to acquire a controlling interest in the common stock, usually with a generous tender offer. Their intent is to oust the current management, break up business segments and sell them for their asset value, confiscate both the excess cash and the proceeds from sale of assets, and to confiscate the company funded employee pension reserves.

This is known as a "hostile takeover," which is completely different from a friendly takeover offer from a company looking for expansion by merger or acquisition. Friendly mergers, or acquisitions, are usually negotiated in private between senior executives of both companies with concurrence of their Boards of Directors. The merger only becomes public knowledge when shareholders of both companies are offered the deal for their vote.

Once targeted by a corporate raider, a company may invoke a number of defenses, most of which are all detrimental to the company regardless of whether or not the takeover is successful. The following defense strategies are typical defenses invoked:

1. using Greenmail, which is paying the raider an enormous amount for its shares that makes it more profitable just to go away instead of proceeding with the takeover attempt that may not succeed

2. using the Poison Pill defense, which consists of issuing existing shareholders a new series of non-dividend paying preferred stock with provisions allowing redemption of shares at an enormously high price after any takeover, the proceeds of which are then used to acquire the takeover company's stock

3. using the Golden Parachute defense, which only protects management by changing the By-laws to require extra generous severance payments for corporate officers thereby making it exorbitantly expensive to replace current management

4. using the White Knight defense, which invites a third, friendly company to merge on favorable terms

5. using the Pac Man defense (named after the one-time popular computer video game in which a video character gobbles up its enemies) where the target company makes a hostile takeover offer for the raiding company

6. effecting the Scorched Earth Policy, which simply beats the raiding company at breaking up the most lucrative business segments, known as the "crown jewels," and then distributing the proceeds to shareholders, thereby eliminating the incentive for a hostile takeover

Current Ratio

Working capital for a particular company is unique for that company. However, a comparison with other companies in the same industry group is near impossible, as each organization will be typically different in capital structure and revenues. Therefore, a comparative evaluation can be made using a value computed by a ratio of current assets to current liabilities. This ratio is called the Current Ratio, which allows companies of different sizes (within reason) to be compared with each other.

Current Ratios that are below 1.0 indicate that the company does not have enough liquid assets to pay current debts, while ratios greater than 2.0 may indicate ineffective application of liquid assets and may well invite a hostile takeover offer. However, the better evaluation is to compare the Current Ratio of the company of interest with other companies in the same business segment, as well as with the average Current Ratio for all companies in that category.

In addition, comparing historical annual values for previous years can give an indication of a trend change. Well-managed businesses should maintain a level value. A decreasing trend may indicate that the business is becoming less efficient with expenses increasing greater than earnings. An increasing trend may indicate that either increased revenue is being accumulating without long-term reinvestment; or else, there may be a problem with inventories not being sold and therefore accumulating on the shelves. The later can be determined by using the Quick Ratio as explained below.

Quick Ratio

This ratio indicates the quality of current assets by eliminating inventory from current assets, and the remaining value thereby called "quick assets." the Quick Ratio, which is also called both the "Acid Test Ratio" and the "Liquidity Ratio," is computed by dividing quick assets by current liabilities. A value less than 1.0 may indicate that inventory has become a problem. Comparison of historical ratios can indicate whether increasing working capital is due to increasing inventories that may be obsolete.

Tangible Net Worth

The tangible net worth is determined by subtracting intangible assets from net worth (shareholder equity). By itself, it has no significant value other than to indicate the collective amount shareholders may receive should the business be terminated. However, it is used as a component in other parameters. When stated as a per share dollar amount, it is called the "book value" (defined below). For the example given previously under "Off-Balance Sheet Transactions," without full disclosure of the unconsolidated entity, the tangible net worth for "Z" corporation would be greatly improved. Prior to the unconsolidated entity being formed, the actual shareholder equity would be shown to be a negative $200 million. Afterwards, it would be shown to be a positive $100 million.

Debt to Equity Ratio

This ratio indicates how much of the capital structure of the company results from using leverage (borrowing). It is typically computed, with some variations, as long-term debt divided by the sum of long-term debt plus tangible net worth. A ratio greater than 0.5 (50%) would indicate that creditors have invested more money into the company than have stockholders.

The Debt to Equity Ratio for the example for corporation "Z," illustrated previously under "Off-Balance Sheet Transactions," indicates that the real ratio is 0.8, but is reduced to 0.6 with the off-balance sheet transaction.

Book Value

The "book value" of a business is the common stock shareholders, tangible net worth. This is determined as the amount remaining after subtracting both the intangible assets (goodwill, intellectual property, and mineral and franchise rights), and the par value amount of preferred stock from the tangible net worth. The dollar amount of the book value has little meaning by itself. Therefore, book value is typically expressed as a per share value by dividing tangible net worth by the number of outstanding common shares. However, book value is a useful valuation parameter when compared with other companies within the same business segment. The comparison is expressed as an additional ratio by dividing the market price of the stock by the book value per share. This is discussed below under "Price-to-Book Ratio."

Book value per share represents the current intrinsic value per share, and is the minimum that shareholders would expect to receive for a merger or buyout. However, if forced into liquidation, the shareholders would likely receive much less. In a forced liquidation, the value of inventories and works in progress could likely be deemed worthless (scrap value only). In addition, machinery and equipment carried at cost less accumulated depreciation may also have little market value.

Income Statement Parameters

The degree of success from business operations can also be indicated with additional parameters using information obtained from the Income Statement. These Income Statement parameters are as shown below.

Earnings per Share

The amount of earnings generated over a given period universally measures the profitability of a business. The net earnings after taxes, as given in a typical Income Statement (as was shown in Table 8-3), can be stated on a per share basis by dividing by the average number of outstanding common shares for the reporting period. This ratio is called the "primary earnings per share" as it gives a quantitative measure of the profits on a per share basis for existing common shareholders.

However, many companies have convertible securities that may eventually be converted into common stock. Conversion will have the effect of diluting the earnings among potential, additional common shareholders. On the conversion of convertible preferred stock, no additional capitalization is received, with the par value of convertible debentures being transferred to common shareholder equity in the Balance Sheet. Conversion of debentures will also improve (lower) the Debt to Equity Ratio. Therefore, these companies are required to also report per share earnings *as fully diluted earnings per share*; dividing the reported net earnings by the total number of common shares that would exist assuming that the convertible securities had all been converted. The purpose is to show the maximum possible dilution of the reported earnings.

Cash Flow

Most analysts believe that a better measure of profitability is the "cash flow" of a business, not net earnings. Cash flow is the actual dollar amount flowing into the business during the reporting period. It is determined by adding the amount written off on the Income Statement for "depreciation" to the net earnings. Depreciation is an accounting fiction created by income tax law that allows business organizations to annually write-off the cost of both acquired property and capital equipment over their assigned lifetimes. Depreciation shields current revenues from taxation. Therefore, cash flow is the actual dollar amount received by the business after expenses and taxes.

Cash flow is also more meaningful when presented on a per share basis. This is computed by dividing cash flow by the average number of common shares outstanding over the reporting period. Cash flow is not a required reporting parameter; therefore, it is rarely reported in financial reports generated by the issuer or its auditors. Most analysts who use cash flow analysis simply determine the value from the Income Statement by adding the depreciation back to net earnings. Whenever reported, it is typically given as "primary cash flow" per share, rarely as "fully diluted."

Profit Margin

The "profit margin" is a measure of the degree of success of management in turning a profit. It is determined by dividing net earnings by net operating revenues (as was shown in Table 8-3), therefore being expressed as a percent of income. It is taken as a measure of the efficiency of management in its ability to turn a profit. Since it is expressed as a percentage, profit margin is one parameter that is not expressed on a per share basis.

Balance Sheet and Income Statement Parameters

Other financial parameters used to evaluate the financial condition of a business combine data from both the Balance Sheet and the Income Statement. The following are typical of such parameters.

Return on Total Equity

The Return on Total Equity ratio measures how effective management has employed the amount of stockholder total equity. It is computed by dividing the net earnings from the Income Statement by the net worth (stockholder equity), and expressed as a percent. It is compared with the value computed for previous reporting periods. Increasing changes indicate that management is annually expanding the return, and is to be expected; a decreasing change trend is unfavorable, and indicates a failure of management to respond to unfavorable or changing business conditions. A flat (unchanged) trend could indicate that something may be amiss, in either management or the business sector.

Return on Common Equity

This parameter is similar to Return on Total Equity, but treats preferred shareholders as creditors, and preferred stockholder dividends as an interest obligation (which they are not). It is computed by subtracting preferred dividends paid from net earnings, and dividing this difference by the difference between the net worth less the par value of the preferred stock. The result is also expressed as a percent. Many analysts insist that Return on Common Equity is a better measure than the Return on Total Equity because it indicates the effectiveness of management's use of common shareholder capital.

Return on Total Assets

The ratio, Return on Total Assets is a parameter that measures the effectiveness of assets employed. It is computed as the ratio of the sum of annual net earnings and long-term debt interest paid, to the total assets listed in the Balance Sheet, and is expressed as a percent. It takes into account assets purchased with shareholder capital as well as those acquired with long-term debt. Adding back the interest paid to net income results in excluding the interest cost on financed assets, which gives a measurement of the effectiveness of assets used.

Inventory Turnover

Inventory Turnover is a parameter that measures how many times the inventory has been sold and replaced. It is computed as a ratio of net operating revenues to yearend inventory, and expressed as a mixed number (such as 8½). Inventory turnover has little meaning by itself; however, high numbers are generally good while low numbers may indicate a problem. It is most useful when compared with both past years' turnover numbers, and when compared with numbers reported for other companies in the same industry sector.

Stock Price Valuation Parameters

Investors constantly try to ascertain the value for a share of common stock in a company. However, establishing value is nebulous at best. For most analysts, value is determined by market sentiment reflecting the current perceptions of the investing community. For others, typically long-term investors, value is determined by estimations of "intrinsic value."

A number of parameters are used to indicate the value of common stock as determined by market sentiment. The discussions in the following paragraphs are typical of such parameters.

Price-to-Earnings Ratio

Businesses that are in the rapid expansion and mature growth stages of the business life cycle will have historical financial data on which the value of the current stock price can be assessed. The most common parameter used is the "Price-to-Earnings Ratio."

The Price-to-Earnings Ratio, otherwise stated simply as "P/E," is reported in the financial media as the ratio of the current, per share market price to the *past* 12 month's earnings per share. It is expressed as a mixed decimal number (such as 10.5), and no value is reported should the earnings for the past year be either zero or negative. The P/E ratio has significance for common stock of growth companies than make no, or nil, dividend payments to investors. It usually is compared with P/E ratios of similar industry companies, and with P/E ratios of an index within the same business sector.

However, financial analysts use anticipated *forward* year earnings to determine growth stock value. Typically, forward P/E ratios reflect collective opinions of investors on expectations of the year-to-year earnings growth for companies in both the rapid expansion and mature growth life cycle stages. A forward ratio higher than the industry sector's past P/E average represents high expectations. Low forward ratios, or ratios lower than the average past P/E for the sector index could indicate that the price may be at a bargain (called an "overlooked" stock). However, there may be a justification for investors having depressed the stock with a sell-off, if it is in opposition with the overall direction of the market. It could indicate a potential problem with the stock, and not the buying opportunity that a low P/E would portend.

Traditionally, most companies in the mature growth stage of the business life cycle would be undervalued at P/Es of about 10, or lower, and overvalued at P/Esover 20. Rapid expansion stage companies where either sales or earnings, or both, are at a multiple of market average growth rates, would support a P/E ratio two to four times that of the averages. However, companies within certain industry groups will have, as a group, P/E ratios that are very different from those of the broad-based stock averages. One example is the typical very low P/E ratios for the U. S. automobile manufacturing industry.

Excluding the market bubble of the 1990s, the average P/E ratio for stocks making up the Dow Jones Industrial Average (DJIA), the granddaddy of all stock indexes, traditionally ranged between 10 and 20. Therefore, market lows occurred at the DJIA P/E low of about 10, and market highs occurred at the DJIA P/E high of about 20. However, with the exuberance for investing money into the equities markets by the public in the 1990s, the traditional norms have all been transgressed. Therefore, in this first decade of the 21st Century, it remains to be seen whether new limits are to be established, or if a return to historical values will occur.

Stock Price Range Estimation Using the P/E Ratio

Stock prices in the marketplace usually are cyclical, and represent changes in short-term investor sentiment. Therefore, P/E ratios may be used to predict the future price range of a stock, based on both recent historical P/E ratio ranges and using consensus estimates for future earnings. This can be performed by first using data from the past five years to establish both the average annual P/E high, and the average annual P/E low. Applying analysts' consensus estimates for the future years, to the 5-year P/E averages will estimating the probable stock range for the future years.

This is illustrated by Table 8-7, "Future Stock Price Estimate Example," as shown below, which indicates the future, 3-year price ranges for a hypothetical common stock using historical data as well as future earnings estimates, everything else assumed to be held constant.

If the current price is near, or above, the high of the price range shown, it would be considered as overvalued. A price near or below the low of the range shown would be considered undervalued. Of course, the price range estimates are only as good as the assumptions made in arriving at the future earnings estimates and depend on continued investor sentiment of those that trade the stock. In addition, changing economic trends can also affect the computed future price estimates, either positively or negatively such as when the economy is changing from recession to expansion, or the reverse.

Table 8-7 Future Stock Price Estimate Example					
Fiscal Year Data					
	'99	'00	'01	'02	'03
Annual Earnings, $:	0.50	0.75	0.80	0.95	1.20
Yearly Price High, $:	12	20	18	28	36
Yearly Low Price, $:	8	10	14	15	24
Yearly P/E High:	24	26.7	22.5	29	30
Yearly P/E Low:	16	13.3	17.5	15.8	20

5-Year High-Low Averages: P/E High = 26.4
                                 P/E Low = 16.5

	Future Year Price Estimate		
	'04	'05	'06
Est. Future Year Earnings	$1.50	$1.90	$2.40
Est. Future Year Price High, (26.4 x Est. Earnings):	**$40**	**$50**	**$63**
Est. Future Year Price Low, (16.5 x Est. Earnings):	**$25**	**$31**	**$40**

Many sources provide historical financial data for individual stocks, as well as giving estimates for the future. However, the most popular is the *Value Line Investment Survey*, which covers 1700 actively traded stocks. This publication can be found in most public libraries and securities dealer's branch offices.

The P/E method of estimating future stock price is not valid for new issue stocks in companies that do not have a historical database. Moreover, securities dealers, as well as their sales representatives, involved in the offering are precluded from making projections on potential business performance (earnings, sales or stock price) during both the offering period and the quiet period after the public offering. In addition, this method requires a sufficient number of annual financial reports after going public before a reasonable historic database can be established to be able to use financial data for price prediction purposes.

Relative Price-to-Earnings Ratio

This parameter measures the value of an individual company's P/E ratio relative to a particular stock index. The index typically chosen for this comparison is the Standard and Poor's 500 Index (S&P 500). It is expressed as a mixed-decimal number, and is computed by dividing the current company P/E ratio by the current average value for stocks making up the S&P 500 Index. The average P/E ratio for the S&P 500 Index can be found weekly in the "Market Week" section of *Barron's*.

Price-to-Sales Ratio

Development stage businesses, as well as recent new businesses issuing capitalization securities, either do not have a historical financial database to assess earnings trends or may have sales growth but have not produced any earnings. The later was typical of many of the "new era" electronic communications businesses utilizing Internet service companies in which the business strategy was to capture market share by strictly concentrating on sales growth and ignoring earnings.

The Price-to-Sales Ratio has occasionally been used over the years; it was uniquely applicable as a valuation parameter for these rapid expansion businesses, such as the former dot-com companies. Businesses that have little or no earnings can then be compared with each other, but more importantly, they can be compared with any company, even with those that have had consistent earnings.

The technique used is the same as that shown in Table 8-7 above, except that net operating revenues (see Table 8-3) per share are used in place of earnings per share, both for historical data and for future year estimates. This valuation method is only as good as the assumption for maintaining sales growth rates and for continuing economic conditions, as well as for the accuracy of the estimates.

Price-to-Book Ratio

The Price-to-Book Ratio is expressed as the ratio of market price per share to book value per share. It is an indicator of the relative value of the common stock compared with other company P/E ratios. The market price is typically higher than the book value, which can be considered its liquidation value. Nevertheless, it has greater meaning when used to detect a change in the annual price-to-book value over a number of years. It can also be compared with the average price-to-book value for other companies in the same business segment.

Generally, a corporation is considered undervalued if this ratio is less than one, and considered as overvalued if this ratio is over two. However, price-to-book values can vary widely over time depending upon economic conditions, and investor anticipation for both the company and the industry group.

Dividend Yield

Dividends are payments of a portion of earnings generated by business operations to the shareholders. Shareholders of common stock in companies in the mature growth stage of the business life cycle, as well as shareholders in utility companies, most likely receive periodic dividends from excess earnings; earnings that are not need for reinvestment into the business. Preferred stockholders receive fixed dividend payments that are *promised* for as long as the stock is outstanding. Preferred stock may be called to refinance at a lower dividend rate, and convertible preferred stock may be called to force a conversion to common stock.

The amount of the dividend distribution is usually expressed as a percent of the current stock price; therefore, it represents a yield on stockholder's investment, called "Dividend Yield." It is computed by dividing the dividend per share by the current share price and expressed as a percent. Therefore, the yield is affected by many different factors, such as:

1. any change in actual dividend distributions

2. a change in a growth company common stock price resulting from an unforeseen earnings change

3. a change in price of preferred stock considered as an income investment as a result being affected by a change in long-term interest rates

Common stocks for development and rapid expansion business life cycle stages will typically pay no dividends, as all earnings are used for expanding the business. Dividends paid by most mature growth stage companies are typically not sufficient to result in being classified as an income investment security: the exception being utility companies. Significant dividend amounts are paid only by companies who have reached large capitalization status with annual growth rates that are less with each succeeding each year.

Dividend yields from common stocks are of interest mostly to income seeking investors who are also looking for growth. They are not of interest to those who are interested only in capital appreciation with explosive growth securities. Dividend yield provides an investment value support level for share prices for the large cap, mature growth stage stocks during periods of economic decline and market uncertainty. Share prices drop to and are supported by investment value levels that result in the current dividend yield being comparable to yields of long-term debt obligations.

Dividend Payout

"Dividend Payout" measures the degree of risk for dividends being paid on common stock held by income seeking investors. It compares the dividends per share to the earnings per share, as a ratio, by dividing the dividend yield by the earnings per share and expressing the result as a percent.

Investors in companies in which the payout is less than 50% can feel that there is a good chance in receiving the same level of dividends in the future, should the current earnings not be maintained. However, future dividends for stocks in which the payout is over 75% may very well be negatively affected by a downturn in earnings. Not only will the stock price be likely to drop as a growth stock because of declining earnings, but also the price decline will be aggravated by the decline in investment value should the dividend be cut.

Relevance of Fundamental Analysis

Investors in equity securities all seek some form of capital appreciation, which is typically called "growth." Capital appreciation is the increase in the price of the security because others, in the future, are willing to pay a higher price for owning the security. Even though many investors seek income from common stock dividend payments, they also look for capital appreciation. An "income only" investor would do better with debt obligations where the yield from interest payments is typically higher than most all dividend paying common stocks.

Risk-taking, growth objective investors seek significant, short-term—less than one year—capital appreciation in stocks that have a unique market niche in a growing industry. They do not necessarily seek value (bargain priced stocks), but are willing to pay whatever price necessary for the potential of being able to realize significant capital appreciation. The stocks of these companies are typically in the development or rapid expansion stages of the business life cycle, and have high P/E ratios, high Price-to-Book Ratios, and nil Dividend Yields.

With the exception of than those who repeatedly invest in initial public offerings, most short-term investors are required to be market "technicians." These individuals use "technical analysis" to determine when to buy or sell based on stock price-volume charts. They attempt to deduce investor sentiment and psychology for individual stocks, and the overall market, from telltale signals that may be indicated by the charts. A discussion of technical analysis could fill volumes. However, since it is not relevant to new issue investing, technical analysis is considered as being beyond the scope of this book.

Investors should realize that most initial public offerings are short-term investments. Most will rise in price after the effective IPO date and will eventually decrease and fall below the offer price. "Turkeys" will decrease in price from the "get-go." Therefore, IPO investments do not require being a market technician. They only require a good story, rudimentary fundamental analysis, and the use of specific tactics for IPOs that are presented in Chapter Ten, "New Issue Investment Tactics."

INTRINSIC VALUE ANALYSIS

Many individuals seeking growth are classified as "value" investors. This type individual takes a long-term approach to investing which assumes that buying stock in a company of value within a growing industry will result in significant growth (capital appreciation) over the long run. Therefore, they typically represent the lump sum "buy-and-hold" type investment strategy, or the "dollar-cost-averaging" strategy with systematic, incremental investment purchases.

Most value investors perform fundamental analyses in a search for companies in a growth industry whose stock prices are relatively low, but have the potential for increased sales and earnings. (Note that the term "relatively low" indicates that value is set by current market sentiment with comparisons made to average parameter values.) These stocks typically have relatively low P/E and Price-to-Book Ratios, and relatively high dividend yields. Share prices can be estimated, as was stated above under "Fundamental Analysis." Accordingly, value stocks will typically be in the mature growth life cycle stage.

However, others seek to determine value by attempting to establish an absolute dollar price based using a mathematical present value computation, which is called "intrinsic value analysis." Benjamin Graham—who wrote *Security Analysis* with David Dowd in 1934 and *Intelligent Investor* in 1949—first introduced this method as a tool for stock value analysis. The intrinsic value for a security is determined by estimates of all future income that can be expected, and discounted by a particular discount (interest) rate. Price valuation using present value is different from the future price estimation shown in Table 8-7. Intrinsic value analysis relies on long-term (10 to 30 year) estimates of future income, rather than the shorter-term (3 to 5 year) estimates of company earnings used in fundamental analysis.

The present value computation is easy to make for securities that have investment value. As previously stated, securities that have investment value are those that offer a specific annual dividend (or interest payment) and a maturity date. For debt obligations, the annual interest amount, maturity date, and par or face value (amount received at maturity) are specified. The discount rate that is typically used is the yield-to-maturity of equivalent duration U.S. Treasury obligations (the conventional investment standard). Long-term debt obligations typically have a call date; therefore, the call date should be taken as the duration along with the call premium value, if applicable.

Preferred stock issues typically have no maturity date; however most do have a call date. Therefore, the period to the call date should be used along with the call premium value, if applicable. When securities have no defined maturity date, a lifetime of 20 years can be assumed for valuation computation purposes along with assuming a discount rate for the current yield-to-maturity for the 10-year Treasury bond (viewed as the riskless investment standard).

Growth securities have little, if any, investment value because of the typical nil dividends. These represent common stocks of companies that have and are expected to increase earnings in the future. Determining an intrinsic value for so-called growth securities is even more nebulous than for investment value securities. Analysts use historical company earnings to estimate future, long-term earnings that are used to determine intrinsic value. The accuracy then depends upon the evaluation of the historical growth performance of the business, and the assumption that management can maintain this growth in the future.

Intrinsic value analysis has no meaningful significance for speculation in initial public offerings of startup and development companies who have no historical performance database. However, value investors may be able to use intrinsic value analysis to establish a quantitative value for a new issue stock price for an established private or closely held company that may finally be going public, although in most instances historical financial data for these corporations may be non-existent.

Estimating Fair Value for Growth Securities

Intrinsic value analysis establishes what is called a "fair value" for a stock. This method can be used for any stock that has a historical database of at least 10 years, and is expected to remain in business indefinitely. This will represent companies in the mature growth stage of the business life cycle. The rational approach is to estimate the fair value for the investment horizon of the individual investor (from 10 to 30 years). A minimum of 10 years is recommended whether or not the investor may have a shorter investment horizon because short periods can result in unreasonably low estimated values. Also, 30 years is suggested as the maximum since the error in estimated fair value over longer periods is likely to be significantly large due to potentially significant differences between actual and estimated income growth and changes in the discount rates over these long periods.

The intrinsic or fair value of a stock can be estimated as the current book value plus the discounted value of the future earnings stream. (The assumption is that future earnings will be retained as shareholder equity.) The mathematical expression for the fair value of a business with a future estimated earnings stream could be given as shown:

$$\textbf{Fair Value} = \textbf{BV} + \sum_{n=1}^{n=N} \textbf{En}/(1 + i)\hat{\ }\textbf{n}$$

Where:

- **BV** = current book value
- **i** = discount rate expressed as a decimal
- **Σ** = sum of quotients of En/(1 + i)^n for years n = 1 to n = N
- **N** = number of years to maturity
- **n** = year number from "1" to "N"
- **En** = estimated earnings for each subsequent year "n"
- **(1 + i)^n** = one + the discount rate to the "n" power

However, one need not be a mathematician to evaluate the fair value of a company. For the average individual, the present value computation can be simplified as shown in Figure 8-1, "Normalized Fair Value Estimate," which gives the present value of the estimated future earnings stream for a 20-year period. "Value," as defined in the chart, is presented as normalized: in **dollars per share, per dollar of *current* earnings per share**, which is given for various estimated annual earnings growth rates. Twenty-years is used as being a reasonable period to estimate of the potential earnings growth rate. Any other duration will require generating a different chart.

An estimate of the normalized, per share fair value from future earnings in dollars per share, per dollar of *current* earnings per share can be read off the vertical axis of Figure 8-1. First, enter the chart on the horizontal axis at the selected value for the discount rate. Then, go up to the point on the graph that represents the approximate level of annual earnings growth rate anticipated for the period. (Note that three annual growth rates are given: 0% per year; 10% per year; and, 20% per year.) Lastly, the present value of future earnings, per dollar of current earnings, can be read from the vertical axis. The discount rate to be used is the current YTM for the 10-year maturity U. S. T-bond, which can be considered the investment standard.

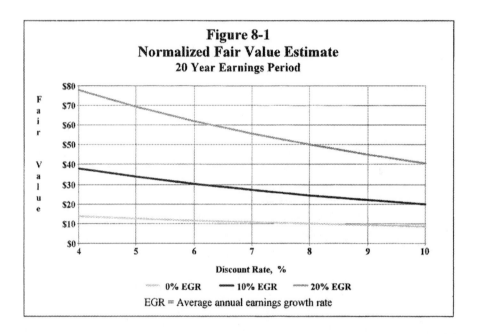

The future annual earnings growth rate can be assumed as the average annual earnings growth rate over the past 10 to 15 years; however, past performance is never a guarantee of future performance. A data source such as the *Value Line Investment Survey* is invaluable because it gives both earnings per share data for at least the past 15 years, and the current book value per share. The estimated, discounted value for the anticipated earnings indicated by Figure 8-1, added to the current book value per share represents the fair value for the stock, otherwise called the intrinsic value.

For example, assume that a new issue offering has a *pro-forma*, annual per share earnings of 25 cents, which can be expected to grow over the next 20 years at a 20% annual rate. Using a 6% discount rate as the value of a T-bond with 10 years to maturity, the present value of expected earnings is then found, from Figure 8-1, to be about $62 per share per $1 of current annual earnings. Multiplying this by the actual $0.25 per share annual current earnings, a fair value for the stock's earnings stream is computed to be $15.50 per share. Assuming that the *pro-forma* book value is $2.50 per share, the fair value for this example would be established at $18.00 per share ($15.50 + $2.50).

Intrinsic value analysis is useful for publicly traded stock having at least 10 years of historical financial data, or for income securities (as is described below under "Estimated Fair Value for Income Securities). The actual offering price for an IPO is set by investor demand. The fair value has little bearing on the offering price, which is likely to be much higher than the computed fair value, should such be able to be computed. When the public offering price is lower, it could well indicate that the investor used an unrealistic annual earnings growth rate, or that the issue could well be a turkey and the price has been set low to attract investors. In such cases look for inducements described in the prospectus, such as bundling warrants with the offering, or mentioning underwriter stabilization during the quiet period after the effective date.

For example, assume that a stock has had an average, earnings growth rate of 10% per year over the past 15 years and there is every expectation that this should continue in the future. Also, assume that the current share price is $60, the per share book value is $15, the current year per share earnings are $3, and the 10 year T-bond yield to maturity is 6%. Figure 8-1 would indicate that the present value per dollar of earnings, over the next 20 years, would be estimated at $30. With $3 per share in current earnings, and a $15 book value, the fair value for the stock would then be computed as 30 x 3 + 15, or $105 per share. The $60 market price offers a "margin of safety" of 75%, (105-60)/60, for a long-term investor who would decide to purchase this stock.

Warren Buffett's Contribution to Intrinsic Value Analysis

The current champion of intrinsic value analysis is Warren Buffett, considered the world's most successful value investor. His reported technique uses present value computation for estimating a fair value for the stock price, but, Buffett uses a term that he calls "owner's equity" (OE) instead of annual earnings. OE is determined by deducting annual capital expenditures from cash flow on a per share basis. The reasoning is that capital expenditures are a legitimate cost of being in business, although not a cost of doing business for accounting purposes. In addition, cash flow, as opposed to net earnings, represents the actual revenue received after operating expenses and taxes. He also uses the current yield to maturity of the 20-year maturity T-bond as the discount rate.

Figure 8-1 can be used with Buffett's OE parameter to estimate a stock's fair value. This can be accomplished by computing past, per share, annual OE values from historical data for a number of years, and then determining the average, long-term, OE growth rate. This value is to be used instead of earnings for the growth rates shown in Figure 8-1, as well as the current yield for the 20-year T-bond (used as the discount rate). The fair value can then be determined by adding the present value of the future, 20-year, estimated OE stream to the current book value.

Estimating Fair Value for Income Securities

Income securities consist of notes, debentures (bonds), preferred stock, REITs, and ownership units in income objective UITs and LPs. These securities typically have a defined maturity where the initial investment (par or face value) is returned to the investor. Indefinite life preferred stock should have a call provision in which the call date can be used as the maturity.

The "fair value" for these securities can be determined by a present value computation of the discounted income stream as well as the discount value of the returned principal at maturity. It is determined by combining (adding) the present values of the discounted income stream and the investment principal returned at maturity. The mathematical expression for this computation is given as shown below.

$$\text{Fair Value} = \sum_{n=1}^{n=N} Dn/(1+i)^{\wedge}n + S/(1+i)^{\wedge}N$$

Where the definitions of the two terms for Fair value are:

$$\sum_{n=1}^{n=N} Dn/(1+i)^{\wedge}n = \text{Present value of the income stream, and}$$

$S/(1+i)^{\wedge}N$ = Present value of the principal amount, S

The definitions for the symbols used are:

Σ = sum of quotients of $Dn/(1+i)^{\wedge}n$
(for years n = 1 through n = N
D = Expected annual income in dollars
S = Expected dollar amount returned at maturity
N = Number of years to maturity or call
n = Number of each year from first year to last year
i = Discount rate expressed as a decimal

One need not be a mathematician to evaluate the fair value of an income producing security. The fair value computation can be simplified as shown below using Figure 8-2 and Figure 8-3 with the suggested discount rate being the yield-to-maturity for the 10-year Treasury bond.

Figure 8-2, "Present Value of a $1 Annual Income Stream," represents the discounted dollar value for a $1 per year income stream for periods from 10 years to 30 years. The present value for a security paying an amount other than a $1 annual return for any given maturity and discount rate can be determined by multiplying the present value from the chart by the actual annual income.

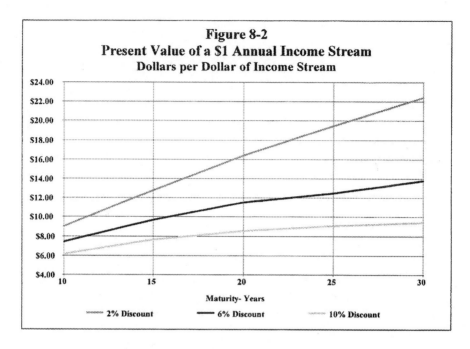

For example, assume a $1000 investment with a maturity of 25 years offers $100 annual income (a 10% coupon), which can be compared with the current YTM for a 10-year T-bond assumed to be 6% for this example. From Figure 8-2, the PV of $1 of income stream is $12.50 per dollar, which represents $1250 for the investment.

Figure 8-3, "Present Value of a $1000 Unit Value Security," shown below, indicates the discounted value of an initial $1000 unit investment made to generate the income stream. It shows that the present value of the investment decreases both with maturity and with discount rate.

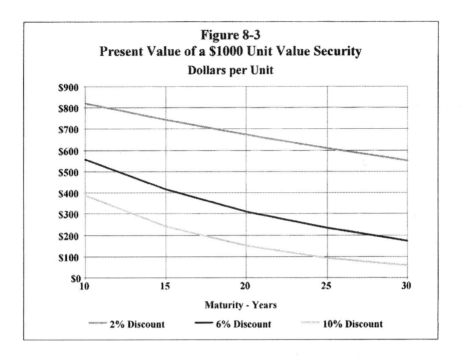

Figure 8-3
Present Value of a $1000 Unit Value Security
Dollars per Unit

For above stated $1000 investment example having a maturity of 25 years and offering $100 annual income, the PV for the $1000 investment is indicated, from Figure 8-3, at about $250 assuming a YTM for a 10-year T-bond at 6%. The fair value for the example investment can then be determined to be the sum of $1250 for the income stream, and $250 for the discounted present value of the return of capital at maturity. The total then gives a fair value of $1500 for the investment.

Fair value can be used for evaluating many variations of fixed-income investments including indefinite life securities and zero-coupon securities. The fair value for indefinite life securities can be evaluated as a 30-year life investment (at a maximum) consisting of the PV of both the income stream and the invested principal. Zero-coupon securities have no income stream; therefore, the fair value is simply the PV of the par value (face value) of the security at maturity. The fair value for REITs can estimated as a 30-year life investment having the PV of both the anticipated income stream, consisting of interest and principal repayments, and considering the invested principal as zero at maturity.

It can be shown that the fair value for a $ 1000 face value investment standard T-bond, for both any maturity and T-bond coupon, is $1000. Therefore, the fair value for any investment other than the riskless investment standard (the T-bond in this case) should be greater than that of the investment standard by at least 130% to provide a margin of safety. (Benjamin Graham suggested using 150% as a margin of safety.)

Other Evaluation Parameters for Convertibles

The conversion feature offered with convertible debentures and convertible preferred stock results in a two-tier valuation for price in the marketplace. The convertible market price will be influenced by the common stock market price when the common stock price is above the conversion price. It will be supported by its "investment value" when the common stock drops significantly below the conversion price.

It would be unfair to evaluate convertibles strictly by a computed fair value for an income security as presented above because the yield for convertible securities can be set lower than that of equivalent straight securities at issue. Therefore, the following method can be used to evaluate convertible securities (either debentures or preferred stock) as a new issue security. Note, that once a convertible has been issued, and has traded in the marketplace for some time, the decision to purchase based on fair value evaluation becomes more arduous since the investor would face a choice or whether to buy the convertible at its market price or simply buy the common stock.

Convertible Security Investment Value

The *investment value* for a convertible is the market price that it would have *if* it were an equivalent quality nonconvertible security with the same lifetime. (This is not the same as the fair value estimation for an income security as was described previously.) The investment value is the lower than the conversion value and is computed either to maturity, or to call.

The investment value can be determined by a variation of the expression presented in Table 2-2, using the yield to maturity computation for equivalent nonconvertible securities. Therefore, the expression given in Table 2-2 can be restated to compute investment value. This is shown in Table 8-8, "Approximate Convertible Security Investment Value."

Table 8-8
Approximate Convertible Security Investment Value
Callable or Definite Lifetime

Investment Value = [2 x P + F x (2/N – Y)] / (2/N + Y)

Where:

P = annual dividend or interest payment in dollars
N = number of years to the first call date (or to maturity)
Y = decimal YTM (or YTC) of an equivalent nonconvertible security
F = par or face dollar value at maturity (or at call)

Most fixed-income securities are issued with a call proviso that allows the issuer to refinance in the future at a lower rate, should interest rates decline. However, a moratorium on calling the issue prevents the issue from being called during the first five or ten years. This gives investors some assurance that they can receive a minimum period of income. The call proviso for convertibles will force a conversion to common stock should the conversion value (conversion ratio times the common stock price) be greater than the convertible's redemption price (par value plus the premium, if applicable) at call. The investment value for the convertible is computed as the lower of either the investment value to call, or the investment value to maturity.

For example, assume that a $100 face value baby bond with a 25-year maturity is offered with an 8% coupon on the face value (representing $8 per year). It can be first called in 10 years at a call price of $105 ($5 premium), but if called after 15 years it will be redeemed at the face value. At the time of the offering, the equivalent quality nonconvertible security YTM is found to be 10%. Therefore, using the expression given in Table 8-8, the investment value is computed as $88.33 to call or as $77.78 to maturity. The lower value should be considered as the offering's investment value. (Note that if a $5 premium were not offered at call, the investment value at call would decrease to $86.67.)

The investment value for a security will change with changes in both duration and in equivalent nonconvertible security yield. It can be shown that longer periods to call, or to maturity, will reduce the investment value when equivalent nonconvertible yields are greater than the convertible's initial yield. However, longer periods increase the investment value when equivalent nonconvertible yields are less than the convertible's initial yield. This is illustrated in Figure 8-4, "Convertible Bond Investment Value Example: 10% Initial Equivalent Nonconvertible Yield to Maturity" for a $100 par value, 8% yield convertible baby bond.

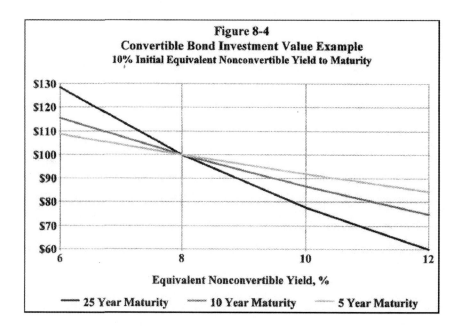

Figure 8-4
Convertible Bond Investment Value Example
10% Initial Equivalent Nonconvertible Yield to Maturity

For securities that have an indefinite life, the term "2/N" of the investment value expression in Table 8-8 becomes equal to zero; but, there will be a significant error owing to the approximation expression from which is derived. Therefore, indefinite life investment values can more accurately be computed by dividing the annual dollar dividend (or interest) payment for the convertible by the current yield of equivalent nonconvertible securities expressed as a decimal.

For example, assume that a $100 per share par value convertible preferred stock is first callable in 5 years at $105, or at par at 10 years, and is offered at an 8% annual dividend ($8.00) when the equivalent quality nonconvertible securities are yielding 10%. The computed investment values are $95.00 if called in 5 years; $86.67 if called at 10 years; and, $80 for the $8 annual dividend considering an indefinite lifetime ($8.00/0.10). Therefore, $80 would be considered as the investment value for this security.

The fair value for the convertible preferred stock example, assuming an arbitrary 6% discount rate for a riskless security, would be determined as $60 for the income stream (from Figure 8-2) plus $40 for the principal (based on $105 per share at call), for a total fair value of $100. Inasmuch as the fair value for the riskless investment standard would also be $100, the issue would not provide the requisite 130% margin of safety for an investment. However, as long as the fair value is above than that of the investment standard, one might be able to justify the investment based on the potential for capital appreciation from the conversion feature.

Conversion Premium

The conversion premium is the amount that the convertible price exceeds its investment value. It is expressed as a percentage paid for the conversion privilege. The conversion premium percentage is computed as, 100 x (par value—investment value)/investment value. The higher the conversion premium, the lower will be the investment value, which may be important if the common stock price were to decline in the future.

For example, assume that an offering for a $100 per share, indefinite life, par value convertible preferred stock is callable in 5 years at $105, or at $100 at 10 years. The yield is 8% (annual dividend at $8.00), and the equivalent quality nonconvertible security is found to yield 10% annually. The convertible's investment value (as was shown above) would be $80. The premium percent paid on purchase for the conversion privilege would then be computed to be 25%, 100 x ($100-$80)/$80.

SUMMARY OF FINANCIAL PARAMETERS

Table 8-9, "Summary of Financial Parameters" is presented below as a guide to parameters stated in corporate financial statements.

Table 8-9
Summary of Financial Parameters

Parameter	Definition
Current Ratio:	Current assets/ Current liabilities
Quick Ratio:	$\dfrac{\text{Current assets} - \text{current liabilities}}{\text{Current liabilities}}$
Tangible Net Worth:	Net worth – Intangible assets
Debt to Equity Ratio:	$\dfrac{\text{Long-term debt}}{\text{Long-term debt} + \text{tangible net worth}}$
Book Value:	$\dfrac{\text{Tangible net worth}}{\text{Number of outstanding shares}}$
Price to Book Ratio:	Book Value/ Stock price
Earnings per Share:	$\dfrac{\text{Net earnings}}{\text{Number of outstanding shares}}$
Cash flow:	$\dfrac{\text{Net earnings} - \text{depreciation}}{\text{Number of outstanding shares}}$
Profit margin:	Net earnings/ operating revenues
Return on total equity:	Net earnings/ shareholder equity
Return on common equity:	$\dfrac{\text{Net earnings} - \text{preferred dividends}}{\text{Net worth} - \text{Par value of preferred stock}}$
Return on total assets:	$\dfrac{\text{Net earnings} + \text{Long-term debt interest}}{\text{Total assets}}$
Inventory turnover:	$\dfrac{\text{Net operating revenues}}{\text{Year end inventory}}$
Price to earnings Ratio:	Stock price/ Earnings per share
Relative price to earnings Ratio:	$\dfrac{\text{Price to earnings ratio}}{\text{S\&P 500 price to earnings ratio}}$
Price to book:	Stock price/ Book value
Dividend yield:	$\dfrac{\text{Dividends per share}}{\text{Stock price}}$
Dividend payout:	$\dfrac{\text{Dividends per share}}{\text{Earnings per share}}$

Nine
Guidelines for New Issues

◆

The Rationale for High-Risk Securities!

There are no magic formulas for evaluating the merits of a new issue security. Every offering should be evaluated using common sense judgments of the information provided in the offering materials, not on touts of friends or acquaintances. Especially not on high-pressure, sales pitches from cold calling securities sales representatives whose sales success depends on stimulating the natural greed of individuals. Greed is what clouds the reasoning of otherwise rational individuals. *If it sounds too good to be true, it usually is!*

Public, new issue, equity security offerings of common stock and limited partnership units should always be considered as speculative investments. Only investors who can afford to lose the amount invested should consider these type securities. In addition, every new issue investor should recognize their individual risk personality, and carefully consider both the probability of success that one is likely to achieve as well as the amount of financial resources that should be made available for speculative investments. Therefore, only a portion of available investment capital should be relegated to speculative securities.

A careful review of the prospectus is a definite requirement. If a quick reading should provoke an interest, the investor should then proceed to carefully evaluate the issue and apply various guidelines, before giving an "indication of interest" to the selling distributor. Understanding the information contained in the prospectus and knowing how to evaluate the merits of the offering, using specified guidelines can help avoid making an investment mistake. However, nothing can guarantee that any particular investment will eventually not become a loser.

UNDERSTANDING RISK, REWARD AND RATIONALITY

Investment risk, for any given security, is not absolute; and should be viewed as the degree of risk from reasonable circumstances. Therefore, individuals should always be rational when considering potential investments. Investments touted to have guaranteed results, or excessively high rates of return with either little downside risk are not realistic and must be suspect. High-pressure sales tactics, or saying "trust me," are telltale signs of malintent in any sales pitch!

Risk is defined herein simply as the probability of a loss in an attempt to achieve a certain goal. *Reward* can be stated as the value received by the amount put at risk. Probabilities are easily computed for games of chance, and the rewards are usually defined. For example, a roulette player will achieve a reward of $35 for a dollar bet on one of 38 possible numbers (numbers one through 36 plus zero and double zero). Therefore, over the long-term, every dollar bet at the wheel will yield $0.92 in reward (1/38 x $35).

The financial markets are considered *rational*, which means that the higher the perceived investment risk, the higher will be the demand for the potential reward. Therefore, demand for investment reward varies directly with risk and inversely with safety. However, the risk for any single investment security is nebulous at best. Numerous papers have been written by academia on quantifying investment risk by using the mathematics of statistics. *Beta, variance,* and *standard deviation* are terms fully understood by both mathematicians and financial professionals, but are meaningless to the average individual. None-the-less, the average individual investor can minimize risk by practicing both investment objective allocation and diversification, both of which are discussed below.

Investment Risk

There are two types of investment risk, *specific risk* and *systematic risk*. Specific risk is the risk taken when investing into securities of a particular company, industry, or geographical location. The price of the securities is therefore sensitive to conditions that are unique to the company, industry, or global region. For example, the share price of a company that plunges drastically when it is suddenly revealed that management has used fraud in its accounting is unique to that company (even though the industry group in which it is classified may be enjoying a business bonanza). Another example of specific risk for an industrial group are the losses suffered by the U.S. semi-conductor industry in the 1980's as a result of the *dumping* (selling below cost) of Japan's semi-conductors on the U.S. market.

Specific risk can be minimized by diversification. To be classified as diversified, mutual funds are limited to a maximum of 5% of fund assets being invested into any one security. However, for individual investors with limited assets, the rule-of-thumb guideline is that no more than 15% of investment assets should be in any one company, industry, or particular geographical region outside the U.S. Assuming a minimum of $3000 for each investment, a reasonable investment amount for diversification would be about $20,000.

Systematic risk is simply market risk, and markets tend to be manic-depressive. They are either overly optimistic, or extremely pessimistic. The best that an individual can do about systematic risk is to not be swept up by the emotions of the market; either selling out completely because of excessive fear in downturns nor be consumed by greed during expansions and buying everything available. For new issue securities, this can be accomplished with a pre-defined investment strategy, which is discussed in Chapter Ten, "Tactics for New Issue Investments." Too many individual investors lose money because they have no tactical plan for taking profits, or that matter, for minimizing losses. The taking of profits when prices increase or minimizing losses when prices decrease appears to be a foreign concept for many.

Individual Risk Personality

The degree of risk for each person varies with what is called the individual's "marginal utility for money." This economic theory states that as a person's earnings increase beyond that needed for necessities—food, shelter, and clothing—more money is then available for discretionary spending. This theory, which is the basis for progressive, income tax structures, essentially defines each investor's *risk tolerance*: how much one can afford to lose. In addition, all investors should be aware of their individual *risk personality* as well as their risk tolerance. Risk personalities can be classified into three categories: risk-taker (or risk-seeker); risk-neutral; and risk-avoider.

A risk-taker derives more pleasure from gaining a dollar than losing one, and typically tries for extraordinary rewards with a lower rate of success. They are likely to lose money more often than they win; therefore, they should employ a securities broker with a full service firm to act as their conscience to attempt to keep from squandering their money. Most brokers will forgo commissions on unsuitable transactions for the benefit of the client, as well as being required by law. Risk-neutral personalities are those that get equal pleasure for $1 gained as pain for $1 lost. These individuals tend to be more balanced in making investments, and occasionally may consider a potentially higher return investment in the attempt to boost their financial goals. Risk-avoiders are the opposite of risk-seekers. They are satisfied with low returns on investments considered to have a high degree of safety, and avoid higher return investments completely.

Reward Probability

The individual with a risk-seeking personality usually will chase any number of investment opportunities (fliers) with extremely high risk in an attempt to seek explosive, short-term returns. The more anxious is the risk-seeker, the less likely that the outcome will be favorable. Therefore, reality for the probability of success can be understood by using a generalized, rule-of-thumb, investment probability of success guideline. An example of such a guideline is shown below in Figure 9-1, "Rule of Thumb Probability of Investment Success."

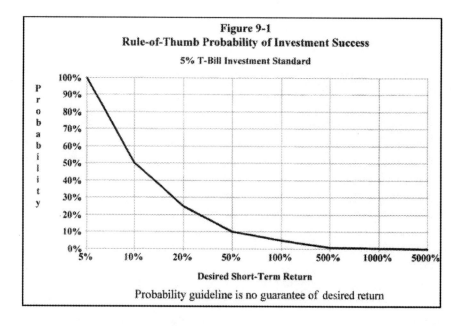

The guideline assumes that the probability of success can be estimated as the yield of a 1-year Treasury bill, used as an investment standard, divided by the percent amount of the desired short-term return. Therefore, this guideline indicates that there is a 100% chance of achieving a 5% return, but higher desired yields with other, more speculative investments will be less likely to be achieved. For example, this figure indicates that there is only a 10% chance for a 50% desired return, and a ½% chance of a 1000% return. If a lower yield T-bill is assumed, then the probabilities of success will be even lower.

Figure 9-1 has no factual basis; however, the validity of the chart is not important. It simply demonstrates that one should realize that potentially high returns have a very low probability of coming to fruition. Whether a 100% desired return could actually be achieved on the average of 1 out of 20 attempts should not be the issue. What is important is that one should realize, and be comfortable with the knowledge, that it may take about 19 or more unsuccessful investment attempts, with significant losses, before being able to obtain the desired goal.

CAPITAL ALLOCATION GUIDELINES

Investment capital should be carefully allocated to prevent going broke. This is especially important for the risk-seeking personality with limited financial resources. Guidelines for capital allocation are presented below for various income classes as a function of investor age. Following these investment allocation guidelines can help to minimize *gambler's remorse*. It should help to avoid investment allocation mistakes from which recovery may not be possible. The guidelines are arbitrary; nevertheless, using rule-of-thumb guidelines can help investors preserve investment capital in their pursuit of wealth.

Middle-Income, Risk Seekers

A guideline for capital allocation is presented in Figure 9-2, "Rule-of-Thumb Investment Objective Portfolio Allocation: Middle-Income, Risk-Seeking Individual." This chart presents an allocation between both fixed-income and growth investment objective securities as a function of investor age.

Middle-income individuals are arbitrarily defined here as those having a ratio of annual income to age between 1000 and 2500. Although the allocation guidelines of Figure 9-2 are arbitrary, they are given to help quantify risk tolerance for the risk-seeking, middle-income, wage-earning investor. The allocation for fixed-income securities should be considered as a minimum amount, whereas the allocation for growth (capital appreciation) and all speculative securities (including IPOs) should be considered as maximum amounts.

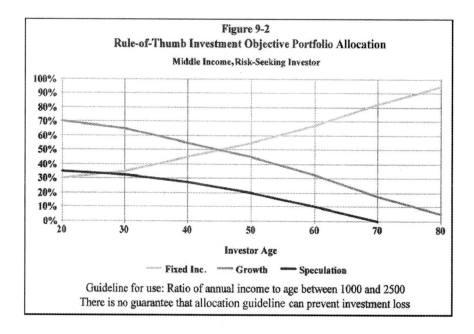

Figure 9-2
Rule-of-Thumb Investment Objective Portfolio Allocation
Middle Income, Risk-Seeking Investor

Guideline for use: Ratio of annual income to age between 1000 and 2500
There is no guarantee that allocation guideline can prevent investment loss

For example, an age 30, risk-seeking individual is encouraged to follow the Figure 9-2 allocation guidelines if annual income is between $30,000 and $75,000. For this person, an income less than $30,000 would indicate that high-risk securities should be avoided, while an income of greater than $75,000 would allow being put in the "higher income" category as shown below. An age 60 individual would be encouraged to follow Figure 9-2 with an annual income between $60,000 and $150,000. It should be noted that retired persons living on either retirement or pension distributions, or both, would most likely fall into the category of those who are encouraged to follow these "middle income" allocation guidelines. Risk-takers may chafe at its *conservatism,* but if followed it should limit the risk-seeking, low-risk tolerance personality from being overextended with high-risk securities.

Lower-Income, Risk Seekers

The rule-of-thumb guideline for defining lower income for speculative investments is someone whose ratio of annual income to age is 1000 or lower. For example, an age 30 individual making $30,000 or less, as well as an age 60 individual earning less than $60,000 would both be considered as having low income as far as speculative investments is concerned, and should avoid IPOs. Even though this is an arbitrary value, it should help to prevent risk-seeking, lower-income individuals from blowing their money on speculative investments.

Higher-Income, Risk Seekers

Risk-seeking investment personalities interested in IPOs who have achieved a high, middle-income status (referred here as *higher income*) should also observe investment allocation guidelines. These types can be allowed to allocate a higher percent of investment capital to speculative issues. Therefore, Figure 9-3 "Rule-of-Thumb Investment Objective Portfolio Allocation: Higher-Income, Risk-Seeking Investor" is presented for individual investors having a ratio of annual income to age that is greater than 2500.

Some individuals may have sufficient means to be able define their own, more aggressive risk tolerance and risk allocation. This includes accredited individuals (individuals having a net worth greater than $1 million and an annual income greater than $200,000), and financially sophisticated investors that have both high incomes and high net worth, although not qualifying as accredited investors. These individuals either have the capacity to recover losses, or have sufficient wealth so that potential investment losses would not affect their future lifestyle. The classic question should always be, Would this investment alter future lifestyle in any way if completely lost? Nevertheless, risk-seeking, accredited or high-income investors would also be advised to follow the guidelines of Figure 9-3. This will help to prevent the gambler's instinct of "never letting a gambling opportunity be passed by" from taking control. While this type person may feel that he or she can afford to take losses, over time cumulative loss can do serious financial damage without the influence of some sort of guideline.

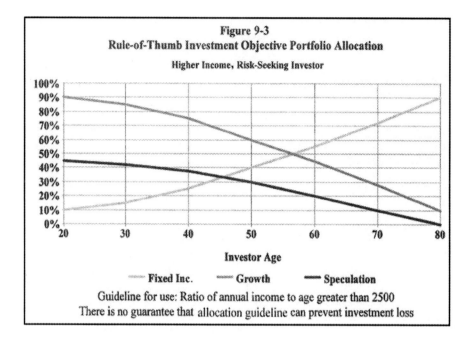

Figure 9-3
Rule-of-Thumb Investment Objective Portfolio Allocation
Higher Income, Risk-Seeking Investor

Investor Age

Fixed Inc.   Growth   Speculation

Guideline for use: Ratio of annual income to age greater than 2500
There is no guarantee that allocation guideline can prevent investment loss

New Issue Investment Category Allocation

Investment capital for new issue investments should be allocated using the guidelines of Figure 9-2 and Figure 9-3. New issue securities can be both growth or fixed-income investments and each type has its speculative category securities. The following paragraphs represent rule-of-thumb investment categories for capital allocation purposes.

Growth Category Speculative Securities

Private placements and IPOs of startup and development stage businesses whose capitalization is under $250 million are to be considered as the highest degree of speculative security. Not far behind is the emerging growth stage, small capitalization company with less than $2 billion, and new issue offerings of mature growth companies seeking business growth through acquisitions (large cap companies with capitalization's greater than $8 billion). Also considered speculative are IPOs that are issued bundled with warrants, as well as new issue ADRs. New issues of both closed-end funds and non-REIT UITs having growth as the investment objective can be considered in the non-speculative growth category.

Fixed-Income Category Speculative Securities

All fixed-income new issues should be considered speculative for companies whose debt obligations are rated as "speculative" (BBB or lower). Also, convertibles and straight preferred stock issued by companies having a capitalization less than $2 billion should be considered speculative. Preferred stock issues of mid cap (between $2 billion and $8 billion) companies and large cap (greater than $8 billion) companies should be placed into the speculative category if dividends are "non-cumulative" (see Chapter Two, "Business Capitalization Securities").

Contrary to conventional wisdom, REITs and UITs investing in mortgage-backed securities should be considered only by higher net worth individuals, not pensioners looking for their next monthly check. Mortgaged-backed securities are considered the safest type of income investment; however, they are categorized as speculative securities to limit the amount on investment capital in these investments. Because they are required to pass through the annual principal repayments to investors, REITs, and UITs with mortgaged-backed securities, must return repaid capital to investors. Consequently, there will be no capital remaining to return to the investor at maturity. No stockbroker could ever explain to an aging client at the maturity of her REIT that her only source of income has stopped, and that she has received her investment principal incrementally over the years.

In addition, the maturity dates for REITS and mortgage-backed securities are not fixed because of early repayment of mortgages (see Chapter Two, "Business Capitalization Securities). Mortgage repayment is accelerated during periods of decreasing interest rates, and lengthened during increasing interest rate periods. Therefore, both duration and payment amount are uncertain. Mutual funds investing in REITs are allowed to reinvest the repaid principal. Therefore, these securities should not be considered as speculative for allocation purposes.

Realities of Speculative Investments

Assume an age 50 single individual with an annual income of $100,000 is interested in speculating with IPO investments to attempt to achieve a short-term return of $20,000 to purchase a compact car. Her self-directed, securities account has a balance of $200,000, and she had previously indicated that speculation was her second investment objective with growth being the first.

The allocation guideline of Figure 9-2 would be appropriate since the income to age ratio guideline for this investor is less than the 2500 arbitrary ratio specified. This guideline indicates that the equity securities in the account be limited to 45% of the account balance, with the speculative amount limited to 20%, which for this example would be $40,000. Therefore, the desired short-term return, expressed as a decimal, would then be 50% ($20,000/$40,000). This type return may be considered easily achievable by a risk-seeking individual that expects this amount of return to be easily achieved within the first few months of an IPO (see Chapter One, "Getting Rich Quickly").

However, the reader should understand the realities of successful speculation. As shown in Figure 9-1, the rule-of-thumb probability of success, for a desired short-term return of about 50% is indicated to be about 10% (one out of ten investments), assuming a riskless one year return of 5%. The investor should expect that it might take up to 10 attempts before a successful return can be achieved. Therefore, no one speculative investment should exceed $4000 (for the example cited) to preserve the amount of speculative capital allocated. Those who are mathematically inclined will quickly observe even if the nine losing position losses were limited to 20% by liquidating positions that drop in price by that amount, the one potential successful position would have to achieve a return of 180% just to break even. For the cited example's 50% desired return on $40,000, the single successful position would need to achieve a return of 680%. Without a "home-run" IPO investment of this magnitude, this example investor's speculative capital will eventually be all depleted with about 20 unsuccessful deals (assuming that the loss for each is limited to 20%).

NEW ISSUE SELECTION GUIDELINES

New issue investments are extremely risky investments for the average individual. The securities industry generally depends upon institutional and high net-worth investors to fund new issue securities. However, many risk-seeking personality individuals (otherwise called gamblers) look for the potentially explosive rewards that can occur. Therefore, a rule-of-thumb guideline for limiting the amount of speculative investment capital for the average working individual as discussed previously should be followed, as well as both general and specific guidelines for new issue offerings.

The different types of new issue security offerings available were described previously in Chapter Two, "Business Capitalization Securities" as: fixed income, debt obligations and preferred stock; equities, common stock, ADRs, and limited partnership units; hybrid securities, convertibles; and derivative securities, warrants. Some have income potential while others have capital appreciation potential. They may also be rated as either investment grade quality or as speculative grade quality. Investment grade securities are deemed relatively safe from default, but are subject to ordinary market risk. Speculative securities are either subject to default, or to price declines due to circumstances that are beyond the control of the issuer, such as currency rate changes with foreign securities.

However, only common stock, limited partnership, and convertible security offerings are discussed herein as being considered within the scope of the risk-seeking investor. Arbitrary investment guidelines are given below, and should be considered as rule-of-thumb guidelines. The general guidelines apply to any new issue offerings described here, while specific guidelines are presented for each of these three different types of new issue securities. Each guideline should be considered along with all other general and specific guidelines stated herein. Guidelines that are stated as an "avoid" guideline should be *avoided absolutely*, regardless of how much enthusiasm is being generated for the offering.

General Guidelines for New Issues

The following general guidelines, described below, should be applied to all new issue offering securities.

Reading the Prospectus

Potential investors, for whom new issue offerings are compatible with suitability requirements and the investor's investment personality, should first read the cover page and the summary. This reading should invoke some degree of excitement about the offering. One may not be able to define exactly what causes such enthusiasm, except that it should be something about the product or service, business sector, market niche, or the management team that is compelling.

If there is insufficient interest in the story, then the offering should be passed up with a "no thanks" answer to the securities sales person. However, should there be an interest in the story, it follows that a more careful reading should be made of the following sections:

1. the business description

2. use of proceeds

3. capitalization disclosure

4. summary of selected financial data

5.   management's discussion

6.   the underwriting agreement

This additional information should provide continued interest in the story, as envisioned by the investor, and indicate a high potential for the success of the business operation.

When the initial excitement has not ebbed after the more detailed reading, the remaining sections should then be carefully studied to make sure that there is likely not to be any future, negative surprises. This specifically includes the sections on risk factors, the financial statements and the accompanying notes, and the auditor's report letter. Lastly, before any commitment is made, the entire prospectus should then be reviewed from cover to cover, and all investment guidelines, both general and specific as described below, should be applied.

Managed Offerings

Investment bankers perform due diligence during the underwriting of a firm commitment, new issue offering and put both their reputation and capital on the line. Therefore, consider only offerings that are managed by an investment banker (underwriting securities dealer). However, managed offerings with an underwriting compensation greater than 10% should be suspect.

Non-Managed Offerings

Non-managed offerings are distributed with the sponsoring securities dealer acting as a sales agent. In addition, many companies decide to distribute capitalization securities by themselves, and simply engage securities dealers to distribute the issue for a fee. This applies especially to new issues being offered over the Internet as a DPO. In order to induce conventional securities dealers to participate in the non-managed distribution, the issuer typically may offer a distribution fee of 20% or more. (The author has observed one LP issue with a 50% distribution fee). These offerings may also encourage securities fraud by the issuer since there is little, if any, due diligence performed. No penetration into the management is ever made, and therefore the offering should be considered as having excessive risk.

Non-managed offerings are utilized for common stocks, but are typically used for exempt securities such as those issued by limited partnerships, general partnerships (working interests), and private placements. However, of the lack of due diligence and high distribution fees of non-managed offerings is more than sufficient justification for the individual investor to avoid these issues.

Underwriting Commitment

Only offerings being underwritten with a firm commitment, or with a firm commitment for the minimum quantity of a "mini-max" offering, should be considered. All *best effort* offerings should be avoided! They may result in a grossly undercapitalized business that will be inadequate for the purposes intended, and may seriously affect the liquidity of the securities in the marketplace after the effective date. Best effort commitments may also have extraordinarily long cooling off periods, which could be as long as 6 months and longer, as the dealers distributing the offering endeavor to find subscribers. These offerings typically require a deposit of those indicating an interest, which will be put into an escrow account until the effective date. Despite what the broker may assure, the deposit essentially will be frozen should disgruntled investors that get tired of waiting for the issue to go public later ask for a refund.

Securities Market Listing

All new issue securities should be listed on one of the public securities markets after the effective date. This will exclude most DPP limited partnerships, private placements, small cap and intrastate offerings. The exempt equity securities (exempt from SEC registration) are considered as illiquid, since they are not listed on a public market, and therefore should be avoided. (This guideline does not apply to exempt Treasury and municipal debt obligation offerings since these securities trade in the dealers' market over-the-counter.) Every investor should be able to immediately sell any securities held, whenever they so decide.

The acceptable equity markets include the NYSE, AMEX, the regional exchanges, or the NASDAQ. Offerings that are to be listed on the OTC Bulletin Board or the Pink Sheets, and exempt private placement, intrastate, and small-cap offerings (SCORs) should all be avoided due to a lack of an adequate market.

Risk Factors

Consideration should be given to any offering that, as described in the risk factor section of the prospectus, is free from potential or pending litigation. It should also be free of all major risks that are out of the control of management. Such as the potential for being in violation of statutory regulations that are in the process of being changed by law. All risk factors must be disclosed in the prospectus. If there is any indication of any such risk, such as a serious environmental hazard liability, the offering should be avoided!

Common Stock Liquidity

Liquidity in the trading market after the effective date is very important. What otherwise would be nominal size market orders may result in moving the market for thinly traded issues (less than 5000 shares daily). Buy or sell orders for quantities larger than those currently available in the marketplace will result in large price swings. In addition, the market makers' spreads are likely to be much higher than the 5% NASD guideline.

To minimize the potential for being trapped into an illiquid position, avoid any common stock offering in which:

1. the floating supply is less than 5 million shares

2. the floating supply capitalization is less than $5 million

3. 60% or more of the outstanding shares are controlled by insiders

4. any single entity controls more than 40% of the outstanding shares

Auditor's Unqualified Opinion

The prospectus for the new issue offering most likely will contain the independent auditor's report rendering an unqualified opinion. The opinion should contain the phrases "the aforementioned statements present fairly" and "in conformity with generally accepted accounting principles" in the opinion paragraph (typically the second paragraph). A third paragraph, which would be unlikely with a new issue offering, would give either a qualified opinion, a disclaimer of opinion, or an adverse opinion. A third paragraph that contains the words "except that" or "subject to" indicates a qualified opinion. A statement about information unavailable to the auditor will be the reason for giving a disclaimer of opinion. An adverse opinion will be indicated if the words "does not present fairly" are included. Anything but an unqualified opinion is to be considered a potential major problem. If the opinion is anything but unqualified, the offering is to be avoided.

Recently, some auditors have been found as not being completely independent. Their objectivity had been tainted by holding seats on the board of directors of, or by engaging in lucrative consulting contracts with companies that they are paid to audit. While this is now illegal under the Sarbanes-Oxley Act, any offerings in which this situation is remotely possible should be avoided.

Shelf Offerings

A shelf offering (an issue that distributes partial offerings over a 12-month period) is a device used when demand for the total amount of securities to be offered may be insufficient. This occurs when the managing underwriter considers the total amount of capitalization desired, to be too much for the market place to bear at one time, and therefore suggests that it be spread over one year. This type offering is used to avoid an initial "turkey" by artificially limiting the supply with limited partial offerings over a year's time. Therefore, shelf offerings should also be avoided by the individual investor.

Exempt Equity Offerings

Exempt equity offerings are those that are exempt from registration with the SEC, therefore full disclosure by prospectus may not available. These include private placements, small cap offerings (less than $5 million), and intrastate offerings (issues sold only to residents of one state, which only requires registration in the state if greater than $5 million). All exempt securities offerings should be avoided because they lack both full disclosure and liquidity.

Retirement Account Securities

IPOs may be purchased in retirement accounts providing that the owner has stated a speculative investment objective, has a history of purchasing IPOs, and has an appropriate financial status (high annual income as well as high net worth). However, it should be understood that losses from speculative IPOs in retirement accounts are doubly treacherous. Losses invalidate the allowable annual contributions made to the account, and any explosive capital gains will not receive favorable capital gains tax treatment on distribution (as it would occur in a regular, self-directed securities account).

Therefore, the average individual investor, regardless of his or her risk personality should avoid buying both IPOs, and DPP limited partnership interests as well as *working interests,* in retirement accounts. The lack of liquidity of DPPs and working interests provide no flexibility should the investor later decide the account needs restructuring. Only standby offerings of financially sound existing public companies and convertibles of companies whose debt obligations are rated as investment grade (see Chapter Two, "Business Capitalization Securities") should be considered in retirement accounts.

Underwriting Firm Success

Some underwriters have greater success with new issues than do others. The large, national firms with thousands of securities brokers can, after the Quiet Period, continue to promote these new issues in the marketplace to clients. The larger the firm, the more "deals" can be underwritten with a greater capitalization per deal. (In the vernacular of *The Street,* "deal" refers to a new issue underwriting.)

Smaller, regional underwriters may be successful with new issues of local companies that are not large enough to be of interest to the national underwriting firms. The individual clients of these firms have a better chance of subscribing to quantities of up to 1000 shares of a new issue, as opposed to clients of the national firms that are likely to be *shut out.* However, to the investors' disadvantage, new issues sponsored by these smaller underwriting firms run a greater chance of inadequate due diligence. Therefore, only the higher income, risk seeker whose income to age ratio is greater than 2500, as a rule of thumb, should consider issues underwritten by the regional securities dealers.

It is important that an underwriter have experience in bringing new issue securities public. However, Table 9-1, "1999 Underwriter Ranking," shown below, illustrates that the success of an IPO is not strictly a function of the number of deals made by the managing underwriter. Of the five underwriters having the most deals in 1999 (and greatest dollar capitalization), only three were in the top five for highest average IPO return (success rate).

Table 9-1
1999 Underwriter Ranking

By Capitalization Amount

Underwriter	Number of Deals	Capitalization Amount ($ Billion)
1. Goldman Sachs	48	$13.5
2. Morgan Stanley Dean Witter	48	$12.9
3. Merrill Lynch	37	$8.3
4. Credit Suisse First Boston	53	$5.8
5. Donaldson Lufkin & Jenrette	37	$3.7

By Yearend Average Return Rate

Underwriter	Number of Deals	Average IPO Return (%) (1)
1. Credit Suisse First Boston	53	320%
2. Morgan Stanley Dean Witter	48	308
3. Dain Rauscher Wessels	4	237
4. Prudential Securities	6	235
5. Goldman Sachs	48	200

Note: (1), Average market price at yearend/IPO offer price
Source: "Gravy Train," by Jack Willoughby, *Barron's*, 12/13/99

Having access to IPOs through any national managing underwriter for the average individual can be a problem if one is not a long time client (see below, "Acquiring Access to New Issue Offerings"). Potential IPO investors should inquire about recent offerings brought public from underwriters of interest, and then determine the current success rate averaging the success rates of all issues offered within the year. The success rate for each issue is computed by dividing the current market price by the offering price, and subtracting one. Multiplying by 100 will result in a percent rate. This average success rate should be at least 130%.

Acquiring Access to New Issue Offerings

Any investor can get easy access to IPOs by investing into a mutual fund, within a large fund family, that specializes in IPOs. High-income, high net worth individuals can consider a hedge fund. To have consistent access to IPOs, average individual investors require a record of IPO investing with significant sums. Institutions, with their financial clout, will get the bulk of IPO shares; however, eventual access to new issue offerings should be able to be obtained if one has a sufficient sum available for speculation (about $25,000 minimum). Keep in mind that the amount of capital used for these speculative issues should be consistent with the allocation guidelines of either Figure 9-2 or Figure 9-3.

The first step is to determine which national underwriter, with a local branch office, has had more than the average number of deals in the past year. (Financial periodicals, such as *Barron's* have frequent articles on new issue underwriters.) For example, the underwriters with five or more deals in 2001 are shown below in Table 9-2, "Major 2001 Managing Underwriters." Note that the number of deals for 2001 was considerably less than the bubble year of 1999, shown in Table 9-1.

Table 9-2
Major 2001 Managing Underwriters

Manager	Number of Deals	Capitalization: $billions
Goldman Sachs	11	$12.2
Morgan Stanley	10	$10.9
Credit Suisse First Boston	13	$9.8
Salomon Smith Barney	6	$8.2
Merrill Lynch	9	$1.6
UBS Warburg	7	$1.5
Lehman Brothers	8	$1.4
Banc of America	5	$0.8
Deutsche Banc Alex Brown	5	$0.6

Source: "Wall Street Wizzards," *Barron's*, 12/10/01

Next, an account should be opened with a local broker from one of these underwriters by calling the branch manager and getting a referral for someone in the firm that specializes in IPO offerings. The account must have "speculation" as the primary investment objective, and the broker must be reminded that the client is interested in IPOs. A reasonable amount of speculative capital should be in the range between $25,000 and $50,000. The greater the amount that is available, the better the chances of getting access. In addition, opening accounts with other underwriting firms will increase chances of having access to IPOs.

However, the total amount deposited for speculation must represent the amount allocated for speculation for the investor. For example, assume that an age 45, higher-income, risk-seeking investor desires to speculate with $50,000. Figure 9-3 guidelines would require that he or she also have an investment portfolio with an equal amount in fixed-income securities as a minimum, and an additional equal amount as a maximum in other growth securities. In other words, this investor's investment portfolio should be worth at least $150,000. If one cannot comply with allocation guidelines, then the desired speculative deposit amount should be cut back appropriately.

Before getting access to IPOs, the investor will have to demonstrate that he, or she, is a serious speculator that generates a substantial amount of commissions for the firm. This is performed by soliciting ideas for trading stock from the broker, and acting on all of the reasonable recommendations. This will establish that the client is a serious short-term trader. In time, through repeated inquiries and hopefully before any serious loss of capital through trading, the investor should be able to have access to occasional IPOs without being shutout (although the quantity requested may be limited).

Market Conditions

IPO securities have greater sensitivity to market conditions than do stocks of established companies. Most new businesses fall under the category of a small-cap, or micro-cap company. These stock prices tend to outperform the market during economic expansions (bull markets). Sales increases grow at a greater rate than those of larger companies, which attracts interest from investors looking for greater than average capital appreciation. However, they under perform the market averages greater price declines during economic contractions (bear markets) as speculative stockholders sell out their positions at the first signs of decreased, or flat, earnings or sales.

The 1990s' IPO bubble peaked with the dot-com issues being representative of a "new era" in valuation: companies with sales but with no foreseeable earnings. Table 9-1 showed that 223 deals were made between the top five underwriters for the bubble year 1999. However, in the recession year of 2001, Table 9-2 indicates that the top five underwriters only made 49 deals.

Market capitalization for new issue securities for the bull market of the 1990s is presented below in Figure 9-4, "Yearly IPO Capitalization." The figure shows the peak capitalization for year 2000 was 16 times the capitalization for 1990. In addition, this 11-year period had seven increasing capitalization years and four down years, with the decline in 2001 being the greatest percent decline of the previous two declining periods.

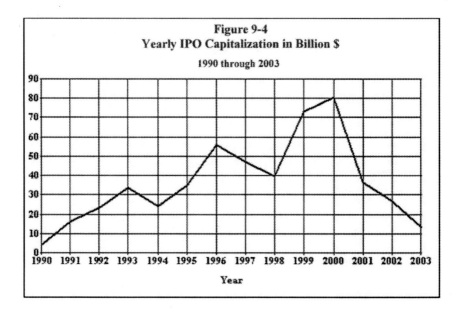

Figure 9-4
Yearly IPO Capitalization in Billion $
1990 through 2003

Investors should be wary of purchasing an IPO going public at what would appear to be a market top. (Although the market bubble was clearly defined by 1999, risk-taking investors would continued to buy IPOs into 2000, to their detriment.) At this stage, the demand for IPO issues will be high, and therefore are likely to be priced at a premium. IPOs of market niche companies can be expected to do well in any type market; however, the demand for these will quickly decline once a bear market is recognized as speculative investors reduce the size of their holdings by exchanging into fixed income securities for safety of principal purposes.

Therefore, guidelines for market conditions for IPOs are that they should be considered after an economic decline, or recession, that has been followed by at least one quarter having a positive Gross Domestic Product, or GDP, change. (Typically, a recession is defined as two or more calendar quarters of negative changes in GDP.) IPOs should be avoided after an economic expansion has "tired," which is typically signaled by a slowing in a broad market index, such as the S&P 500 Index, following an explosion in common stock price.

Shutout IOIs

IPO investors frequently find that they are shutout of an offering in which they have given an indication of interest (IOI). These incidents typically happen to individual investors who desire to purchase small quantities (1000 shares or less). When this occurs, the shutout client should realize that the securities broker is not responsible, because allocation is usually made on a lottery basis with the firm's principals. (Of course, long-time clients would expect to get their IOIs filled.)

The normal reaction is to place a market order to purchase shares in the marketplace at the start of public trading. However, this tactic for purchasing IPOs is flawed even with a hot issue. The average IPO does not respond with a continual explosion in stock price. As reported by William Powell in the *Wall Street Journal*, 3/17/94, the average IPO peaks in stock price at about three-months after the effective date, and thereafter declines.

The study results that were reported by Powell are shown graphically below in Figure 9-5, "Average IPO Stock Price Performance" (reproduced from Figure 1-1). This indicates the peak average IPO return is about 15%, which occurs at about three-months after the effective date, and subsequently declines to only a 3% return at 24-months.

In contrast, the peak average return for investors purchasing IPOs at the 1st day's closing price was found to be about 3% at 3 months, and declining to a negative 7% at 24-months. Although the information database for Power's article is dated (1994), it does show typical average IPO market price characteristics prior to the manic market of the late 1990s.

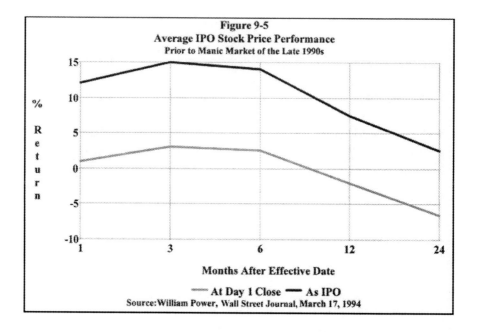

Figure 9-5
Average IPO Stock Price Performance
Prior to Manic Market of the Late 1990s

One example is the IPO of VA Linux Systems (see Table 1-1) that had a first day return of over 600% in December 1999. However, at two years, IPO investors still holding shares would have a loss of 90%. First day purchasers of Linux would have never seen a positive return, and at two years would have had a loss of 98% should they have held onto their shares.

Another example is the successful IPO of United Parcel Service Class B stock (also see Table 1-1) that had a 175% return on the first day in November 1999, but gradually declined to only 114% return at two years. However, one purchasing the stock at the first days close would never have realized a profit, and at two years would have had a loss of 28%.

Therefore, the general guideline for equity IPOs is that anyone that has been shutout of an IPO offering, as well as any other interested investors, should pass up the opportunity to purchase shares in the marketplace after the effective date. The strong probability of an eventual loss with such a purchase is balanced only by the potential of a limited short-term gain.

Specific Guidelines for New Issue Equity Offerings

Many new issue common stock offerings (simply called a "public offering") are used by existing public companies to raise additional capital. This typically occurs with companies in the stability and decline stage of the business life cycle looking for capital to restructure or to "buy growth." They may also occur for companies in the rapid expansion stage and mature growth stage, but less frequently for the mature growth stage since other capitalization options are available (such as issuing debt obligations or preferred stock). Public offerings can be either a different class common stock or same class shares with a standby rights offering.

Latter Business Stage Public Offerings

Generally, there is no compelling reason for investors to participate in Mature Growth and Stability & Decline stage offerings if they do not presently own stock in these companies. Even if one does own shares, there is no reason to expect significant price appreciation for the new issue offering. Therefore, new issue offerings for these companies should be considered as a value play, and evaluated as a value stock as indicated in Chapter Eight, "Financial Evaluation of Business Organizations." The estimated fair value, for a 20-year period, should be computed at 1.5 times the offer price as a minimum to assure an adequate margin of safety. In addition, a new issue offering of a different class common stock with limited voting rights should be avoided.

The attractiveness of new issue offerings can be determined by scrutinizing the prospectus for use of proceeds. The majority should be applied toward new business opportunities. However, the offer should be avoided if management is seeking additional capitalization to achieve a turnaround by reducing debt, or to purchase growth through an acquisition. Evidence of this could include either of the following:

1. more than 50% of the proceeds are to be used to pay down long-term debt

2. proceeds are to be used to acquire growth by a major acquisition of another company

The management of companies that become burdened by too much debt should not be encouraged to repeat their errors in the future. In addition, mergers and acquisitions typically result in problems trying to consolidate the businesses under one management. Warren Buffett's admonition, *"turnarounds seldom turn"* should be taken seriously.

Rights holders (current shareholders who receive rights to purchase additional stock in a rights offering) must decide about exercising their rights and purchase additional shares. The conventional wisdom dictates that if the investor liked these shares enough to initiate and hold a position, then they should be willing to exercise the rights to maintain their ownership share. As stated in Chapter Ten, "New Issue Investment Tactics," if one decides not to exercise the rights, he or she should sell them. (Rights will trade in the same market in which the stock trades.) Inaction will result in losing the market value of the rights upon expiration (the rights expire worthless).

As explained previously, the underwriter will purchase new issue shares covered by expired rights and offered to the public with a standby offering. Investors who have no previous ownership position need not be compelled to purchase shares in a standby offering.

The *pro-forma* financial statements offered in the prospectus should show a healthy financial condition. The Current Ratio should be about 1.5 and the Quick Ratio should be 1.0 as a minimum. The Debt to Equity Ratio should not exceed 1.0; otherwise, the creditors would "own" more of the company than would the shareholders. Historical data on working capital, cash flow, and profit margin should show annual increases over the past five years. High dividend paying companies should have a Dividend Payout Ratio of less than 50%. Avoid issues where the dividend payout is 75% or greater.

Rapid Expansion Stage Business Public Offerings

Occasionally, a company that has successfully completed an IPO will decide to issue additional shares within the year with an additional public offering (which should not be confused with an IPO shelf offering). The demand for shares in the marketplace encourages the issuer to offer additional shares with a primary offering that can provide additional capital for even greater expansion than initially anticipated. However, the key adjective for the offering is "primary." A "secondary" offering should be avoided because no capital will be applied to business expansion, only to enrich inside shareholders tendering shares to the public.

In the main, primary public offerings of existing public companies in the rapid expansion phase can be as successful as the IPO itself. However, they should not be confused with public offerings of companies, which have previously distributed an IPO during an economic bubble expansion that no one can expect to be sustained. An example of the first type public offering is Callaway Golf, and an example of the second type public offering is Sycamore Networks Inc.

Callaway Golf designs and manufactures high quality, innovative golf clubs and balls. An IPO for 2.6 million shares at $20 was made in February 1992, followed by a public offering for an additional 1.4 million shares at $27 in November. Three, two-for-one stock splits were made in March of 1993, 1994, and

1995. The split adjusted percentage return on shares purchased as an IPO was: 18% at 6 months (indicating a decline from the first day's close); 215% at one year; and 1,045% at five years, which is computed as a 62% per year return on average. In addition, the split adjusted percentage return on shares obtained as a public offering in November 1992 was, 171% at 6 months, 286% at one year, and 418% at five years. These healthy returns, which would represent an annual 39% per year, would satisfy the desired return any speculative investor.

However, the success of the IPO for Sycamore Networks was chiefly the result of a manic market devouring all new issues. Sycamore develops voice and data traffic networks over existing optical fiber. In October 1999, the company's IPO distributed 7.5 million shares at $38 per share. The IPO return at the first day's close was 430%, which increased to 629% at three months. A public offering for an additional 10.2 million shares at $150 was then issued in March 2000—the peak of the manic market bubble—after a three for one stock split the previous month (February). The first day's return on these new issue shares was only 14%. Thereafter, the returns were negative (Wall Street rhetoric for a loss) with a 31% loss at three months, an 89% loss at one year, and a 96% loss on December 31, 2001. In addition, holders of shares acquired at the IPO price would also have experienced a loss of 57% at the end of year 2001.

Initial Public Offerings of Startup Companies

IPOs are the first time offering of common stock to the public. However, IPOs are all different. Some have a good probability of success, but the majority is doomed to eventual failure *as an investment*. The specific guidelines, given below, will not guarantee a successful investment, but should help avoid making mistakes.

Startup companies typically have a business concept, but do not have sufficient capital to be able to be in business. More than two thirds of startup businesses fail within the first five years, many because of a lack of capitalization, but mostly because of bad management. The management and key personnel are typically experts in their field, but their business acumen has never before been challenged. Individual investors in startup companies that raise capital from the public with only a business plan are disadvantaged. They have neither the opportunity nor the expertise to penetrate management's ability to run a business, as would venture capitalists. Individual investors should avoid such offerings because of the excessive risk of failure by inept management.

Therefore, successful startup companies will likely have been privately capitalized as a startup company by a venture capitalist. The venture capitalist will personally meet with management to evaluate their ability to run a successful business. They will also seek a majority interest in the organization to ensure that management's decisions are for the benefit of the company, and provide assistance by making recommendations on operating the business. Within five years, these privately held, development stage companies will have offered shares to the public through a split offering (see Chapter Seven, "New Issue Offerings").

Initial Public Offerings of Ongoing Businesses

Ongoing businesses that are in the development stage of the business life cycle, and possibly rapid expansion stage, will often offer IPOs. This type offering is the best type to evaluate since it will have a historical financial record. However, one can still be trapped into a bad investment, which may look good on paper, if the guidelines listed below are ignored.

The proceeds of these primary offerings should be applied to expanding the business. Secondary offerings should be avoided as the venture capitalists and other principals are simply taking profits from their initial investments. Split offerings should be avoided if more than 40% of the proceeds are major private shareholders offering their shares to the public through the offering process.

Primary, and split offerings, where more than 50% of the proceeds are used to pay off accrued debt should be avoided. Recapitalization of floundering businesses typically does no good with the existing management. How can the previously unsuccessful management be expected to become more successful at running the business with an infusion of capital? What should be expected is a continued floundering of a public company.

The current working capital shown in the financial statements must be positive. If it is negative and the *pro-forma* financial statements indicates that they will be positive (as it most assuredly will be), the company is still likely to continue to be a floundering business. The *pro-forma* current ratio should be at least 2.0, and the profit margin should be at least 10%. Previously floundering businesses that cannot pay current bills without new capital should be avoided.

Current earnings, or at least the cash flow, should be positive. Development stage businesses engaged in research and development of new technology may expect explosive earnings in the future with a new product even though rate of spending may be in excess of revenues. However, it may require additional capitalization in the future. Therefore, these offerings should be avoided because at best, they indicate that the current finances could be in jeopardy without future additional capitalization, and it could take years for significant earnings to occur.

Any investor can make a safer, long-term value investment with existing blue chip (large capitalization, investment grade) securities.

Historical income statements should show a history of growth over the last five years. Earnings, cash flow, or revenues can all be used to measure growth. The rule of thumb is for only one down year in the last 5 years. On the other hand, this can be modified to only one down year out of the last 3 years if the organization has not been operation for five years. If earnings have been negative, revenues can be used to measure growth, as long as the current cash flow is positive. Avoid all offerings in which the down years number either three of the past five, or two out of the past three.

Companies issuing IPOs typically carry little long-term debt. However, many will carry some long-term debt as a leverage tool used by management. Therefore, any offering in which the total debt represents more than 40% of the *pro-forma* capitalization (shareholder equity of at least 150% of total debt) should be avoided as having excessive debt for a new public company.

Specific Guidelines for Limited Partnership Units

Limited partnership organizations were discussed in Chapter Two, "Business Capitalization Securities" as limited life business organizations. Most LP units offered to the public are registered with the SEC, and do not allow units to be freely exchanged to permit them from enjoying certain tax advantages; thereby coming under the category of what is called a "direct participation program," or DPP. Some DPPs are not registered with the SEC, but are still offered to the public as an *exempt* security under the small-cap exemption provision (less than $5 million), or as an intrastate offering. Intrastate offerings require state registration, unless it falls under the small-cap umbrella.

However, a few LPs are offered with publicly traded units and act like tradable common stock securities in the marketplace. These type organizations are also discussed later in this chapter under "Publicly Traded Limited Partnerships."

New issue offerings of LP units are all IPOs that typically provide capitalization for specific business projects having a limited lifetime. These typically offer a promise of future annual income, but many also offer tax advantages to the limited partners by passing through depreciation and amortization tax write-offs on property, or on oil and gas resource depletion. Having no public market for partnership units, these type new issue securities cannot provide explosive capital appreciation as is anticipated for corporate IPOs. None-the-less, guidelines for these securities are given here since a great many of these securities are offered to accredited investors, as well as to non-accredited, higher income investors who meet nominal financial requirements that are established for each issue.

The securities representative and dealer distributing the new issue LP units have legal liability for determining investor suitability. However, sales reps of underwriters offering LP units as DPPs typically solicit non-accredited individuals to fill their sales quotas. Most cold callers will be distributing unmanaged offerings, or offerings that are exempt from registration, as well as those strictly touting tax advantages.

The risk for any securities investment is always taken by the investor. Therefore, every potential investor must be completely aware of the risks. The business must make sense, and the promised returns should be reasonable. A statement by a tax attorney on the potential tax liability, or tax shelter, will be contained in the prospectus. Even though the sponsor is bound to find someone who will provide a favorable tax opinion, the final determination on tax matters is the responsibility of the IRS. Therefore, LP investments should not be made based on touts of tax advantages or tax shelters. They should only be based on the fair value estimation with a margin of safety of at least two times the offer price. (Note, LP investments are passive activity interests and are subject to IRS passive activity rules, which allow losses to offset only passive activity income, not the investor's earned income.)

Evaluating a LP is not very easy for the average individual. Unless one has direct knowledge of the business, there is little that one can do, apart from trusting the salesperson to assess the validity of the numbers and projections that will be stated in the prospectus. However, this is never recommended, ever! Therefore, partnership agreements should be read very carefully before subscribing, even though the prospectus may contain up to 100 pages of dry reading. The following basic questions must be able to be answered as is shown below.

How will the capital raised be used?

It must be fully disclosed and reasonable, make sense to the individual. Avoid offerings where use of capital is not specifically disclosed.

What is the profit-expense sharing arrangement between limited partners and the general partner?

The arrangement should be reasonable with the general partner receiving a fair compensation for managing the partnership. Avoid disproportionate partnership sharing arrangements, such as the general partner receiving all income and limited partners allocated all expenses (see oil and gas sharing arrangements below).

Can the LP maturity date be extended at the whim of the general partner without a vote of the limited partners?

Many investors will enter a limited lifetime investment expecting that the project will end at the specified maturity date. There may be good reasons to extend the life of the partnership, but it should be upon a vote of authorization from the limited partners, not at the whim of the general partner. Therefore, avoid LPs that allow the sponsor to make such decisions.

Are limited partners responsible to indemnify the general partner for any liabilities?

The basis for limited partnerships is the limited liability of the subscribing partners only to that amount which in invested. However, an indemnification clause in the agreement opens up the limited partners to any liabilities incurred by the general partner in managing the partnership. Therefore, LPs with indemnification clauses should be avoided.

How easily can ownership units be re-sold and to whom?

Units cannot be traded publicly, but partners should be able to dispose units privately (typically with the approval of the general partner).

As mentioned previously under "General New Issue Guidelines," DPP limited partnership units should never be purchased in a retirement account.

Real Estate Partnership Guidelines

LPs in real estate are common, and typically allow income from rentals to be off-set by real estate expenses. These securities are offered by LPs that list specifically targeted, existing, income producing real property that the LP has or will acquire. The estimated fair value of these units (as described previously) should be 2 times the offer price to provide a 100% a margin of safety for these illiquid securities.

Some real estate LP projects should be avoided. These are new construction projects, undeveloped land projects, and blind pools. New construction projects have no income against which expenses can be applied. Undeveloped land projects are very speculative because the intent is for eventual appreciation in land value, while in the interim there is no income against which partnership expenses can be charged, and land itself cannot be depreciated. Lastly, blind pools are typically large, multi-property, partnership projects in which the general partner does not disclose specific properties that it intends to acquire; a "trust me" deal.

Equipment Leasing Partnership Guidelines

These LPs promote equipment-leasing programs that produce partnership income for the limited partners. The depreciation allowance offsets income from leasing. Two types of leasing arrangements are used. Full-payout leases provide payback to the partners in full. Operating leases renders the partnership with a substantial interest in the equipment at the end of the lease term. These LPs should have an estimated fair value of 1.5 times the offer price.

Oil and Gas Partnership Guidelines

Oil and gas partnerships can be very complicated to understand. Essentially, there are three types of oil and gas LPs: exploratory, developmental, and income programs. Exploratory programs are the most speculative with the hope of bonanza strike; however, wildcat drilling statistically produces dry holes. There is no way to establish a fair value for these units; therefore, exploratory programs should be absolutely avoided by anyone not considered an accredited investor.

Developmental programs have less risk than exploratory programs. They have a good chance of an income producing well, but low chance for a bonanza with exploration being made in proven oil or gas fields. Fair values that are estimated from existing wells should be 2 times the offer price; however, only higher income, risk-seeking individuals should consider these programs.

Income program LPs usually acquires existing producing wells that provide immediate income to the partnership. With production data being available, the fair value for these programs can readily be determined, and should be considered if the fair value estimate is at least 1.5 times the offer price.

It should be noted that oil and gas LPs have an additional advantage for the limited partner, which is called the "depletion allowance." The IRS allows the recovery for cost of acquiring drilling rights for oil and gas with a depletion allowance. The large, oil and gas producers are required to use the "unit rate" depletion method. The depletion is determined by dividing the total natural resource cost basis by the number of resource units in the reserve. The resource cost is then depleted over the reserve's lifetime as it is withdrawn from the ground.

However, small, independent producers and royalty holders are allowed to use the "percent rate" depletion method regardless of the lifetime of the producing well. Here the IRS defined percent rate (dependent on resource type) can be annually applied as the depletion allowance, which for small oil and gas producers is 15% annually. Accordingly, the accumulated total depletion amount allowed for small producers will be greater than the cost after eighty months. This will allow for continued sheltering of partnership income until the partnership is terminated. This benefit dictates that only oil and gas LPs that can qualify as a "small producer" should be considered.

General Partner Guidelines

The general partner, sometimes called the sponsor, should have been successful with previous similar projects. Therefore, offerings that are a new venture for the general partner should be avoided.

In addition, the partnership should be free of any encumbrances that may pose a conflict of interest for the general partner, such as other similar projects that are also being simultaneously managed by the general partner. Therefore, LP offerings should be avoided if:

1. the proceeds will be commingled with funds from other projects

2. the partnership calls for limited partners to indemnify the general partner for any liabilities incurred in running the partnership

There are a variety of sharing arrangements: the methods of sharing revenues and costs between the limited partners and the general partner. A few of the typical arrangements are discussed in the following paragraphs.

The *overriding royalty interest* arrangement is typically favored by the general partner. In this arrangement, the limited partners are allocated all costs and the majority portion of the net revenues. The general partner receives from 5% to 12% of gross revenues. Avoid offerings that allow more than 15%.

The *functional allowance* arrangement is used mostly in oil and gas programs. This arrangement allows the limited partners to bear all deductible (expensed) costs, while the general partner bears all capitalized costs. In return, the general partner receives a share of net revenues. Avoid offerings where the general partner's share exceeds 30% of revenues.

Disproportionate sharing arrangements typically will allow the general partner to receive a much larger share of revenues than the share of expenses allowed. These typically allow the general partner a 50% share of revenues, with a 25% share of costs (a 2 to 1 disproportionate ratio). Therefore, a rule of thumb guideline is to avoid offerings in which the disproportionate ratio exceeds 20% (1.2 to 1).

DPP Income Offering Guidelines

Investors that are promised income over the life of the DPP partnership should compare the offering price with the estimated fair value. The offering price of the units should be substantially less than the fair value (see "Intrinsic Value Analysis" presented in Chapter Eight, "Business Life Cycles, Financial Statements and Analyses"). Any offering in which the fair value is less than 1.5 times the offering price should be avoided. This arbitrary value should give a margin of safety of 50% for the investment. (However, some would argue that a higher margin of safety is required for an illiquid security.)

As mentioned previously, DPP limited partnership units being considered for a retirement account should definitely be avoided.

Publicly Traded Limited Partnership Offerings

Other LPs are not offered as DPPs, but have ownership units that trade in the securities markets the same as common stocks. In fact, they are typically indistinguishable from common stock. Units offered to the public are registered with both the SEC and the different states in which offered, as applicable (see Chapter Four, "Securities Regulations"). The limited partnership form of business organization is typically chosen by a management (the general partner) that desires public support for capitalization but does not want to either be controlled by, or have to answer to, stockholders of a corporation.

The profit/expense sharing arrangements between the sponsor and investors are defined in the prospectus. Income received by the investors is considered as dividend income and taxed by the IRS as such. The IRS will treat the organization as a corporation, and all profits will therefore be subject to corporation tax, before distribution to investors. This differs from the DPP type of limited partnership where income net of DPP expenses and depreciation is reported as "passive income."

There are many examples of this type of organization: LPs of many large city sports franchise teams, and some franchised restaurant chains. These publicly traded LP unit offerings should be treated as common stock offerings. Therefore, both the previously stated general and specific guidelines for equity offerings apply.

Specific Guidelines for Convertibles

New issues of convertible securities (convertible preferred stock and convertible debentures) attract the conservative leaning risk-taker who seeks potential long-term growth, but in the interim can receive income. However, convertibles should be considered as a growth security, and not strictly a fixed-income security. The forced conversion because of a call, as well as the possibility of a redemption call when interest rates drop, can result in a double whammy for the individual who is strictly looking for income. Therefore, the guidelines for convertibles are:

1.   the estimated fair value should be at least 1.5 times the offering price

2.   the conversion premium should be a maximum of 25%

As mentioned previously under "General Guidelines for New Issues," convertible securities placed in retirement accounts should only consist of issues of companies in which the debt obligations are rated as "investment quality" (see Chapter Two, "Business Capitalization Securities").

CHAPTER SUMMARY

Every investor should limit the total amount of speculative and growth category capital assets by using guidelines presented in Figures 9-2 and 9-3.

Recognize that the following "growth" category new issue securities should be considered as speculative:

1.   private placements

2.   IPOs of "startup" and "development" stage businesses, or offerings less than $250 million in capital stock

3.   IPOs of "emerging growth" stage businesses with capitalization less than $2 billion

4.   new issues of "mature growth" stage businesses seeking growth through acquisition

5.   IPOs bundled with warrants

6.   ADRs

Recognize that the following "fixed-income" category new issue securities should be considered as speculative:

1. preferred stock and convertibles from companies whose debt is rated "speculative" (see Table 2-3)

2. preferred stock whose dividends are "non-cumulative,"

3. mortgage backed REITS and UITs

New Issue Equity Offering Guidelines

Avoid "non-managed" offerings.

Avoid "managed" offerings that have an underwriting compensation greater than 10%.

Avoid "best efforts" managed offerings.

Avoid offerings in which the stock is to be listed on the OTCBB or on the NQB Pink Sheets.

Avoid all "shelf" offerings.

Avoid "secondary" offerings.

Avoid "small cap" offerings with a floating supply capitalization less than either $5 million, or 5 million shares.

Avoid offerings in which "insiders" control greater than 60% of the outstanding supply and any single entity controls more than 40%.

Avoid IPOs in manic markets.

Avoid placing IPOs in retirement accounts.

Avoid IPOs from managing underwriters whose average annual success rate is less than 130%.

Avoid turnaround offerings where greater than 50% of capital raised is to pay down long-term debt, or when proceeds are to purchase growth through an acquisition of another company.

Avoid "split" offerings if greater than 40% of the proceeds go to previously private placement shareholders.

Avoid all "private placement" offerings.

Avoid offerings whose *pro-forma* financial statements show that either the:

1. total debt is greater than 40% of the capital raised

2. current ratio is less than 1.3 (2.0 if an ongoing business)

3. quick ratio is less than 1.0

4. debt to equity is ratio greater than 1.0

5. profit margin is less than 10% (if an ongoing business)

6. dividend payout is greater than 50% (for an ongoing business)

7. cash flow is negative

8. down profit years represent 3 of past 5, or 2 of past 3 years (for an ongoing business)

New Issue Limited Partnership Offering Guidelines

Avoid DPP securities because they have no liquidity.

Avoid units in which the lifetime of the partnership can be extended by the GP without a vote of the LPs.

Avoid units in which the partnership agreement calls for the LPs to indemnify the GP for any liability incurred in managing the partnership.

Avoid projects in which the GP has no demonstrated previous success with similar projects.

Avoid units in which the partnership agreement calls for the GP to have a "sharing arrangement" greater than 1.2 (sharing in revenues 20% greater than sharing in expenses), or allowing the GP to receive more than 15% of gross revenue.

Avoid units in real estate projects engaged in new construction, undeveloped land, and blind pools.

Avoid all "exploration" oil and gas projects.

Avoid oil and gas development projects whose estimated fair value is less than 2 times the offering price.

Avoid "income" projects in real estate and oil and gas partnerships in which the estimated fair value is less than 1.5 times the offering price.

Avoid offerings in which the proceeds are to be commingled with funds of other partnerships.

Avoid oil and gas income projects that cannot qualify as a "small producer."

New Issue Convertible Securities Offering Guidelines

The following are selection guidelines for new issue convertible securities, preferred stock or debentures.

Avoid offerings whose estimated fair value is less than 1.5 times the offer price,

Avoid offerings whose conversion premium is more than 25%.

Ten
New Issue Investment Tactics

✦

Playing the Trump Card!

Strategy can be defined as the art of employing skillful plans to meet an objective. Achieving capital appreciation through new issue securities requires a progressive strategy that includes:

1. being completely aware of all the various business capitalization securities that are offered to investors

2. recognizing the roles of the participants: the types of investors; and securities dealers who act as investment bankers, or who may simply by participating in the offering as selling dealers

3. understanding the securities industry's rules and regulations

4. realizing the differences between the various markets on which securities trade

5. establishing an appropriate securities account for holding new issues

6. understanding the new issue process and the different types of new issue offerings

7. properly evaluating each recommended new issue offering

8. use defined allocation guidelines to limit the amount of capital at risk

9. determine which offerings to pass up to avoid potentially disastrous mistakes

The success of a new issue purchased for potential explosive growth will depend on the demand for the issue in the marketplace after the issue becomes public on the effective date. Generating public demand is an underwriting strategy that depends on the strength of the underwriting group. However, explosive price growth will only be achieved by IPOs of companies having a good story (a unique product or service that will eventually receive widespread demand) as well as having strong underwriting support.

In the best case offering, the underwriting group will have thousands of securities brokers across the country attempting to generate enormous demand with the public for the new issue having a compelling story. Principals from the underwriting securities dealers at the same time attempt to interest institutional investors into subscribing to the issue. The stratagem is to convince the institutional investors, and the public, to oversubscribe to the offering by submitting IOIs for many more shares than is available. The tendency is then to nearly fill the institutional investors orders, and shutout most of the public IOIs. Therefore, on the effective date, public investors who have been shutout will be encouraged to place market buy orders for the shares, thus creating a demand with the only supply being those willing to sell their newly subscribed shares and the underwriter's over allotment.

On the other hand, an offering devoid of a good story will do well by not being a turkey. The device used to create demand for this type issue is with a shelf offering, issues that distribute partial offerings over a 12-month period. This type offering is used not to generate a "hot" issue, but to avoid a "turkey" by artificially limiting the supply with limited partial offerings made over the period of a year.

However, no strategy can be successful if the individual investor fails to use tactics appropriate for new issue securities. Tactics can be defined as the art of employing skillful maneuvers to accomplish the objective established by the strategy. Tactical maneuvers for new issue equities are different from other securities investments. The formula investing plans, such as the dollar-cost-averaging or constant-dollar investment plans will not work for most securities offered as a new issue.

Of the hundreds of IPO deals brought public each year, those whose price explode out of the "box" and continues to skyrocket in price are rare. Therefore, IPOs should be considered short-term "investments" (an oxymoron), and the tactics required are not the conventional wisdom that are typical for securities investments, especially when the stock offering is bundled with warrants. Therefore, this chapter defines tactics that should be followed by those who have purchased new issue securities. They are classified with regard to investment objective and security type.

TACTICS FOR NEW ISSUE, GROWTH SECURITIES

The following recommended tactics for growth securities, with the exception of convertible securities, provide guidelines for maneuvering with a new issue position to attempt to either protect potential profits, or minimize losses. They are devised based on the potential for success as indicated by the perceived demand in the marketplace. Tactics for convertible security are discussed separately under "Convertible Security Offerings."

Initial Public Offerings

In view of the previous discussion on IPO supply and demand, tracking the market price, hour by hour for the first 10 days and then daily thereafter over the next 30 days, is critical in assessing what type tactic should be used, if any. This period will indicate whether or not substantial profits may eventually be achieved, or if the investor should cut losses and run.

Turkeys

It is not a good sign if, within the quiet period, the stock or unit price remains unchanged at the offering price, or decreases. Shares traded at the offering price indicate that the underwriter is stabilizing the issue by fixing the bid at the offering price as a market maker. However, stabilization can be terminated by the underwriter at any time. A declining market price indicates that the underwriter is no longer stabilizing the price, or never has been. An insufficient demand in the marketplace indicates a lack of sponsorship by the underwriters.

The conventional wisdom for IPOs is to minimize the loss realized with a market price decline after the effective date. As a tactical move, the position (stock or units) should be sold completely if the price declines by 10% in a bull market, or 20% in a bear or uncertain market. Individual investors should be agile and get out of a losing position before institutional investors pull the plug and dump their shares, thereby accelerating the price decline.

If the issue initially consists of stock bundled with warrants that has been subsequently unbundled before the decline limits have been reached, then the tactic would be to sell the stock, and hold onto the warrants. Since the warrants would have no meaningful dollar value, the attempt is to try to recover as much of the bad play as possible from the stock and to bank on an eventual recovery in stock price that would provide some value to the warrants.

However, the recommended loss-minimizing tactic should not be applied blindly. It may require a deeper penetration into an apparent failed offering to avoid premature selling in the attempt to minimize a loss. For example, in March 1994 an IPO for 1.5 million shares of Hi-Shear Technology Corp. (stock symbol HSR), an ongoing spin-off company, were offered at $5 per share and listed on the AMEX by Baraban Securities Inc., formerly a regional West Coast securities dealer (see Figure 7-1, "Tombstone Ad Example"). At the time, the company had been manufacturing high reliability, electronic, pyrotechnic, and mechanical devices for the aerospace industry as well as for commercial use. During the first five weeks after the effective date, 1.2 million shares were traded at a consistent minimum bid of $5.00, and asked prices varied between $5 1/8 and $5 3/8. After the 5-week quiet period, the price declined to a low of $3 3/8 at six months—a 32% loss from the offer price—as demand continued to wane.

The conventional wisdom for IPOs would have dictated that IPO investors should have sold out when the bid price for HSR fell to $4¼. However, a careful reading of the prospectus would have indicated that the IPO represented about 25% of the issued and outstanding shares, the remaining 75% being held by control persons who were not very likely to tender shares in a marketplace sell-off at this price level. In addition, the consistent $5 minimum bid price for the first five weeks suggested that price was being stabilized, and therefore, the bulk of the 1.2 million shares traded during the period probably were being accumulated by the underwriters.

Underwriters making firm commitments cannot afford to end up owing a majority of the shares offered to the public. Therefore, a sophisticated investor would expect that the next major price move should be a significant price increase. At eight months, the patient investor then would observe the market price for shares shoot up from a low bid of $3 ½ to nearly $15, a 200% profit for initial subscribers. This sudden price increase indicated that the brokers of the underwriting group had likely engaged in a massive marketing campaign to stimulate public interest in the stock. As demand increased, the shares acquired by the underwriters during the stabilization period were distributed at a substantial profit.

The astute IPO holder could then have sold a portion, if not all, of the subscribed shares of HSR, turning a turkey into a profitable investment. The ensuing history of the returns for HSR can be shown to have been 85% at 1-year, 77% at 2-years, 0% at 5-years, and a loss of 60% at 7-years. The impatient IPO investor invoking the loss minimization tactic would have taken a loss from 15% to 20%, depending when the decision to pull the plug was made, and gone on to another potential investment opportunity. Minimizing losses to an acceptable amount is never incorrect, and it should typically help to avert losing the entire dollar amount invested. However, in this example, it would have prevented turning the initial loss into a short-term profit.

Hot Issues

There is an adage that "no one ever went broke taking profits." While this applies to any investment, it is essential for IPO investments. Most institutional investors seeking IPOs are not long-term investors, and will immediately take some profits when prices increase. Selling large quantities of institutionally, owned shares might temporarily depress prices of small-cap offerings because of a temporary oversupply of shares. This decline may precipitate an even steeper decline as worried investors rush to dump shares to capture whatever profit may be left. Therefore, IPO investors must discipline themselves to take profits incrementally.

Hot issue prices will immediately increase after the effective date as those that were shutout of the offering purchase shares in the marketplace. There is no way to determine initially how high the stock price will rise before the demand for the stock is satisfied. Therefore, one should look to retrieve the initial investment as soon as possible within the first three months after the effective date. For instance, if the price should double during this time, then 50% of the shares should be sold. If the price skyrockets to three or four times the offering price within this period, then a third or a fourth, as applicable, of the subscribed shares should be sold.

After the initial investment is retrieved, incremental profits should continue to be taken by selling off, round lot quantities to keep the current dollar value equal to the initial investment amount. However, when the price appears to have peaked and then experiences a throwback of about 30% from the price peak value, the position should be closed out taking a final profit (albeit a reduced one).

This tactic can be illustrated by the following hypothetical example. Assume that 2000 shares were purchased at an offering price of $10 per share (a $20,000 initial investment). The share price after a month increased to $20 where 1000 shares were sold to recover the initial dollar investment amount. At two months, the share price increased to $25 and another 200 shares were sold to take an incremental profit of $5000 while leaving 800 shares at a value of $20,000. The price, at three months, still continued to increase to $33, and 200 more shares were sold taking an additional $6,600 profit while leaving 600 residual shares. However, at one year from the effective date the price had decreased to $23. At this point, the investor sold the remaining 600 shares and close out the position taking a final $13,800, totaling $25,400 in profits on an initial $20,000 investment.

The tactic described above can be called the Constant Dollar Investment Plan. Incremental selling, as the stock price increases, to keep the dollar value of the position constant will provide the discipline to take profits. However, as shown above, it should be abandoned for new issues when prices decline appreciably following a significant price run up. The historical probability is that the market price will continue to decline in time to the level of the offering price, or lower. This represents profit taking by the initial subscribers, as well as those who bought shares at the higher prices attempting to limit losses.

A successful IPO investment can be transformed into a long-term investment objective position, after taking out both the initial investment amount and an appreciable amount of incremental profits. Holding some residual shares in the securities account will permit participation in any future price increase with the shares remaining. However, should the price decrease to penny stock levels, the nearly worthless residual shares can be sold to offset the tax liability on previously generated capital gains. The IPO investor who continues to keep a constant dollar amount invested as prices decline, after reaching a peak price, by repurchasing shares with profits previously taken incrementally can eventually lose all profits previously taken as well as the initial investment amount.

The terms "bundled unit" and "hot issue" are oxymora. No underwriter would suggest bundling an offering with warrants if they believed that the issue could be classified as "hot." However, bundled units can achieve success in the marketplace. Therefore, holders of successful unbundled units should first sell the warrants, then a sufficient number of shares to recapture the initial investment amount.

Using Leverage

All new issue securities must be purchased 100% in cash. However, issues that are listed to trade on the NYSE, AMEX, or the NASDAQ National Market (see Chapter Five, "Securities Markets" for explanations of the different markets) may be margined. Therefore, after the required quiet period—defined in Table 7-1—IPOs and other new issue securities held in a cash account can be placed into a long margin account (explained in Chapter Six, "Securities Accounts"). This doubles the buying power for purchasing the same or other securities. However, future price declines on margined securities can also have a double negative effect. Only risk-seeking accredited individuals who *feel* that they can afford to lose the entire invested amount should use the leverage of margin with new issues.

An example of an appropriate, yet damaging, use of leverage can be illustrated with the IPO for Pixar (see Table 1-1); a digital animation studio creating animated feature films. In November 1995, an IPO for 6.9 million shares was distributed by underwriter Robertson, Stephens & Co. at $22 per share. The first day, price appreciation was 86% to nearly $41 per share at market close. Within the next four weeks, the end of the quiet period, the share price had declined to nearly $37, but still 68% above the offering price.

Assume a subscriber of 1000 shares decided to take back the initial $22,000 investment amount, after the price decline, by selling 600 shares. In addition, the investor placed the remaining 400 shares into a long margin account, and immediately purchased another 400 shares on margin using the equity from the residual 400 shares, thereby acquiring a $14,700 debit balance: a perfectly legitimate and appropriate tactic once the initial investment has been reclaimed. However, at three months after the effective date, the share price had declined to $20 (a price 10% below the offering price). By the time this price level was reached, the securities dealer would have demanded a $3500 immediate deposit (a margin call). The astute investor, fearing additional price declines, would then act appropriately by selling all 800 shares. After paying off the $14,700 debit balance, the net profit would have been $1,300. Should margin not have been used with the residual shares after reclaiming the initial investment, an $8000 profit would have been generated on selling the residual 400 shares at $20. In fact, the share price would continue decline to about $15 at one year, indicating that taking profits, as they occur to capture the initial investment, is a valuable tactic.

However, an inappropriate use of margin can be illustrated with the same Pixar IPO example given above. Assuming that at one month, the investor inappropriately placed all 1000 shares into a margin account (instead of reclaiming the initial investment amount as shown above), and then margined another 1000 shares that generated a debit balance of $36,800. In this case, at three months, the margin call would have amounted to $8,800, and selling all 2000 shares at $20 would leave only $3200 after paying off the debit balance. The bottom line for this investor would have been a loss of $18,800: a typical example of how greed can run amuck.

The previous examples hopefully show clearly the benefit of taking back the initial IPO investment for successful offerings as they occur. After that, using leverage may result in a huge reward, and at worst, it can result in breaking even. Inappropriate use of leverage can result in significant losses.

Rights Offerings

Shareholders are issued subscription rights to purchase additional shares when a new issue of same class stock is offered. If shareholders liked the stock, and had purchased shares prior to the new issue offering (either as a new issue or in the marketplace), they should be willing to exercise the rights to purchase additional shares to maintain their position. However, those who do not desire to exercise the rights should take specific action to avoid incurring a loss on the previously purchased shares. The recommended action depends on the type of rights issued.

Transferable Rights

Transferable rights can be sold in the same market on which the stock trades. The investor that desires not to subscribe will suffer a loss of the value of the right if left to expire, therefore they should be sold before the expiration date. Recall the example presented previously under "Subscription Rights," Chapter Two, "Business Capitalization Securities": stock price of $33 cum-rights, $15 subscription price, and 5 rights required per new share issue indicated a rights value of $3 per right. Selling the rights issued in the marketplace would recover the loss in value of the previously purchased shares to the extent of the dealer's commission.

Assuming that a shareholder of 1000 shares of the hypothetical example sells the 1000 rights issued to the account at $3 each, the full-service dealer's commission would be about $170. The $170 cost is acceptable compared with the $3000 loss that would occur if rights were left to expire worthless.

Non-Transferable Rights

Holders of non-transferable rights desiring not to purchase additional shares through the subscription rights offering can use an alternative, and more complicated tactic. The technique is to sell a number of shares equivalent to the quantity that can be subscribed in the marketplace. Next, the shareholder would inform his broker to exercise the rights issued to replace these shares. This recovers the loss that would occur by letting the rights expire.

Using the previous hypothetical example, a holder of 1000 shares would sell 200 shares at the ex-rights share price of $30, and exercise the issued rights to purchase 200 shares at $15. The net loss would then be only the commission on the sale of previously owned shares, about $136 for a full service security dealer, and the investor would still own 1000 shares at about the same value.

Convertible Security Offerings

Convertible preferred stock and convertible debentures that are purchased for income also offer an opportunity for capital appreciation. However, long-term income is more ambiguous than that offered by an equivalent, nonconvertible security because of the conversion feature. Therefore, these must still be considered as capital appreciation objective securities.

A convertible may be called by the issuer for two reasons: to refinance at a lower dividend or interest rate; or to force a conversion. Either reason will result in a loss of the capital appreciation that had been achieved with an increase in the market price of the convertible. Therefore, incremental profits on the capital gain should be taken to prevent its evaporation whenever it may be in danger of being called. This requires a minimum investment of $10,000 (assuming a $1000 face value convertible debenture, or a $100 face value convertible preferred stock) in convertible securities be held in street name in a brokerage account so that single debentures, or odd-lot shares of preferred stocks can be sold when appropriate.

Call Issued to Refinance

The company may choose to call the issue to either eliminate or significantly reduce the dividend or interest payments of the convertible when the moratorium period for calling the convertible has expired and interest rates have declined. For calls issued when the conversion value is less than the call value, the convertible holders should then tender the securities called for the call value. (Note that should the conversion value be greater than the call value, the issuer would be forcing a conversion. This is described below.) If the company has insufficient retained earnings to cover the redemption, it would then be required to finance the call by offering another type or share class security to the public. The rate of return that would be demanded for the new issue would then have to compete with that demanded of equivalent quality and maturity securities.

The best tactic for calls on convertible securities to refinance is to tender the securities for the call price—the par value plus the premium, if applicable. There would be no compelling reason for subscribing to the new convertible issue offering a reduced rate of return, unless the conversion premium were low, about 10% or less. The new issue investor would be better to take the money, and look for a new speculative opportunity.

For example, assume a $100 par value, convertible preferred stock with a 5:1 conversion ratio and callable in 10 years at par. It is issued at an 8% dividend yield when the yield for equivalent nonconvertible securities is 10%. This example has previously been shown, using Figure 8-4, to have an initial investment value of about $87. It was shown that should the equivalent nonconvertible security yield later decrease to 6% after its offering, the investment value for this convertible would then increase to about $115, which can be compared to the $133 investment value the issue would have if it were an indefinite lifetime security. Assuming all else remains constant, including the common stock price; the investment value will decrease with time such that at five years it will be about $109. As the call date nears, the investment value will approach the par value (or call premium price) should the equivalent yield remain below the convertible's initial yield. At this point, the security is most likely to be called and a new series of preferred stock issued at a lower dividend rate.

For the above convertible stock example, should equivalent yields have increased to 12% after issue, the investment value would have dropped to about $67, which is determined as an indefinite life security that is not likely to be called. This investment value will remain constant at $67 (assuming everything else remains constant as well as the stock price), a 33% paper loss, as the call date is approached and passed. However, the fair value, assuming a discount rate of 6%, to the 10-year call date can be shown to be near the $100 per share par value established by Figure 8-2 and Figure 8-3. The income stream from Figure 8-2 indicates a fair value of about $7.50 per dollar annual dividend, or $60 per share. The fair value of the principal amount at call in 10 years would be $0.56 per share of dollar value, which with a market value of $67 is computed as about $38 per share. The total fair value is therefore $98 per share.

The point of this exercise is that the market price of a convertible security will reflect the investment value if it is not set by its conversion value. Investors looking for capital appreciation from convertible securities should avoid taking a nominal profit or locking in a capital loss when interest rates dictate the price of the security. Holders of the above-illustrated convertible security examples could have either taken a 15% profit in the first year when the interest rates decreased, or sold out with a 33% loss if interest rates increased. Even though one could make an argument for taking a 15% profit within the first year, it would normally be considered as insufficient for the risk-seeker.

Selling the issue and taking a 33% loss to avoid the possibility of even greater losses in the future would be an understandable reaction for the case of increased interest rates, but it would be a mistake. Selling to limit the losses is conventional wisdom in securities trading; however, in the case of new issue convertible securities, it prevents the possibility for making a substantial profit in the future. A substantial increase in conversion value in the future due to common stock price increases should be possible, which is the reason for subscribing to the offering in the first place. In this example, the convertible cannot be called for 10 years; therefore, the paper loss of the lower investment value would be offset by the fair value of the security because of the 10-year call date.

Call Issued to Force a Conversion

Common stock prices are established by company fundamentals, the state of the economy, and investor perception of the potential for future earnings growth (called "expectations"). The price of the common stock is therefore independent of, and is not affected by, the market price of the convertible security. Since the convertible is a hybrid security, is established either by its investment value, or by the conversion value (conversion ratio times the common stock price). Consequently, the market price for a convertible will be the investment value when the conversion value is less than the investment value; otherwise, it will be the conversion value.

The company may choose to call the issue to force a conversion to common stock when the moratorium period, if there is one, for calling the convertible has expired. However, the conversion value must be significantly higher than the par value (plus the call premium if any) at call. This will force a conversion of convertible preferred stock, or the convertible debenture (as applicable), to eliminate future dividend or interest payments. Convertible security holders will then order conversions before the conversion date, and sell the newly acquired converted shares in the marketplace to take a profit. Since the majority of the converted shares will be offered for sale on the marketplace at about the same time, the market price for shares could be depressed because of this oversupply, especially if it is a thinly traded stock.

For the above-cited example, assume that the market price for the common stock increases from $16 at the offering of the convertible, to $32 after 10 years. With a 5:1 conversion ratio, the convertible's market price would then be about $160. The investment value would be equal to the par value of $100 if equivalent interest rates were down to 6%, or the investment value would be about $67 if the equivalent interest rates were up to 12%. The convertible owner can convert the security at any time and doesn't require a call to be issued. It only depends upon whether the owner thinks that an appropriate profit has been achieved.

There is an adage on The Street that "Bulls make money, bears make money, but pigs just get slaughtered." The best tactic for a convertible issue is to take profits *before* the issue is called, not to try to squeeze every dollar of possible profit. This can be accomplished by selling 2/3 of the position when the conversion value (CV) indicates a 50% profit over the convertible's offering price. Other alternatives are to sell 4/7 of the position when the CV indicates a 75% profit, or 1/2 for a CV profit of 100%. However, selling a portion of the convertible securities held in the marketplace—instead of exercising the conversion feature and selling the converted shares—could keep common stock shares from depressing market prices, especially thinly traded stocks. The investor then would still maintain a partial position in the convertible security.

Waiting until a call is issued may likely be to the investors' detriment if the holder has no interest in owning the common stock. When a company forces a conversion, the convertible's bid price will drop to a discount of about 15% of the CV as scalpers accumulate convertible securities that they will convert and then sell the stock in the marketplace. In addition, all converted shares being dumped on the market at one time may force the market price down substantially.

TACTICS FOR NEW ISSUE, FIXED-INCOME SECURITIES

New issue securities purchased as tradable, straight (nonconvertible), income vehicles—such as preferred stock, closed-end income mutual funds, or debt obligations—usually require no special tactical maneuvering. These securities will produce a relatively constant income stream with quarterly, or semi-annual, dividend or interest payments. After the effective date, the market price for these fixed-income securities will vary based on changes in yield rates for equivalent quality and maturity securities. However, income objective investors should not be too concerned about market price changes. Preferred stock and debt obligations of investment grade companies should make consistent income payments. Although anything may occur over time, securities of investment grade quality are generally expected to be safe from default.

Investing into a closed-end income mutual fund should produce consistent income, and the value of the account will vary with interest rates. The periodic payments for income producing mutual funds will change over time, as portfolio securities are turned over, either by selling in the marketplace or being redeemed by the issuer at call or maturity. Each turnover will result in a different yield because of changes in interest rates over time. Mutual funds are required to distribute annually all capital gains made on each turnover, but the fund manager can reinvest the principal amount. (Only UITs are required to return invested capital, since the trustee's role is to act as custodian and is precluded from acting as an investment manager.)

When the issuers of straight preferred stock or debt obligations exercise the typical call provision, typically to refinance, the income investor has no choice but to tender these securities for the par, or face, value (or at the premium price if applicable). Absent a call, the investor should maintain the position until maturity. Unless an investor desires a tax loss, it would be ludicrous to sell previously purchased new issue securities in the marketplace in order to purchase new issues that may be offering higher yields. The market price for the securities held would have decreased reflecting the higher return rates demanded by the financial markets.

Non-Tradable Income Securities

DPP limited partnership and other non-tradable, or non-redeemable income securities do not offer the holders of these securities any opportunity for tactical maneuvering. Once purchased, these can only be held to maturity because of the lack of liquidity. Therefore, only accredited investors, or those who feel that they can afford to lose all of the capital invested in these type securities without affecting their future life style should own these type securities.

CHAPTER SUMMARY

Tactics for new issue securities will differ with the type of security held. These can only be used with liquid securities: those that can be traded on the AMEX, NYSE, or the NASDAQ. Owners of private placements, DPP LPs and various other types of illiquid securities have no wiggle room to maneuver with their "investments." The following paragraphs offer tactical maneuvers that should be considered as conventional wisdom for new issues.

Tactics for IPOs

Market prices for IPOs should be carefully monitored during the trading day especially for the first 30 days after the effective date. There are three possible scenarios: 1, prices increase on the effective date and continue to do so during the quiet period; 2, prices remain at the public offer price for a number of days or weeks; and 3, prices decline on the effective date and thereafter.

Prices Increase on the Effective Date and Thereafter

This is what is hoped for with all IPOs. The conventional wisdom dictates that between the period of one and six months, the holder should sell, incrementally if necessary, sufficient numbers of shares to recapture the initial investment. Should the offering had been bundled with warrants; the warrants should be sold first. In addition, a limited number of shares should be sold so that between warrants and shares the initial investment is recaptured.

After the Quiet Period, the risk-seeker can place the IPO shares purchased in a cash account into a long margin account. This would permit purchasing additional securities of the same or other margined stock to take advantage of leverage. Of course, this tool is a double-edged sword; it will result in doubling the share price loss when prices decline (and they most likely will).

Prices Remain at the Offer Price on the Effective Date

This indicates that the managing underwriter is stabilizing the offering by making a bid for shares at the offer price. The good news here is that the underwriter has sufficient conviction in the issue to buy shares in the marketplace at the offer price so that the price is likely not to drop significantly. The bad news is that the investing public has not yet embraced the new issue as something that they should own. As a rule of thumb, after five days of stabilization with no price improvement, the issue should be sold completely. The danger is that after some time, the underwriter will stop stabilizing the issue thereby allowing the share price to drop if insufficient interest still exists.

Prices Decrease after the Effective Date

The conventional wisdom is that any price decline of 10% in a bull market or 20% in a bear or uncertain market is sufficient cause to sell all shares to limit losses and move on to other potential opportunities. If shares are initially bundled with warrants and have been unbundled, the stock should be sold but warrants should be held, since they would have no real market value at this point. Eventually, perhaps years, the stock price may recover at which point the warrants may be worth a substantial amount.

Tactics for Rights Offerings

Rights are offered to existing shareholders of companies that seek additional equity capitalization by issuing the same class of common shares. Shareholders should be willing to exercise the rights to buy additional shares. If not, transferable rights should be sold prior to expiration. Non-transferable rights should be exercised, and an equivalent number of shares should be sold.

Tactics for Fixed Income Securities

New issues purchased strictly for an income portfolio—open-end or closed-end mutual funds, straight preferred stock and debentures—should have no need for using any tactical maneuvering. However, as with any security, the credit rating of the individual issuer's debt obligations should be monitored to determine whether any particular issue might need liquidation to preserve capital. A downgrade in quality grade is instantly followed by a price reduction. Selling after a downgrade only preserves further price declines.

Convertible Securities

Convertible preferred stock and convertible debentures require tactical maneuvering on occasion to avoid significant investment losses that can occur when a call is issued for these securities. Once the moratorium on a call has expired, a call may be issued for either of two reasons. The first reason is to refinance when interest rates decline significantly, permitting dividend or interest payments to be reduced with a new issue. The second reason is to force the conversion to common stock when the stock price is above the conversion price. This avoids paying future dividends or interest payments completely.

When a call is issued to refinance, the typical tactic is to tender the convertible securities, take the proceeds and move on to other opportunities. The investor should only consider subscribing to the new convertible being offered if the conversion premium is less than 10%.

When a call is issued to force a conversion, the conventional wisdom is to convert the securities and sell shares in the marketplace.

Epilogue

◆

Reviewing the Endgame

Teaching has played a large part in my life. Consequently, it has taken ten chapters of detailed descriptions and explanations to explain carefully new issue investment securities, the securities industry, securities regulations, and the underwriting process. I have also provided details on new issue securities of interest to investors seeking income, but the focus has been on IPOs for short-term capital appreciation. It would be unreasonable for me to have tried to condense the material presented so that this book might have been titled *Five Simple Steps to IPO Riches.* Anyone who believes that success with high-risk securities can be made that simple should never consider these investments. IPO investors must also realize that besides having knowledge of these unique securities, it also requires having basic analytical skill, clarity of thought, patience, and self-reliance. The first can be learned, and the others need to be developed.

Each security offering is considered as a new issue. However, the new issue security of primary interest to the risk-seeking individual is the initial public offering. This represents common stock shares being offered to the public for the very first time. Though IPOs are perceived as being able to achieve instant capital appreciation, this distorted view has typically been generated by intense media hype of the first day's price increases of occasional "hot" IPOs. The widely reported explosive price increases for IPOs represent a small fraction of the new issues offered to the public. The average IPO market price typically will peak at three to six months after going public, with losses occurring at two years.

IPOs are theoretically available to suitable clients of the underwriting securities dealers. However, chances that the average individual will have ready access to popular IPOs, especially hot issues, at the offering price is next to nil. Readily available Internet IPO offerings should be avoided because they typically have no market on which they can be traded. Nonetheless, it may be possible to have access to legitimate IPOs by opening an account with one or more underwriting firms, and then establishing a trading history. In addition to hard-to-get IPOs, clients of these firms have a variety of other types of new issue securities readily available, which can offer both long-term growth as well as income. It cannot stressed enough, that new issues offered to individual investors, either on the Internet or by cold-calling sales persons, are typically unsuitable for the average individual, and may likely be fraudulent offerings.

SETTING THE STAGE FOR NEW ISSUES

The type of security offered the public depends upon the type of the business organization issuing the securities and the life cycle stage of the business organization. Not all business organizations are public corporations offering common stock, and many new issue securities are unsuitable for average working individuals. Therefore, it is important that the new issue investor understand the type of business organization seeking capitalization and the type of security that is being offered to the public.

Life cycle stages are identified as startup, development, rapid expansion, mature growth, and stability and decline. Startup phase capitalization is typically provided by venture capitalists, or by private placements, which are unsuitable for the average individual. IPOs are most likely to be offered in the development and rapid expansion phases, but investors should be wary of secondary offerings that do not provide any capital for the company. Fixed-income securities are typical offerings used by businesses in the last two life cycle phases.

Federal, state, and local municipal governments, as well as business organizations offer new issue debt obligations to raise capital to fund particular projects. Debt obligations typically pay semi-annual interest to the owner as a legal obligation of the issuer. Along with preferred stock (an equity security), these types of new issue securities are of interest only to those seeking income, not capital appreciation. However, both convertible preferred stock and convertible debentures provide the opportunity for capital appreciation with the potential for conversion into common stock if the price of the stock increases significantly.

Anyone considering marketable securities as investment vehicles should have knowledge about the business organization and the type of security being offered. They should also be acquainted with the different functions of the securities industry, and its laws and regulations. Knowledge of these regulations can prevent investors from being caught in fraudulent situations. Existing securities laws and regulations evolved out of necessity. Securities offerings were first regulated in 1933 by requiring that all public offerings be registered. This was followed by establishing the SEC in 1934, whose primary responsibilities are to enforce all securities laws, as well as register and regulate all participants working within the industry. The NASD was created, in 1938, as a self-regulating organization, consisting of all registered securities dealers, whose duties are to enforce compliance with all regulations and fair practice rules. Over the next 60 years, the securities industry would grow and once more become the investment of choice for individuals. However, Congress saw the need to enact Sarbanes-Oxley in 2002, to prevent a recurrence of practices of senior management (such as those of Enron, WorldCom, and Tyco) from "feeding at the company trough" by constructing schemes involving accounting irregularities to hide debt, and siphoning cash for personal use through various devices. Many of these companies had auditors as accomplices, who were not exactly "independent," as well as Board Members, who never required management to be accountable for these questionable practices. They were also assisted by securities dealers who, because of being engaged in the investment banking business, "encouraged" their financial analysts to give glowing analytical reports in anticipation of future investment banking business.

Another factor that can indicate the potential success of an IPO is the securities market on which it is to be traded after its issue. The only securities markets of interest to the IPO investor are the national and regional exchanges, and the NASDAQ. The recent rapid changes within the securities industry, which have been brought about by technology advances in electronic communications over the last 20 years, are transforming these different markets into connected markets, as well as evolving toward becoming linked with global securities markets. However, issues that are to be listed on either the OTC Bulletin Board or the NQB's Pink Sheets are to be shunned.

MAKING NEW ISSUE INVESTMENTS

The probable success of many new issue equity securities, especially initial public offerings can also be detected from the required disclosure material presented in the preliminary prospectus. The type of legal relationship between the issuer and the underwriters participating in the offering is a key factor. The most probable success can be expected when the underwriters guarantee that the issuer will achieve the desired capitalization level with a firm commitment type of agreement. The least probable success is indicated when the underwriter only makes a best effort commitment. If the underwriter will not take the risk of guaranteeing the level of capitalization desired with a firm commitment, public investors should not feel compelled to subscribe to the issue in spite of touts from sales representatives. In fact, investors of many best efforts offerings may have to wait a better part of a year, after submitting a subscription check, before the issue becomes public. In contrast, firm commitments go public in less than 30 days.

Business organizations seeking public capitalization use investment bankers: securities dealers that offer capitalization securities to the investing public for a fee. They also continue to promote these securities in the marketplace to other suitable clients. Some securities underwriters underwrite offerings that are, on average, more successful than others. National firms have thousands of brokers in branch offices located throughout the country. Regional firms have a local focus that serves local businesses seeking capitalization. In recent years, Internet securities offerings have become exceedingly popular with risk-taking individual investors. However, these offerings typically benefit only the issuer and the online offering dealer. Online offerings lack required due diligence efforts, typically because they come under the small cap exemption. Exempt securities fall under the heading of *let-the-buyer-beware,* instead of the intended requirement, which is for *full and fair disclosure.*

Understanding the financial condition of any business organization is required before subscribing to an offering. The more traditional method for financial evaluation of a business is called Fundamental Analysis. This method is made easier by reducing various financial parameters to ratios, and then evaluating the financial condition by making comparisons with the financial parameters reported for past years, as well as with different organizations within the same industry sector. For many investors, determining the financial condition of an organization may appear to be beyond their comprehension. However, the financial condition can easily be assessed by applying deductive reasoning to a number of financial parameters given in disclosed financial statements. Financial data for all public businesses are disclosed to the public by law. The only difficult task is becoming acquainted with, and understanding the terms used in these statements.

Another method for evaluation is called "intrinsic value" analysis. Though the short-term trading public largely ignores intrinsic value analysis, it can be a valuable tool for the long-term investor. The benefit is that the method yields a theoretical dollar value for the stock, which can then be compared with the current offer price. However, it requires historical data on annual earnings, depreciation, and capital expenditures. One also must assume the earnings growth for the next 10 to 30 years. Although this requires a leap of faith for nonbelievers, the method can indicate a theoretical price range based on past performance, and on anticipated long-term performance!

New issue equity securities (common stock and limited partnership units) should always be considered as speculative investments. Only investors who can afford a complete loss of the amount invested should consider these type securities. In addition, every new issue investor should understand that the probability of success of any particular investment would be fractionally small. Therefore, the amount of financial resources made available for speculative investments must be limited to only a portion of available investment capital. I have presented allocation guidelines, which varies the allocation of investment objective categories with age and income. Admittedly, these guidelines are arbitrary, but they will help to prevent risk-seekers from "betting the farm" and losing all by limiting the amount of speculative capital to a fraction of that available.

INVESTMENT GUIDELINES REVISITED

Using investment guidelines can also help avoid making an investment mistake. However, one must realize that nothing can guarantee that any particular investment will eventually not become a loser.

Guidelines for investments into new issue equity securities are summarize below.

Avoid "non-managed" offerings.

Avoid managed offerings that have an underwriting compensation greater than 10%.

Avoid "best efforts" managed offerings.

Avoid offerings in which the stock is to be listed either on the OTCBB or on the NQB Pink Sheets.

Avoid all "shelf" offerings.

Avoid "secondary" offerings.

Avoid "small cap" offerings with a floating supply capitalization less than either $5 million, or 5 million shares.

Avoid offerings in which "insiders" control greater than 60% of the outstanding supply and any single entity controls more than 40%.

Avoid all IPOs in manic markets.

Avoid placing IPOs in retirement accounts.

Avoid IPOs from managing underwriters whose average annual success rate is less than 130%. Avoid "split" offerings if greater than 40% of the proceeds go to previously private placement shareholders.

Avoid turnaround offerings where greater than 50% of capital raised is to pay down long-term debt, and when proceeds are to purchase growth through an acquisition of another company.

Avoid all "private placement" offerings.

Avoid offerings whose *pro-forma* financial statements show:

1. total debt is greater than 40% of the capital raised

2. current ratio is less than 1.3 (2.0 if an ongoing business)

3. quick ratio is less than 1.0

4. debt to equity is ratio greater than 1.0

5. profit margin is less than 10% (if an ongoing business)

6. dividend payout is greater than 50% (for an ongoing business)

7. cash flow is negative

8. down profit years represent 3 of past 5 or 2 of past 3 years (for an ongoing business)

Guidelines for limited partnership units are given as follows:

Avoid DPP securities because they have no liquidity.

Avoid units in which the lifetime of the partnership can be extended by the GP without a vote of the LPs.

Avoid units in which the partnership agreement calls for the LPs to indemnify the GP for any liability incurred in managing the partnership.

Avoid projects if the GP has not demonstrated previous success with similar projects.

Avoid units in which the partnership agreement calls for the GP to have a "sharing arrangement" greater than 1.2 (sharing in revenues 20%

greater than sharing in expenses), or allowing the GP to receive more than 15% of gross revenue.

Avoid units in real estate projects engaged in new construction, undeveloped land, and blind pools.

Avoid all "exploration" oil and gas projects.

Avoid oil and gas "development" projects whose estimated fair value is less than 2 times the offering price, and only by higher income investors.

Avoid "income" projects in real estate and oil and gas partnerships in which the estimated fair value is less than 1.5 times the offering price.

Avoid offerings in which the proceeds are to be commingled with funds of other partnerships.

Avoid oil and gas income projects that do not qualify as a "small producer."

The following two guidelines are given for new issue convertible securities, preferred stock or debentures.

Avoid offerings whose estimated fair value is less than 1.5 times the offer price

Avoid offerings whose conversion premium is more than 25%.

TACTICAL MANEUVERS REVISITED

Of the hundreds of IPO deals brought public each year, those whose price explode out of the "box" and continue to skyrocket in price can be counted on only one hand. Tactics for new issue securities differ with the type of security held, and can only be used with liquid securities—those that can be traded on the NYSE, AMEX, or the NASDAQ.

There are three possible scenarios for IPO market prices after the effective date: 1, prices increase on the effective date and continue to do so during the quiet period; 2, prices remain at the public offer price for a number of days or weeks; and 3, prices decline on the effective date and thereafter.

When prices increase on the effective date and thereafter, the conventional wisdom for IPOs dictates that the holder should sell a sufficient number of shares to recapture the initial investment. If the offering had been bundled with warrants, the warrants should be sold first, and a limited number of shares should be sold so that between warrants and shares the initial investment is recaptured.

When the bid price remains at the offer price, the managing underwriter is stabilizing the offering. If stabilization continues for more than five days, the holder should consider selling to recover a lost hope. After some time, the underwriter will stop stabilizing the issue thereby allowing the share price to drop should insufficient interest still exist.

The conventional wisdom for offerings that decrease on the effective date and beyond is that any price decline of 10% in a bull market, or 20% in a bear or uncertain market is sufficient cause to sell all shares, or bundled units containing warrants, to limit losses to that which has occurred. If units have been unbundled, the warrants should be held, since they would have no real market value at this point. Eventually the stock price may recover at which point the warrants may be worth a substantial amount.

Convertible preferred stock and convertible debentures may require tactical maneuvering to avoid significant investment losses when a call is issued for these securities. Once the call moratorium for the issue has expired, a call may be issued when interest rates decline significantly. This permits dividend or interest payments to securities holders to be reduced by refinancing with a new issue; or forcing the conversion when the stock price is above the conversion price in order to eliminate paying dividends or interest payments.

The typical tactic, when a call is issued to refinance, is to tender the convertible securities, take the proceeds and move on to other opportunities. The investor should only consider subscribing to a new convertible being offered if the conversion premium is less than 10%.

When a call is issued to force a conversion, the conventional wisdom is to convert the securities, then sell the shares in the marketplace.

Rights are offered to existing shareholders of companies that seek additional equity capitalization by issuing the same class common shares. Shareholders should be willing to exercise the rights to buy additional shares. If not, transferable rights should be sold prior to expiration, and non-transferable rights should be exercised and an equivalent number of shares held should be sold.

CONCLUDING REMARKS

There are no magic formulas for finding, evaluating the merits of, and obtaining access to a new issue security at the offer price. Deciding to invest into an IPO requires a careful review of the prospectus. If a quick reading should provoke some interest, the investor should then proceed to carefully evaluate the issue and apply applicable guidelines before giving an indication of interest to the selling distributor. The offering should be evaluated using common sense judgment of the information provided in the offering materials. Investors should disregard touts of friends or acquaintances, and especially high pressure, sales pitches from securities sales representatives whose sales success depends on stimulating the natural greed of individuals. Greed is what clouds the reasoning of otherwise rational individuals. *If it sounds too good to be true, it usually is!*

Bibliography

✦

Additional Resources

New issue offerings available to the public are reviewed and discussed in a number of periodicals, and in a variety of Internet domains. The two most common periodicals are *The Wall Street Journal* and *Barron's*. Both are information sources for all securities and financial markets, and they cover new issues being offered to the public. The *Journal*, being a daily publication, is likely to provide an information overload for the average individual, as daily issues stack up waiting to be read. *Barron's*, being a weekly publication, would be better for those who find that weekends are typically the best time for concentrating on investments. *Barron's* presents reviews and articles about current IPOs available, as well as frequently covering significance events in the new issue markets and various underwriters. A yearly subscription to *Barron's* is herein recommended for every investor, whether or not they are interested in new issues.

Additional resources on new issue securities can be found in bookstores. Some of these books are:

Investing in IPOs, Version 2.0, Tom Taulli, Bloomberg Press,

The Ernst & Young Guide to the IPO Value Journey, Ernst & Young LLP, Stephan C. Blowers, Peter H. Griffith, Thomas L. Milan, John Wiley & Sons Inc.

Trade IPOs Online, Matthew D. Zito, Matt Olejarczyk, John Wiley & Sons Inc.

IPOs and Equity Offerings, Ross Geddes, Elsevier Science & Technology

Initial Public Offerings, Richard P. Kleeburg, South-Western Educational Publishing

IPOs for Everyone: The 12 Secrets of Investing in IPOs, Linda R. Killian, William K. Smith, Kathleen S. Smith, John Wiley & Sons Inc.

Going Public: Everything You Need to Know to Take Your Company Public, Including Direct Public Offerings, James B. Arkebauer, Dearborn, a Kaplan Professional Company

Information about new issues on the Internet is voluminous. Most websites allow free access, many allow free access after registration, and some require a subscription. The following websites represent a small fraction of domains that result from a Keyword search on IPOs, and are shown in no particular order:

IPOs on NASDAQ,
http://www.nasdaqnews.com/news/news-3f.html
http://www.nasdaq.com/reference/ipos/

EDGAR Online,
http://www.edgar-online.com/brand/earnings/ipoexpress/

Yahoo! IPOs
http://biz.yahoo.com/ipo/

CBS MarketWatch,
http://cbs.market.com/news/ipo/

IPO pricing—Investor Guide,
http://www.investorguige.com/ipopricings.html

Hoover's Online—IPO Central,
http://www.hoovers.com/global/ipoc/index.xhtml

123Jump,
http://www.ipomaven.com/

IPO Research and Analysis
http://www.ipoguys.com

IPO Home,
http://www.ipohome.com/default.asp

IPO Monitor
http://www.ipomonitor.com

Index

0-595-31118-0

Printed in the United States
76693LV00005B/25

9 780595 311187